Pressure
Perfect

OTHER BOOKS BY LORNA SASS

The New Vegan Cookbook

The Pressured Cook: Over 75
One-Pot Meals in Minutes

The New Soy Cookbook

Lorna Sass' Short-Cut Vegetarian

Great Vegetarian Cooking Under Pressure

Lorna Sass' Complete Vegetarian Kitchen
(formerly titled Recipes from an Ecological Kitchen)

Cooking Under Pressure

In Search of the Perfect Meal:
A Collection of the Best Food Writings of Roy Andries
de Groot (Selected and Edited)

Christmas Feasts from History

Dinner with Tom Jones

To the Queen's Taste: Elizabethan Feasts and Recipes

To the King's Taste: Richard II's Book of Feasts and Recipes

Pressure
Perfect

Two Hour Taste in Twenty Minutes
Using Your Pressure Cooker

Lorna Sass

wm

WILLIAM MORROW
An Imprint of HarperCollins*Publishers*

HarperCollins books may be purchased for educational, business, or sales promotional use. For information please write: Special Markets Department, HarperCollins Publishers Inc., 10 East 53rd Street, New York, NY 10022.

FIRST EDITION

Printed on acid-free paper

Library of Congress Cataloging-in-Publication Data

Sass, Lorna J.
    Pressure perfect : two hour taste in twenty minutes using your pressure cooker / Lorna Sass.—1st ed.
        p. cm.
    Includes index.
    ISBN 0-06-050534-6 (hc)
    1. Pressure cookery.   I. Title.

TX840.P7S36326   2004
641.587—dc21   2003052738

04   05   06   07   08   WBC/QW   10   9   8   7   6   5   4   3   2   1

This book is dedicated to my beloved grandmother

Edith Sailon
1900–1994

*who enthusiastically embraced the telephone,
the television, the pressure cooker, and me.*

Contents

Acknowledgments

With a daunting title like *Pressure Perfect,* I needed a calm and creative assistant to help develop and test recipes. It was my good fortune to find the gifted food stylist Dan Macey, who commuted from New Hope, Pennsylvania, to cook under pressure with me on a weekly basis. Thank you, Danny, for all of your great ideas, unflagging enthusiasm, kind patience, and endless generosity.

This cookbook has a very special friend: Cathy Roberts. Cathy cooked every last recipe, often more than once, and e-mailed her results and suggestions to me on a daily basis. Our ongoing dialogue continually nourished my creative spirit and energized me to do the problem-solving that most recipes require. Thank you, Cathy, for giving of yourself so bountifully to me and to this project. (And special thanks to husband, Neil, for cheerfully eating so many dishes in progress.)

As a cookbook author, I am grateful to be standing on the shoulders of culinary giants who set high standards of excellence and have been a source of inspiration throughout my career. I am blessed to have one such colleague, product specialist Elizabeth Schneider, as a longtime friend. Thank you, Elizabeth, for the countless explanations and enhancements and, most especially, for finding order in the chaos.

Many friends, old and new, volunteered to retest the recipes. Heartfelt thanks to Claire Anacreon, Ned Babbitt, Rita Baird, Heather and Gerhard Boch, Becky Brabrook, Joyce Curwin, Christian Dorbandt, Erin Elliot, Kathi Elliot, Martine Gerard,

Heidi Holzer, Ron Leve, Linn Lindert, Dana Lipkin, Viviana Padial, Sarah Saulson, Rosemary Serviss, Sandra Shapiro, and Cathy Walthers.

Rousing cheers for the hard-working HarperCollins team and associates, who contributed their considerable talents to make this book happen: editor Harriet Bell, for embracing the project with such enthusiasm; art director Roberto de Vicq de Cumptich for such a striking jacket; photographer Beatrice da Costa and food stylist Anne Disrude for such an irresistible chicken; designer Leah Carlson-Stanisic for such readable recipes; senior production editor Ann Cahn for such careful attention to details; production manager Karen Lumley for keeping us on schedule; and assistant Katie Connery for such good cheer when doing favors large and small.

Heartfelt gratitude to Sarah Jane Freymann for invaluable support and guidance at the beginning of this project. Special loving thanks to Richard Isaacson, who bought a pressure cooker a few days after we met in 1995 and has been a dear friend ever since.

"There is a gadget on the market that
permits a cook to scoff at time. It is a pressure cooker . . .
The hurry-up cook in possession of this steamer may serve
many dishes denied her by any other method."

—IRMA S. ROMBAUER
The Joy of Cooking (1946 edition)

Introduction

If you are one of those "hurry-up" cooks who dreams of getting a fork-tender beef stew on the table in half an hour, you've discovered the right book. For healthy, homemade fast food, the pressure cooker can't be beat.

Pressure cooking first became popular in America during the Second World War when Rosie the Riveter came home from her shift and had to make dinner for the kids. The cooker's popularity waned during the fifties when America discovered frozen food and TV dinners. But, by the late eighties, with the introduction of newly designed, 100-percent safe cookers from Europe, pressure cooking started making an impressive comeback. Who could resist a pot that produced soul-satisfying soups and stews in one-third the standard cooking time?

I certainly couldn't. I was first introduced to pressure cooking by my mom, who had carted a cooker back from India where she had eaten curries and dals prepared in minutes rather than hours. After eating a few of her delicious creations, I bought my own pressure cooker and began experimenting. My excitement with the results inspired me to write *Cooking Under Pressure,* published in 1989.

Between then and now, I've continued to cook under pressure. (Who doesn't nowadays?) I love good food, but I'm not patient about waiting for it to be done. If I can make that fork-tender beef stew in thirty minutes rather than ninety, there's a good chance I'll make the beef stew.

Pressure Perfect is really two books in one: it teaches you how to make the most of your pressure cooker and also offers you over two hundred recipes to add to your repertoire. I had a lot of fun creating new recipes for this book, largely because I dropped any preconceived notions about what the cooker could and could not do. As a result, I was able to create enticing recipes for pasta, fish, risottos, meatloafs, and cheesecakes (yes, cheesecakes!), in addition to all of the splendid soups, stews, ribs, and pot roasts that the pressure cooker is known to do so well.

And we're not talking about fifties food here: gray pot roast and limp string beans. Glance through the recipes and you'll discover contemporary dishes with vivid color and flavor on every page.

Since the pressure cooker came into my life close to twenty years ago, I've eaten better and saved money as well as time. Now I'd like to share with you all that I've learned. I invite you to experience the surprise and delight that awaits every cook who unlocks the lid of a pressure cooker and sees what magic has transpired within.

Happy Cooking!

Lorna Sass
New York City

If you need information on purchasing a pressure cooker or would like to share your recipes or reactions, I'd be happy to hear from you. (Please enclose a self-addressed, stamped envelope if requesting a response.) Write to me c/o Cooking Under Pressure, P.O. Box 704, New York, NY 10024.

The World of
Pressure Cooking

Welcome to the world of pressure cooking, where soups and stews develop two-hour taste in twenty minutes. To many cooks of my acquaintance, the pressure cooker has become as useful a tool as the desktop PC, so I've taken the liberty of using these initials to refer to my favorite appliance.

HOW THE PC WORKS

Once you've locked the lid in place and set the cooker over high heat, the liquid inside comes to a boil and produces steam. Because the lid has an airtight seal, the steam gets trapped inside the pot and forces the internal pressure to build up to 15 pounds per square inch (PSI).

When the cooker is operating at high pressure (15 pounds PSI), water boils at 250 degrees Fahrenheit rather than the standard 212 degrees. Since the water is 38 degrees hotter than usual, food fibers break down and flavors mingle in one-third the standard cooking time. That's why a pot roast becomes fork-tender in one hour instead of three, and split peas dissolve into a puree in twenty minutes rather than sixty.

Do you think that this is all too good to be true? Or are you beleaguered by the fear that your pressure cooker will blow up before your dinner is ready? Please read on. . . .

COOKERS, THEN AND NOW

If you were born before 1950, chances are you've heard your family's version of the story about Aunt Tillie's pressure-cooked split pea soup ending up on the ceiling. Such family legends began during the forties when pressure cookers had simpler designs. If a food particle clogged the vent or the cook forgot to turn down the heat once high pressure was reached, the pressure kept building inside the cooker. Eventually the jiggle-top pressure regulator blew off, taking the contents of the pot along with it.

Nowadays that accident couldn't happen because the redesigned cookers on the market have multiple safety mechanisms. If, for example, the cook forgets to turn down the heat once high pressure is reached, one or more vents will automatically release excess pressure. In addition, most cookers have cutout windows on the sides of their lids. In the unlikely event that the safety vents do not function properly, the increasing pressure will force the rubber sealing gasket to extrude through one of the windows, creating another opening for the steam pressure to escape.

Now that pressure cookers typically have three backup safety mechanisms built into their designs, it seems fair to call them foolproof!

BUYING A NEW PRESSURE COOKER?

There are over a dozen brands of pressure cookers on the market, and most brands sell two or three different designs in various sizes. It's nice to have such a wide range of choices, but it can be a bit confusing. Here are some guidelines to help you select a new cooker. Contact the manufacturers or distributors listed on page 319 to obtain design details and to locate retail outlets.

Lid

Contrary to what they say about books, you *should* judge a pressure cooker by its cover. The lid reveals how the cooker functions and what safety features are built into the design.

First make sure that it's simple to lock the lid into place and remove it after cooking. Then determine what kind of pressure regulator the cooker uses and how easy it is to know when high pressure is reached. There are three types of pressure regulators (so named because they regulate the amount of pressure in the cooker).

The most sophisticated type is a spring-valve pressure regulator, used in many cookers imported from Europe. Although designs vary, most spring-valve regulators have a small brightly colored rod or cylinder that pops up as the pressure builds. When the rod comes up high enough to reveal a designated mark, the cook knows at a glance when high pressure is reached. (See Advantages of Second-Generation Cookers on page 7.)

The second type of pressure regulator is a removable, round metal weight that sits on top of the cooker's vent pipe. This design is used in American pressure cookers and in some imported brands. When high pressure is reached, the weight rocks gently back and forth, a motion that gives this cooker the nickname "jiggle-top." It is quite easy to know when high pressure is reached.

The third type, called a developed-weight pressure regulator, is used in many imports. Think of it as a jiggle-top in disguise since the regulator sits on top of the vent pipe but gets locked into position before cooking begins. This regulator lifts up slightly when high pressure is reached, but since it rarely jiggles, the cook must observe it carefully.

Safety Backups

Make sure the cooker has at least three backup safety mechanisms for releasing excess pressure. See Cookers, Then and Now, on page 3 for details.

Pounds Per Square Inch (PSI)

Look for a cooker that operates at 14 to 16 pounds per square inch when it reaches high pressure. Cookers that reach high pressure at 12 or 13 pounds PSI don't get the job done as quickly.

Bottom

A well-constructed, heavy bottom distributes heat evenly and prevents sticking and scorching. Opt for an 18/10 stainless-steel cooker that has a three-ply bottom with an aluminum or copper sandwich.

Handles

Select a cooker with heat-resistant plastic handles so you won't have to reach for pot holders when you move it from stovetop to sink. Some cookers come with two short handles; others have one short and one long handle. Choose the shape you find more comfortable; keep in mind that the pot can be heavy to lift when it is full.

Liquid Minimum

Choose a cooker that requires 1 cup liquid or less to reach high pressure. A cooker that demands more liquid may result in excess gravy or a watery sauce.

Size

Since you cannot fill a pressure cooker more than two-thirds full, for maximum flexibility, it is wise to buy the biggest cooker you have room to store. Even if you plan to cook for just two, I recommend an 8-quart (7-liter) cooker and certainly nothing smaller than a 6-quart (5-liter) model. Some companies sell sets: an 8-quart and a 4-quart pot with a shared lid. It's handy to have a second small cooker for preparing vegetables or risottos, but your primary cooker should be large.

Advantages of Second-Generation Cookers

Cookers that operate with a spring-valve pressure regulator are commonly referred to as "second generation" since they use a more recently developed technology than jiggle-tops. Second-generation cookers cost two to three times more, but offer numerous advantages.

Versatility: The design of the spring valve reduces concerns about clogging the regulator's vent, which makes it possible to cook foaming foods like beans and grains without careful monitoring.

Quiet: There is little to no hissing and an absence of the *chug-chug* sounds typical of jiggle-top cookers.

No Guesswork: It is very easy to determine when the cooker has reached high pressure. Just watch for the colorful rod or disk to pop up.

Stovetop Quick-Release Option: There is a way to release pressure quickly without setting the cooker under cold running water. This option is particularly convenient when the pot is full, thus heavy to move.

CAN I USE MY OLD JIGGLE-TOP COOKER?

The answer is yes, provided that it is designed for safety and all of the parts are in good working order.

First, check the Owner's Manual to determine if there are at least three backup safety mechanisms built into the design. (See Cookers, Then and Now on page 3 for details.)

If so, do a test run. Pour 2 cups of water into the cooker. Bring the cooker up to high pressure. If the pressure doesn't rise or if water drips down the sides, purchase a new gasket. (Check the directory of manufacturers on page 319; use only the gasket made for your model.)

Then take the cooker through the trial run described on page 9. If you are satisfied with the results, use the cooker.

Pressure Cooking
Perfected

As with any new appliance, it takes a small investment of time to become acquainted with your pressure cooker. Start by reading the Owner's Manual, which should provide the necessary information for filling in the blanks below. You'll be glad to have this information at your fingertips when you start cooking.

GETTING TO KNOW YOUR PC

Size
My cooker holds ___8___ quarts.

Pressure cookers come in sizes ranging from 2½ to 8 quarts. Imported cookers are sized in liters: a 5-liter cooker holds approximately 6 quarts, and a 7-liter cooker holds about 8 quarts.

Capacity
For most ingredients, the maximum capacity is _2/3 solids_. 1/2 liquids
For foaming ingredients, like beans and grains, the maximum capacity is _1/2_.

The maximum capacity is usually two-thirds, but only one-half for foaming ingredients.

Pressure Regulator
My cooker has (check one)

_____ a removable "jiggle-top" pressure regulator
_____ a developed-weight pressure regulator

_____✓_____ a spring-valve pressure regulator
Refer to page 5 for descriptions of each type.

Liquid
The minimum liquid requirement is __2 ½__ cups.

Most cookers require 1 cup liquid to come up to pressure. A few models require as little as ½ cup or as much as 2 cups.

Pounds Per Square Inch at High Pressure
High pressure in my cooker is __12__ pounds per square inch (PSI).

You may have to contact the manufacturer to ascertain this information. For most cookers, high pressure is 15 pounds PSI.

Next consult the Owner's Manual and learn how to do the following:

1) Lock the lid in place.
2) Recognize when the cooker has reached high pressure.
3) Quick-release the pressure.
4) Unlock the lid once all of the pressure has been released.

Finally, do a trial run to determine how much liquid your cooker loses while under high pressure. Some cookers don't lose any liquid during the course of an hour-long test. Others lose as much as 3 cups through released steam.

There is very little work involved in this trial run, but you will need to stay near the kitchen for one hour and use a timer. For detailed explanations of key phrases used in these steps, see The Language of Pressure Cooking, page 10.

1) Pour 4 cups water into the cooker.
2) Lock the lid in place.
3) Over high heat bring to high pressure.
4) Reduce the heat just enough to maintain high pressure and cook for 20 minutes.

9

Pressure Cooking Perfected

5) Quick-release the pressure under cold running water.

6) Remove the lid, tilting it away from you to allow the steam to escape.

7) Pour the remaining water into a measuring cup to see how much water the cooker has lost during 20 minutes under pressure.

8) Note how much water was lost in the blank space(s) below.

9) Return the remaining water to the cooker.

10) Repeat steps 2 through 9 two more times, noting water losses below. Don't be tempted to assume that after 40 minutes your cooker will lose twice the water it lost in 20 minutes. It doesn't always work that way.

After 20 minutes, my cooker lost ___*0*___ cups water.
After 40 minutes, my cooker lost ___*1/3*___ cups water.
After 1 hour, my cooker lost ___*1/2*___ cups water.

If your cooker loses more than $1/2$ cup of liquid during the time span that a dish is cooking, you will have to add extra to prevent scorching and to end up with sufficient gravy. In other words, if a dish cooks for an hour and the test reveals that your cooker loses 1 cup of water in an hour, add an extra cup of liquid before you start cooking. The recipes will always direct you when adding extra liquid is necessary.

THE LANGUAGE OF PRESSURE COOKING

The phrases explained below are used repeatedly in the recipes. For a clear picture of the step-by-step process involved in cooking under pressure, read them carefully. Refer to the diagrams in your Owner's Manual as needed.

If you're using an electric cooker or cooking on an electric or high-BTU stove, please see supplementary instructions in Special Situations, page 20.

In a 6-quart or Larger Cooker: There is an important relationship between the size of your cooker and the amount of food you can cook at one time since the top third of the cooker must be left empty to allow room for the steam pressure to build. The recipes are designed so that ingredients do not exceed the two-thirds limit in a 6-quart cooker since that is the most commonly used size. When preparing foods that expand or foam—like beans and grains—the suggested ingredients fill a 6-quart cooker only halfway.

Those with a 4-quart cooker will find special instructions in recipe footnotes called Pressure Points. Those with an 8-quart cooker can increase quantities as space allows.

Do Not Stir: Tomatoes and other ingredients that have a high sugar content are prone to scorching the bottom of pots when cooked over intense heat. Since the cooker is brought up to pressure over high heat, I've designed the recipes so that such ingredients are added last and set on top. You will be reminded, "Do Not Stir," after adding tomatoes and other ingredients that could cause scorching.

Lock the Lid in Place: After the ingredients are assembled in the cooker, lower the lid onto the pot, using the arrows or other visual markings provided by the manufacturer. Then rotate the lid until the lid and pot handles line up. Some cookers have an additional locking mechanism that involves pushing a small lever into place. Check your instruction booklet for specifics. Cookers are designed so that pressure won't rise if the lid is not properly locked in place.

Over High Heat: Place the cooker on a burner that is the same diameter or a bit smaller (never larger). Turn the heat to high.

Bring to High Pressure: Typically it takes less than 5 minutes for the cooker to reach high pressure; however, if it's filled to capacity, it can take as long as 20 minutes. The time it takes for the cooker to come up to pressure is not calculated as part of the cooking time and rarely impacts the minutes required under pressure for the ingredients to become tender.

As the cooker comes up to pressure, a fair amount of air, then steam, is released from one or more vents. Some of the steam may condense on the lid. This is normal.

Lower the Heat Just Enough to Maintain High Pressure: Once high pressure is reached, you must lower the heat immediately. If you don't lower it enough, the pressure will continue to rise and the cooker will hiss more loudly than usual or make a warning noise. If this happens, turn off the heat and quick-release excess pressure by one of the methods described in the Owner's Manual, then continue cooking over lower heat. After using your cooker a few times, you'll learn just how much heat is required to maintain (but not exceed) high pressure. For most cookers, a flame akin to simmering is just right.

If you notice that the pressure has fallen, assume that you've lowered the heat too much or that the cooker isn't full enough to dependably maintain the pressure at high. In either case, simply bring the pressure back up to high over high heat and lower the heat to maintain pressure again—only this time don't lower the heat quite so much. A brief period of reduced pressure is not likely to affect the timing or the quality of the finished product.

Cook Under High Pressure for X Minutes: Cooking time is calculated from the moment high pressure is reached. Above each recipe is a phrase such as "3 minutes high pressure." This means that as soon as the cooker reaches high pressure, you should set the timer and cook under high pressure for 3 minutes.

Quick-Release the Pressure: When the cooking time is finished, turn off the heat. Bring down the pressure by setting the cooker under cold running water until all of the pressure has been released— usually between 30 and 60 seconds. It's best to tilt the cooker at a 45 degree angle and run water down one side of the cover, directing the water away from the pressure regulator. Second-generation cookers offer the option of a quick-release method that can be performed without removing the cooker from the stovetop. Check the Owner's Manual for details.

Quick-Release the Pressure by Setting the Cooker Under Cold Running Water: If the recipe specifically recommends that you release pressure this way, assume that a stovetop quick-release method will cause sputtering at the vent. Sputtering generally occurs when the cooker is very full or contains ingredients that foam, such as barley or split peas. It can be messy and potentially dangerous since the ingredients are quite hot.

Let the Pressure Drop Naturally: When cooking time is completed, turn off the heat. Let the cooker sit until the pressure drops of its own accord, which usually takes about 10 minutes, but can take as long as 25 minutes if the cooker is very full.

The food continues to cook as the pressure drops, and this period of time is needed for some foods to finish cooking. The natural release is preferred for certain foods, such as beans and beef, whose textures can be compromised with a quick-release.

Remove the Lid, Tilting It Away from You to Allow Steam to Escape: Even after all pressure has been released, there is still a significant amount of steam left in the cooker. Take care to tilt the lid away from your face when you remove it. Get into the habit of placing the lid upside down on a heatproof surface away from the burners.

Replace the Lid and Cook for a Minute or Two in the Residual Heat: When delicate foods such as rice, pasta, or fresh vegetables are only slightly underdone after the pressure is released, set (but do not lock) the lid in place and let the food cook in the heat that remains in the pot.

Let the Dish Rest: Pressure-cooked foods benefit significantly from some "breathing time" after pressure release. If you stir well and then let the dish sit uncovered in the pot for 3 to 5 minutes, you will be rewarded with enhanced flavor and texture. The food will remain hot enough to serve without reheating.

TRANSFORMATIONS AND BEYOND

Accompanying each recipe, you'll find entries labeled Variations, Cook-Alongs, Transformations, and Pressure Points. This bonus information is intended to expand the usefulness of this book in various ways, detailed below.

Variations: These are simple ways to modify the recipe by substituting or adding an ingredient or two.

Cook-Alongs: Optional ingredients—usually potatoes, carrots, or Casserole Rice—that you can cook with the recipe as space in your cooker permits. Suggestions for Cook-Alongs are listed under Variations.

Transformations: Transformations go a few steps beyond Variations and dramatically expand the repertoire of recipes offered in this book. By making a few simple changes, you can transform the basic recipe into a substantially different dish.

For example, scan the recipe for Goulash with Potatoes, page 122. Then look at the Chicken Paprikash Transformation. You can see that by using chicken broth instead of beer, substituting chicken for the meat, adding mushrooms, and blending in sour cream rather than using it as a garnish that you end up with an entirely different dish.

When preparing a Transformation, I suggest that you note the changes and substitutions to one side of the basic ingredients list and draw a faint pencil line through any omitted items. Make a small mark in the instructions to remind yourself when there is an altered procedure. (If you were taught never to write in a book, please consider cookbooks an exception. Try thinking of them as workbooks.)

Since this approach to following a recipe is unusual, I'd like to walk you step-by-step through the process of cooking the Chicken Paprikash Transformation.

As you reread the Transformation instructions, jot down "chicken broth" next to beer and "4 pounds chicken" next to meat in the Goulash ingredients list. Then write "+ mushrooms" next to "4 pounds chicken" and "+ lemon juice" next to sour cream. Note down the altered cooking time in the margin of the instructions next to the suggested meat timing. Then make a little mark after the words "fat separator" to remind yourself that at this point you blend in the sour cream.

The main thing to remember when doing a Transformation is to keep referring back to the basic recipe. Do everything the recipe says except when the Transformation deviates. The Transformation always starts at the point where the changes from the basic recipe begin, so when making Chicken Paprikash, you do everything in the basic recipe up to the point of adding the beer. After adding the chicken broth (instead of the beer), you add the bay leaves and salt. After that, you add the chicken (instead of the meat) and toss in the mushrooms. You then return to the basic recipe, which tells you to set the potatoes on top.

After pressure release, you again follow the basic recipe instructions to degrease and season the stew. Then blend the sour cream into the cooking liquid, add lemon juice to taste, and garnish with dill.

This process is much easier than it may sound. After you've done a few Transformations, you'll get the hang of it. Along the way, you'll develop a more intuitive understanding of how cooking works and how new recipes are born.

Pressure Points: Look here for tips that guarantee success and for any adjustments suggested for cookers of different sizes. If you are using a 4-quart cooker, make a habit of checking this section for special instructions.

OTHER USEFUL THINGS TO KNOW

Cutting to Size: Since you need to release the pressure before adding ingredients, it's easiest to have everything in the cooker from the start. To ensure even results among foods with different timing requirements, the recipes will direct you to cut slow-cooking ingredients smaller than quick-cooking ones. For example, when making the Minestrone with Pesto, you'll be asked to cut the potatoes (slow cooking) into 1/2-inch slices and leave the zucchini (quick cooking) whole.

Foil Packets: An excellent way to avoid overcooking and maximize flavor is to wrap ingredients in aluminum foil. For example, if you wrap carrots in foil and float the foil packet on top of a long-cooking stew, the carrots remain firm and full of flavor. On the other hand, if you cook unwrapped carrots in a stew, they become meltingly soft and sacrifice their flavor to the cooking liquid.

To make a foil packet, cut a 1 1/2-foot length of standard width, heavy-duty aluminum foil. Place the prepared vegetables in the center. Bring together the cut ends of the foil and fold over several times to seal. Then fold the two remaining open sides to seal.

Maximizing Seasoning: The high heat in the cooker mutes the flavor of ground spices, dried and fresh herbs, and chopped fresh garlic. To maximize flavor, use whole spices in cooking and add herbs and ground spices after pressure release. When you need to cook ground spices such as curry or chili powder under pressure, use about 30 percent more than you would in a standard recipe. Keep in mind that the taste of granulated or powdered garlic survives much better under pressure than the taste of fresh garlic. If you have a preference for fresh garlic, remember that whole cloves contribute more flavor than chopped.

Liquid Assets: All cookers require liquid to produce sufficient steam to bring up the pressure. Since the minimum liquid requirement for most cookers is 1 cup, the recipes always call for at least that amount. The liquid is usually water or broth but can be juice, wine, or beer.

To save time when preparing large quantities, turn the heat to high as soon as you have added the liquid. The closer the liquid is to boiling, the faster the cooker will come up to pressure once you've locked the lid in place.

Often a cooked dish will contain more liquid than you added initially because ingredients with a high water content—such as onions, celery, and mushrooms—give up at least 50 percent of their volume in liquid as they cook. In addition, because of their tightly sealed lids, most cookers lose relatively little liquid through evaporation.

If the cooking liquid or gravy is thinner or more copious than you'd like, reduce it by boiling vigorously or thicken it as suggested in the recipe. You can also drain some of the liquid off and put it aside for another use.

Getting Out the Fat: Many of the recipes suggest that you degrease the cooking liquid using a fat separator (see page 17) because that is the quickest way to get the job done. However, if you have time to refrigerate the dish overnight, the fat will rise to the top and congeal, making for easier and more complete removal. Another bonus of overnight refrigeration is that most dishes taste better the next day.

USEFUL ACCESSORIES

A good **timer** is indispensable to successful pressure cooking. Buy a three-way electronic timer if you are likely to be cooking more than one dish at a time. If you are satisfied with your oven or watch timer, you'll do fine with those.

An **instant-read thermometer** is essential for judging when meat is sufficiently cooked.

You will need a **steaming basket** for pressure cooking vegetables and making meatloaf (yes, meatloaf!, see page 133). Many cookers come with a steaming basket, but they usually don't have legs to raise them above the water, rendering them useless for proper steaming. This problem can be rectified by setting the basket on a **three-legged trivet**. (If your cooker didn't come with a trivet, you can improvise by crushing aluminum foil into a 1-inch-thick log and shaping the log into a ring that fits snugly around the interior perimeter of the cooker.) An excellent alternative is an inexpensive collapsible **vegetable steaming basket**, available in most kitchen shops. It has built-in feet that raise it above the water. Look for one with a base diameter of about 6 inches.

To make Casserole White Rice (page 182) and bread puddings, you'll need a porcelain or glass 1½- or **2-quart soufflé dish** or **heatproof casserole.** Check to be sure that the dish fits comfortably inside the cooker with at least ½ inch to spare around the perimeter. To make cheesecakes, you'll need a **7-inch spring-form pan**.

If the bottom of your cooker scorches on a regular basis, purchase a **heat diffuser,** an inexpensive disc that evenly distributes heat. Set the diffuser between the burner and cooker. When using one, the cooker will take a few minutes longer to come up to pressure, but recommended cooking time should still be reliable. When releasing pressure, remember to move the cooker off the heat diffuser onto a cool burner. Heat diffusers are available in any well-stocked kitchen store.

An **8-cup Pyrex measuring cup** is the ideal receptacle for large quantities of strained broths. Pour the liquid from the Pyrex cup into a **fat separator** to degrease when you wish to serve a dish soon after it is made. The fat separator's long spout extends from the base and is designed so that you can easily pour off degreased liquid, leaving behind the fat that has risen to the top.

An **immersion blender** is a very handy tool as it allows you to puree all or part of a soup or gravy right in the cooker, saving you the bother of transferring the ingredients to a standard blender or food processor.

You'll need a **kitchen scale** to weigh vegetables and pasta. **Long-handled tongs** are the best tool for removing individual ingredients from the cooker.

A **food mill** does an excellent job of pureeing cooked fruits and vegetables. It is especially useful when pureeing potatoes, which become gummy in the food processor and blender.

If you have trouble finding any of these items locally, they are all available from Zabar's by mail-order (see page 317).

SOME HANDY TECHNIQUES

The following tips are given in alphabetical order by main ingredient.

Roasting Garlic: Remove any loose, papery skins from a whole head of garlic. Set the garlic in a shallow baking dish and roast in a toaster oven or standard oven preheated to 375 degrees Fahrenheit until soft, 20 to 30 minutes. Squeeze the soft flesh out of each clove as needed. Refrigerate in a sealed container for up to 10 days.

Grating Fresh Ginger: Use a porcelain grater (available in Asian groceries) or the side of a box grater with rice-sized holes. Better yet, use the microplane, a terrific rasp sold in many kitchen shops (or call 800-555-2767). It's not necessary to peel ginger before grating. A 1-inch chunk yields about $1^{1}/_{2}$ teaspoons grated ginger. (Ground, dried ginger has quite a different flavor and does not make a good substitute.)

Making Italian Herb Blend: In a small jar, combine 1 tablespoon each dried oregano and basil leaves, 2 teaspoons each dried thyme and rosemary leaves, $1^{1}/_{2}$ teaspoons whole fennel seeds, and 1 teaspoon crushed red pepper flakes (optional). Shake well. Store in a cool, dark place and use within 4 months.

Cleaning and Chopping Leeks: Trim off the root end. Begin slicing from the root end upwards, discarding bruised outer leaves as you go. Even the dark green inner leaves may be used since the cooker does a fine job of softening them. Swish chopped leeks vigorously in several changes of water to release all sand.

Zesting Lemons, Limes, or Oranges: Wash the fruit thoroughly. The best tool for zesting is the microplane, a rasp designed for this purpose, available in many kitchen shops (or call 800-555-2767). You can also use a standard zester or the finest side of a box grater.

Juicing Limes or Making Lime Wedges: To maximize the yield of juice, slice the lime lengthwise a little off-center to avoid the core. Continue slicing wedges around the core. Squeeze wedges to extract juice. Discard core.

Toasting Nuts and Seeds: Toast nuts on a baking pan in a toaster oven (most convenient) or standard oven set to 375 degrees Fahrenheit until nuts are fragrant and lightly browned, 2 to 4 minutes in a toaster oven and slightly longer in a standard oven. Toast seeds in a skillet set over medium-high heat; stir them frequently. Nuts and seeds burn easily, so watch them closely.

Roasting Red Peppers: Set each pepper on a grid raised above a gas burner and turn the heat to high. Rotate with tongs until thoroughly charred. (If using an electric oven, cut the peppers in half, remove the seeds, and core. Press firmly to flatten. Set cut side down, under the broiler, as close to the broiling element as possible.) Wrap each charred pepper in a wet paper towel and enclose in a plastic bag to steam. When cool, use the paper towel to rub off the skin. Remove core and seeds. If not using the peppers immediately, toss in olive oil and refrigerate in a tightly sealed container for up to 5 days.

Toasting Spices: Toast spices in a small skillet over medium-high heat until you can detect their aroma, usually a minute or two. Stir from time to time. When done, transfer immediately from the skillet to avoid burning.

SPECIAL SITUATIONS

Cooking on an Electric Stove

Electric coils create intense heat and are slow to respond to adjustments in temperature. The adjustments you've learned to make for standard stovetop cooking carry over to pressure cooking, but there are a few special considerations:

> The cooker is traditionally brought up to pressure over high heat. If utilizing the highest setting causes scorching, try bringing up the pressure using a slightly lower setting. Alternatively, place a heat diffuser (see page 17) under the cooker before bringing it up to pressure.
>
> Once the cooker reaches high pressure, the heat must immediately be lowered or the pressure will continue to build. To accommodate the coil's slow response, lower the heat a few minutes before high pressure is reached. Alternatively, transfer the cooker to a burner preset to low—or whatever you've determined to be the correct setting for maintaining high pressure.
>
> When the recipe calls for natural pressure release, move the cooker to a cool burner.

Cooking over a High-BTU Flame

To avoid scorching, bring up the pressure over medium heat—or whatever flame you consider equivalent to high on a standard gas range. Alternatively, place a heat diffuser (see page 17) under the cooker before bringing it up to pressure.

Cooking on an Induction Range

Check with the manufacturer to be sure that the cooker will function properly. If so, place the cooker in the middle of a marked heat zone that is the same size or smaller than the base of the cooker. Follow instructions for Cooking on an Electric Stove.

Using an Electric Pressure Cooker

Use the BROWN setting to do any cooking required before
bringing up the pressure.

Program the cooker for HIGH PRESSURE.

If the recipe calls for natural pressure release, reduce cooking
time by 2 minutes to adjust for the longer time it takes for
the electric cooker to release pressure.

If the recipe calls for quick-releasing the pressure by setting the
cooker under cold running water, ignore this instruction.
Instead, subtract 4 minutes from cooking time and allow the
pressure to come down naturally for 4 minutes. Then press
the quick-release button in very short spurts while averting
your face from the steam. If any liquid is ejected from the
valve, wait about 30 seconds before proceeding.

Use the BROWN setting to do any final cooking after the pressure is released.

Pressure Cooking at High Altitudes

Increase cooking time by 5 percent for every 1,000 feet above sea
level. For further information about high-altitude cooking,
check the web site at www.ext.colostate.edu/pubs/columncc/
cc970123.htm.

TAKING CARE OF YOUR COOKER

Pressure cookers require a little more maintenance than the average pot. The pots themselves are usually dishwasher-safe, but the
lids are not. Check your Owner's Manual for details.

Removing and Cleaning the Gasket: To preserve the life of
the rubber gasket (sealing ring), remove it from the lid and rinse
it after each use. Allow the gasket to air-dry thoroughly before
setting it back in the lid. Although gaskets usually last for years,
it's wise to have a backup on hand for the moment when it gives
out.

Cleaning the Vent/Valve Areas: Whenever you wash the lid,
examine these areas and, if necessary, scrub them free of debris
with a soapy, nonabrasive scouring pad or a toothbrush. If you

own a jiggle-top cooker, you may need to poke a toothpick through the vents to be sure they are clear. If you use a second-generation cooker, you will occasionally need to unscrew the pressure regulator and wash the parts well. Look for detailed cleaning instructions in your Owner's Manual.

Scouring the Bottom: If the bottom is encrusted with scorched food, sprinkle with some nonabrasive cleanser such as Bon Ami. Add about 2 cups water and bring to a boil. Let sit for a few hours or overnight. Scrub clean with a scouring pad.

If the bottom interior or exterior become stained, scrub it with a nonabrasive product called Bar Keepers Friend, available in some supermarkets and many housewares stores. To locate a source in your area, call 800-433-5818.

Tightening the Handles: If the handles become loose, tighten them with a screwdriver.

Storing: Rest the lid against the side of the cooker or set it upside down on top. If the gasket isn't thoroughly dry, drape it loosely on the lid. Don't lock the lid in place for storage, or you'll be greeted by a strong whiff of your last meal when you next open the cooker.

Soups and Broths

For additional soups and broths, consult the Index.

As soon as the air turns crisp in early fall, I get a yen for soup. A half hour later, I find myself sitting in front of a steaming bowlful—thanks to the pressure cooker.

In this chapter, you'll find soups to fit all moods and seasons. There are hearty beef and chicken soups, creamy pureed vegetable soups (that are low fat and have no cream), and luscious bean soups. Since the cooker excels at making broths, the chapter closes with a few easy recipes for preparing them.

Hearty Beef Borscht with Sour Cream–Dill Topping

SERVES 6 TO 8

Glorious crimson beets steal the show in this beefy meal-in-a-bowl. Grate some of the beets to intensify the flavor and color of the broth. Dice the rest to enjoy concentrated bites of their unique sweetness.

---

10 minutes high pressure plus 10-minute natural pressure release

---

FOR THE SOUP

1¹/₂ pounds beets (2 pounds if weighed with greens attached), scrubbed and trimmed

1 tablespoon butter or oil

1 cup chopped onions

1 teaspoon caraway seeds

2 cups beef broth

1¹/₂ pounds beef chuck, trimmed and cut into ¹/₂-inch chunks

³/₄ pound green cabbage, coarsely chopped (6 to 7 cups)

3 to 4 tablespoons apple cider or red wine vinegar

1 teaspoon salt (use ¹/₂ teaspoon if broth is salty)

2 large bay leaves

1 pound Yukon Gold or other waxy potatoes, peeled and cut into 2-inch chunks

One can (28 ounces) peeled plum tomatoes (with liquid)

1 to 2 tablespoons sugar (optional)

FOR THE SOUR CREAM–DILL TOPPING

1 cup sour cream

1 teaspoon dried dill

Grate half the beets, using the coarse side of a box grater or the coarse grating disc of a food processor. Cut the remaining beets into ¹/₂-inch dice.

Heat the butter in a 6-quart or larger cooker. Add the onions and caraway seeds and cook over high heat for a minute or two, stirring frequently. Stir in the broth, beef, beets, cabbage, 3 table-spoons of the vinegar, salt, bay leaves, and potatoes.

Pour in the tomatoes and their liquid, breaking the tomatoes into pieces by squeezing them in your hand. Do not stir after adding the tomatoes.

Lock the lid in place. Over high heat bring to high pressure. (This may take longer than usual since the pot is so full.) Reduce the heat just enough to maintain high pressure and cook for 10 minutes. Turn off the heat. Allow the pressure to come down naturally for 10 minutes, then quick-release any remaining pressure by setting the cooker under cold running water. Remove the lid, tilting it away from you to allow steam to escape.

Remove the bay leaves. Slash the potatoes into smaller pieces, if you wish. Add salt to taste. Adjust the sweet-sour balance by adding sugar and additional vinegar, if needed. (The soup should have a slight acidic edge.)

Prepare the Sour Cream–Dill Topping: Blend the sour cream and dill in a small bowl. Let sit for a few minutes.

Serve the borscht in large soup bowls with a dollop of Sour Cream–Dill Topping in the center of each portion. Pass remaining topping at the table.

Tips: Leftovers are likely to need another jolt of vinegar or lemon juice. The soup also tastes good cold.

Variations

• VEGETARIAN VERSION: Omit beef and use vegetable broth instead of beef broth. Serve hot or chilled.

• Adjust the sweet-sour balance with freshly squeezed lemon juice instead of vinegar.

• After releasing pressure, stir in $1/2$ to 1 cup finely chopped beet greens and simmer until they are tender, 2 to 3 minutes.

• Add a few tablespoons of minced sweet pickle to Sour Cream–Dill Topping.

Transformations *(Follow basic recipe except as noted.)*

• UKRAINIAN-STYLE BORSCHT: Substitute pork shoulder for beef chuck.

• PUREED SUMMER BORSCHT: Do not follow basic recipe. Instead, combine 5 cups water, ¼ cup distilled white vinegar, 3 tablespoons sugar, and 1½ teaspoons salt in cooker. Add 2 pounds whole, scrubbed, trimmed beets and 1 small, peeled onion. Cook under high pressure according to size (see Vegetable Timing Chart, page 333; when done, beets should be easy to pierce with a skewer). While beets are still warm, slip off skins. Finely chop beets and onion in food processor. Blend in ½ cup sour cream and 1 cup cooking liquid and process until smooth. Stir beet puree and 2 tablespoons lemon juice into remaining cooking liquid. Chill well. Garnish with lots of snipped fresh dill or chives.

Note: You can cook whole, unpeeled, waxy potatoes along with beets. Serve them cold, one per portion of borscht.

PRESSURE POINTS

• If using a 4-quart cooker, divide recipe in half.
• No need to peel beets: The pressure cooker softens their skins. *Do* peel potatoes, as their skins' texture and color are not pleasing in this context.
• Beets take longer to cook than potatoes. To ensure even cooking, beets are cut smaller than potatoes.
• Do not be concerned if ingredients exceed cooker's maximum recommended fill line: the cabbage will shrink as pressure comes up.

29

Beef, Mushroom, and Barley Soup

This homey old-world soup is simple and satisfying. Bright carrots and verdant dill add a fresh finish. Serve for lunch or dinner, accompanied by black bread and a big salad.

---

10 minutes high pressure plus 10-minute natural pressure release

---

2 tablespoons butter or oil

1 1/2 cups chopped onions or leeks

1 cup diced celery

4 cups beef broth

1 cup water

1 pound beef chuck, trimmed and cut into 1/2-inch chunks

10 ounces button or cremini mushrooms, halved if large, then cut into 1/4-inch-thick slices

1/2 cup pearl barley, rinsed

2 large bay leaves

1 teaspoon salt (omit if broth is salty)

3 medium carrots, peeled, trimmed, halved lengthwise, and wrapped in a foil packet (see page 15)

1/4 cup chopped fresh dill

Heat the butter in a 6-quart or larger cooker, add the onions and celery, and cook over medium-high heat for a minute or two, stirring frequently. Stir in the broth, water, beef, mushrooms, barley, bay leaves, and salt. Float the foil-packed carrots on top.

Lock the lid in place. Over high heat bring to high pressure. (This is likely to take longer than usual since the cooker is so full.) Reduce the heat just enough to maintain high pressure and cook for 10 minutes. Turn off the heat. Allow the pressure to come down naturally for 10 minutes, then quick-release any remaining pressure by setting the cooker under cold running water. Remove the lid, tilting it away from you to allow steam to escape.

Remove the foil-packed carrots with tongs and set on a plate. Open carefully. Slice the carrots and add them to the soup. Remove the bay leaves. Stir in the dill and add more salt, if needed.

Variations
• Instead of fresh dill, add 1 to 2 teaspoons dried dill.
• Make Sour Cream–Dill Topping by combining $\frac{1}{2}$ cup sour cream with $\frac{1}{2}$ teaspoon dried dill. Top each portion with a dollop.
• Cook soup with $\frac{1}{2}$ cup dried baby lima beans that have been soaked overnight and drained.
• After releasing pressure, stir in 1 cup frozen (Fordhook) limas. Gently boil soup until limas are tender, about 5 minutes.

Transformations *(Follow basic recipe except as noted.)*
• DOUBLE-MUSHROOM BARLEY SOUP (Vegetarian): Use vegetable broth instead of beef broth. Omit beef. Instead of adding 1 cup water to soup, soak 1 ounce (about 1 cup loosely packed) dried mushrooms in $1\frac{1}{2}$ cups hot water until soft, about 10 minutes. Add reconstituted mushrooms and soaking liquid after stirring in broth. (When you pour soaking liquid into pot take care to leave behind any grit that has settled on bottom.)
• TURKEY, BARLEY, AND VEGETABLE SOUP: Use chicken or turkey broth instead of beef broth. Instead of chuck, use boneless, skinned turkey thighs. After pressure release, remove thighs, shred meat, and stir it into soup. Add $\frac{1}{2}$ cup frozen peas or corn (or a combination) and simmer until they are defrosted, a minute or two.

PRESSURE POINTS
• If using a 4-quart cooker, divide recipe in half.
• Don't be tempted to omit butter or oil. It's necessary to prevent foaming barley from clogging an excess-pressure vent.
• Carrots are steamed in a foil packet to avoid overcooking.

Chunky Chicken Noodle Soup

Chicken soup made from scratch is healing for body and soul, but takes hours to make by the traditional stovetop method. With this quick pressure cooker recipe, you can use commercial broth and still achieve a soup that tastes homemade.

7 to 8 minutes high pressure plus 4-minute natural pressure release

1 tablespoon butter or oil
1 medium onion, chopped
1 medium carrot, diced
1 rib celery, diced
4 cups chicken broth
2 cups water (or additional broth if using a low-salt version)
2 large bay leaves
4 pounds bone-in chicken breasts or thighs, skinned
4 ounces fine egg noodles
2 tablespoons chopped fresh parsley
Salt
1 to 2 tablespoons freshly squeezed lemon juice (optional)

Heat the butter in a 4-quart or larger cooker. Stir in the onion, carrot, and celery, and cook over medium-high heat until the onion starts to soften, about 2 minutes. Add the broth, water, bay leaves, and chicken.

Lock the lid in place. Over high heat bring to high pressure. Reduce the heat just enough to maintain high pressure and cook for 7 minutes (breasts) or 8 minutes (thighs, or a combination of breasts and thighs). Turn off the heat. Allow the pressure to come down naturally for 4 minutes, then quick-release any remaining pressure. Remove the lid, tilting it away from you to allow steam to escape.

Set a colander over a large bowl, preferably one with a pouring spout (a 2-quart Pyrex measuring cup is perfect), and strain the soup. Return the broth to the cooker. When the chicken is cool enough to handle, chop or shred the meat. (Reserve the bones to make Chicken Broth, page 57.) If you wish, reserve the strained vegetables for the soup.

Bring the broth to a boil. Add the noodles and cook according to package directions until just short of done, usually about 4 minutes. Lower the heat. Stir in the chopped chicken, cooked vegetables (if using), parsley, and salt to taste. Simmer until the noodles are done and the chicken is hot. Stir in lemon juice, if desired, for a bright finish.

Variations
• Instead of fresh parsley, use 1/2 teaspoon dried dill.
• Instead of fine egg noodles, use broad egg noodles or another pasta with a standard cooking time of 9 to 13 minutes. Instead of boiling, cook under high pressure for 4 minutes and quick release.

Transformations *(Follow basic recipe except as noted.)*

• CHUNKY CHICKEN SOUP WITH TORTELLINI AND PEAS: Instead of noodles, add 1 pound fresh or frozen tortellini. Along with chopped chicken, stir in 1/2 cup frozen peas. Simmer until peas are tender, about 1 minute. Instead of parsley, add 2 tablespoons chopped fresh basil. Sprinkle each portion with grated romano or parmesan.

• CHUNKY MEXICAN CHICKEN SOUP WITH AVOCADO AND CORN: Omit noodles. Along with chopped chicken, add 1 cup frozen corn and simmer for 1 minute. Just before serving, stir in 1 ripe, diced Hass avocado. Instead of parsley, add 1/4 cup chopped fresh cilantro. Use lime juice instead of lemon.

• CHUNKY CHICKEN SOUP WITH SQUASH AND BEANS: Omit noodles. Add a 12-ounce package of frozen, unseasoned, cooked winter squash (puree) to the boiling broth. Cover and cook until defrosted. (You can hasten process by breaking up block of squash with a fork.) Stir well to thicken soup. Along with chopped chicken, add 1 cup cooked beans (try black beans or red kidney beans for color), 1 1/2 cups frozen corn, 1/4 cup thinly sliced scallion greens, and 1/2 teaspoon dried tarragon or oregano.

Omit parsley. Simmer until tarragon scents soup, usually a minute or two.

• CHUNKY TURKEY NOODLE SOUP: Instead of chicken, use 3 pounds boneless, skinned turkey thighs. Cook for 8 minutes high pressure, then let pressure drop naturally.

Tip: You can prepare any of the chicken soup Transformations above using boneless, skinned turkey thighs instead of chicken.

PRESSURE POINT

• Even in a brief time under pressure, enough gelatin is extracted from chicken bones to give the soup good body.

Curried Coconut, Chicken, and Sweet Potato Soup

SERVES 5 TO 6

What a beautiful soup! The sweet potato chunks partially dissolve, thickening the broth and tingeing it a glorious autumn orange.

I favor bone-in chicken thighs for this recipe. They remain moister than breasts and shred very easily. Use a mild curry powder to avoid a tongue-lashing. I recommend Sun Brand Madras Curry Powder prepared by Merwanjee Poonjiajee & Sons, available in ethnic groceries and many supermarkets.

The soup is good for a light lunch or as a first course for dinner.

7 to 8 minutes high pressure plus 4-minute natural pressure release

4 cups chicken broth
One can (about 13.5 ounces) coconut milk
2 tablespoons mild curry powder, plus more if desired
$1^{1}/2$ pounds bone-in chicken thighs or breasts, skinned
$1^{1}/2$ pounds sweet potatoes, peeled and cut into $1^{1}/2$-inch chunks
2 scallions, thinly sliced (keep white and green parts separate)
$^{1}/2$ cup frozen peas
2 to 3 tablespoons chopped fresh cilantro
Salt
2 to 3 tablespoons freshly squeezed lime juice

In a 6-quart or larger cooker, blend the broth, coconut milk, and curry powder. Taste and add more curry, if needed, so the broth has a distinct curry taste. Add the chicken, sweet potatoes, and white parts of the scallions.

Lock the lid in place. Over high heat bring to high pressure. Reduce the heat just enough to maintain high pressure and cook for 7 minutes (breasts) or 8 minutes (thighs). Turn off the heat. Allow the pressure to come down naturally for 4 minutes, then quick-release any remaining pressure. Remove the lid, tilting it away from you to allow steam to escape.

Transfer the chicken to a cutting board. When cool enough to handle, shred or chop the meat.

Stir the soup to partially dissolve the sweet potatoes. (If they resist dissolving, use an immersion blender to partially puree the soup, or mash a few chunks against the side of the cooker and stir them in.)

Stir in the scallion greens, peas, cilantro, shredded chicken, and salt to taste. Bring to a simmer and cook until peas are tender, about 1 minute. Stir in enough of the lime juice to give the soup a distinct citrus edge. Ladle into soup bowls.

Variations
- Add cayenne to taste after cooking.
- Stir in 1 to 2 teaspoons freshly grated ginger along with lime juice.
- Top each portion with a dollop of yogurt.
- Before adding scallion greens, stir in 2 cups small cauliflower florets and simmer until almost tender, about 2 minutes.

Transformations (*Follow basic recipe except as noted.*)
- CURRIED COCONUT SOUP WITH SWEET POTATOES AND CHICK-PEAS (Vegetarian): Instead of chicken broth, use vegetable broth. Omit chicken and substitute 1½ cups (15-ounce can) cooked chickpeas. Cut sweet potatoes into ½-inch dice and reduce cooking time to 4 minutes high pressure. Quick-release pressure under cold running water.
- THAI-INSPIRED COCONUT CHICKEN SOUP: Instead of mild curry powder, use 1½ to 2 tablespoons Thai Kitchen brand yellow curry paste. (Watch out: it's hot!) Substitute chopped fresh basil for cilantro.

PRESSURE POINT
- If using a 4-quart cooker, divide recipe in half.

Sage-Scented Butternut Squash Soup with Herb Croutons

SERVES 4 TO 6

This soup celebrates the exuberant color and silken texture of squash. When pureed, the squash develops a rich creaminess—quite a trick for a vegetable that is fat-free.

Herb Croutons are easy to make and punctuate the smooth soup with their pleasing crunch. The soup makes an elegant first course.

---

5 minutes high pressure

FOR THE SOUP
1 tablespoon butter or oil
1¹/₂ cups coarsely chopped onions
2 cups chicken broth
1 cup water
1 teaspoon salt (omit if broth is salty)
3 pounds butternut squash, peeled, seeded, and cut into 1-inch
    chunks
¹/₄ to ¹/₂ teaspoon dried sage

FOR THE HERB CROUTONS
2 tablespoons olive oil
¹/₄ teaspoon dried sage
¹/₄ teaspoon chopped dried rosemary
¹/₄ teaspoon dried thyme
Pinch of salt
1 cup ¹/₂-inch bread cubes (white or whole-wheat)

Heat the butter in a 4-quart or larger cooker. Add the onions and cook over medium-high heat for a minute or two. Add the broth, water, salt, and squash.

Lock the lid in place. Over high heat bring to high pressure. Reduce the heat just enough to maintain high pressure and cook for 5 minutes. Turn off the heat. Quick-release the pressure or allow the pressure to come down naturally. Remove the lid, tilting it away from you to allow steam to escape.

Stir in the sage. If the squash is not very soft, cover and simmer for a few minutes. Let cool slightly. Pass the soup through a food mill (for smoothest texture) or puree using a standard or immersion blender. Reheat and adjust seasonings.

To make the Herb Croutons: Heat the oil in a nonstick skillet over medium-high heat. Stir in the sage, rosemary, thyme, and salt. Add the bread cubes and toss to coat with the oil. Cook, stirring from time to time, until the croutons become crisp, 3 to 5 minutes.

Tip: Prepare Herb Croutons whenever you have stale bread. Freeze until needed.

Variations
- VEGETARIAN VERSION: Instead of chicken broth use vegetable broth in basic recipe or any of the Transformations below.
- Instead of sage, add a pinch of freshly grated nutmeg.
- Instead of Herb Croutons, garnish with snipped chives.
- To add heat and smokiness, cook soup with 1 teaspoon of chipotle in adobo or 1 dried chipotle.
- For a richer finish, stir 1 tablespoon butter into pureed soup.

Transformations *(Follow basic recipe except as noted.)*
- SWEET POTATO SOUP: Instead of squash, use 2 pounds peeled, sweet potatoes. Season with 1/4 teaspoon ground cinnamon instead of sage. (If using a blender to puree, avoid overprocessing or soup could become gummy.) Instead of Herb Croutons, garnish with chopped toasted hazelnuts or pecans.
- CURRIED CARROT SOUP: Add 1 teaspoon whole cumin seeds along with onions. Omit squash and substitute 2 pounds peeled carrots, cut into 1-inch chunks (or use baby-cut carrots), and 8 ounces peeled russet (Idaho baking) potatoes, cut into 1-inch chunks. Cook soup with 4 teaspoons mild curry powder. Increase cooking time to 6 minutes high pressure. After pressure release, omit sage. Add more curry powder to taste plus a pinch

of sugar, if needed, to enhance sweetness of carrots. Instead of Herb Croutons, garnish each portion with a dollop of plain yogurt and a sprinkle of chopped fresh cilantro.

• CREAMY CELERY SOUP WITH FENNEL: Add 2 teaspoons whole fennel seeds along with onions. Eliminate water. Instead of squash, use 1 medium bunch (about 1½ pounds) celery that's been trimmed and cut into 1-inch chunks (include some of leaves), and 8 ounces peeled russet potatoes cut into 1-inch chunks. After cooking, omit sage.

Note: Celery is fibrous. For a supremely silky texture, pass soup through a food mill.

Rustic Leek and Potato Soup

SERVES 6

Potatoes and leeks bring out the best in each other, a point memorably made in this simple, classic soup.

For best results, use starchy russet potatoes and don't stint on salt or the leeks. For 8 cups sliced leeks, you'll need either 4 large (2-inch diameter) or 6 medium (1½-inch diameter) leeks. For slicing instructions that maximize the useful portion of each leek, see page 19.

---

4 minutes high pressure

---

1 to 2 tablespoons butter
8 cups sliced leeks (see headnote)
4 cups chicken broth
2 cups water
2 pounds russet (Idaho baking) potatoes, peeled and cut into
   ½-inch dice
1 large bay leaf
Salt
½ cup heavy cream, half and half, or milk

Heat 1 tablespoon of the butter in a 6-quart or larger cooker. Stir in the leeks, broth, water, potatoes, bay leaf, and salt to taste. (If using unsalted broth, you may need as much as 1½ teaspoons.)

Lock the lid in place. Over high heat bring to high pressure. Reduce the heat just enough to maintain high pressure and cook for 4 minutes. Turn off the heat. Quick-release the pressure by setting the cooker under cold running water. Remove the lid, tilting it away from you to allow steam to escape.

Remove the bay leaf. Stir in the cream and remaining tablespoon butter, if needed, for added richness and flavor. Adjust salt and serve.

Variations

• VEGETARIAN VERSION: Substitute vegetable broth for chicken broth.

• Garnish each portion with a heaping tablespoon of diced slab bacon that has been fried until crisp then drained.

• Omit cream. Instead of a final tablespoon of butter, stir in 2 to 3 teaspoons rosemary-infused olive oil.

Transformations *(Follow basic recipe except as noted.)*

• VICHYSSOISE: After cooking, pass soup through a food mill or puree in a blender or food processor. (Avoid overprocessing, which makes potatoes gummy.) Serve hot or cold, garnished with snipped chives.

• POTATO CORN CHOWDER: Before adding cream, stir in 1½ cups fresh or frozen corn and ½ teaspoon dried thyme leaves. Simmer until corn is tender, about 1 minute. After stirring in cream, add salt and freshly ground pepper to taste.

• POTATO-CHEDDAR SOUP: Instead of leeks, use 2 cups coarsely chopped onions. Stir in 1 cup grated sharp cheddar along with cream.

• CHUNKY FISH CHOWDER: Reduce leeks to 2 cups and potatoes to 1½ pounds. Use 6 cups Fish Broth (page 59) or bottled clam juice instead of chicken broth and water. Cook for 3 minutes under pressure. Before adding cream, stir in ½ teaspoon dried thyme leaves and 1 pound scrod (or other firm-fleshed white fish), cut into 1-inch chunks. Simmer until fish turns opaque and flakes easily, 2 to 3 minutes. Add freshly ground pepper to taste.

PRESSURE POINTS

• If using a 4-quart cooker, divide recipe in half.

• Use all but toughest leek greens in this soup. The cooker does a great job of tenderizing them, and the dark leaves add nice color.

Minestrone with Basil Pesto

This hearty Mediterranean vegetable soup is a meal in itself. For a burst of fresh herbal exuberance, spoon a small mound of pesto on top. If fresh basil is not available, make the pesto with parsley or use storebought pesto.

4 minutes high pressure

FOR THE SOUP

4 cups chicken or vegetable broth

3 cups water

1¹/₂ cups chopped leeks or onions

2 large ribs celery, halved lengthwise and cut into ¹/₂-inch slices

1¹/₂ cups cooked cannellini or navy beans (see page 331) or one can (15 ounces), drained and rinsed

¹/₂ pound green cabbage, coarsely chopped (about 4 cups)

¹/₂ cup small pasta, such as ditalini, tubettini, or orzo

2 medium carrots, peeled and trimmed (leave whole)

1 large or 2 medium zucchini, trimmed (leave whole)

One can (15 ounces) diced tomatoes (with liquid)

1 tablespoon olive oil

¹/₄ cup freshly grated pecorino romano or parmesan cheese, plus more to pass at the table

1 teaspoon dried thyme

¹/₄ to ¹/₂ teaspoon crushed red pepper flakes (optional)

Pinch of sugar (optional)

Salt and freshly ground pepper to taste

1 to 2 teaspoons balsamic vinegar (optional)

FOR THE BASIL PESTO

1 clove garlic (optional)

1 teaspoon whole fennel seeds (optional)

3 cups tightly packed basil leaves

Generous ¹/₂ cup toasted pine nuts or walnuts (see page 19)

$^1/_2$ cup grated pecorino romano or parmesan cheese (or a
combination), plus more to pass at table
$^1/_2$ teaspoon salt, or to taste
4 to 6 tablespoons olive oil

Combine the broth and water in a 6-quart or larger cooker. Over high heat, stir in the leeks, celery, beans, cabbage, and pasta. Add the whole carrots and zucchini. Pour the tomatoes and their liquid on top. Do not stir after adding the tomatoes.

Lock the lid in place. Over high heat bring to high pressure. (This may take longer than usual since the cooker is so full.) Reduce the heat just enough to maintain high pressure and cook for 4 minutes. Turn off the heat. Quick-release the pressure by setting the cooker under cold running water. Remove the lid, tilting it away from you to allow steam to escape.

Use tongs to transfer the carrots and zucchini to a cutting board. Stir the oil, cheese, and thyme into the soup. Season to taste, if desired, with the red pepper flakes, sugar, and salt and pepper. Add the vinegar, if needed, to sharpen the flavors. Dice the carrots and zucchini and stir them back into the soup.

Prepare the Basil Pesto: If using the garlic and fennel, pass them through the feed tube of a food processor while the motor is running. Scrape down the bowl of the processor and add the basil and nuts. Process until finely chopped. Scrape down the bowl again and add the cheese and salt. With the motor running, pour enough of the oil into the feed tube to create a thick (but not stiff) paste. Add more salt to taste, if needed.

Ladle the soup into large bowls. Spoon a dollop of Basil Pesto on each portion. Pass additional grated cheese at the table.

Variations
• Cook soup with 4 or more cloves peeled garlic.
• Instead of water, use broth left over from cooking beans.
• Omit beans and add $^1/_2$ pound russet (Idaho baking) potatoes cut into 1-inch cubes (peeling optional).
• Substitute chopped kale or escarole for cabbage.

• Omit pasta and add 1 cup cooked rice or wheat berries after releasing pressure.
• Instead of zucchini, add 10 ounces fresh or frozen cut string beans.
• Cook soup with an imported parmesan rind. Dice after cooking and stir into soup.

Transformation *(Follow basic recipe except as noted.)*
• CHICKEN VEGETABLE SOUP WITH BASIL PESTO: Cook soup with 1 pound boneless, skinned chicken breasts or thighs that have been cut into 1-inch chunks.

PRESSURE POINTS
• If using a 4-quart cooker, divide recipe in half.
• Cook zucchini and carrots whole to prevent overcooking.

44

Southern Split Pea Soup
with Ham

SERVES 6

Making split pea soup in the pressure cooker is a special treat: the peas dissolve into a comforting puree, saving you the nuisance of using a blender.

When shopping for split peas, look for ones with bright color. Faded peas mean faded flavor.

---

10 minutes high pressure plus natural pressure release

---

1 tablespoon butter or oil (needed to control foaming)
2 cups coarsely chopped onions
2 large ribs celery, diced
8 cups water
1 pound (2¹/₂ cups) green split peas, picked over and rinsed
1 pound smoked ham steak or pork butt, cut into ³/₄-inch chunks
2 large bay leaves
1 teaspoon salt, plus more if needed
¹/₂ to 1 teaspoon dried thyme (optional)

Heat the butter in a 6-quart or larger cooker. Stir in the onions, celery, water, split peas, ham, bay leaves, and salt.

Lock the lid in place. Over high heat bring to high pressure. Reduce the heat just enough to maintain high pressure and cook for 10 minutes. Turn off the heat. Allow the pressure to come down naturally. Remove the lid, tilting it away from you to allow steam to escape

Remove the bay leaves. Add the thyme (if using) and simmer until its flavor pervades the soup. Stir well, taking care to blend in the peas that have sunk to the bottom. Add additional salt to taste, as much as 1 teaspoon, if needed.

Tip: The soup thickens and develops a surface "skin" after standing. Stir well and thin with water or chicken broth, as needed.

Variations

• VEGETARIAN VERSION: Use vegetable broth instead of water, and omit ham. Cook soup with 2 large whole carrots, peeled, trimmed, and foil-wrapped (see page 15). After cooking, slice carrots and stir into soup. Serve with a dollop of Sour Cream–Dill Topping (pages 27 and 28).

• Instead of a ham steak, use a smoked ham hock. After cooking, shred meat and garnish soup with it.

• Add 2 to 3 teaspoons dried dill instead of thyme.

Transformations *(Follow basic recipe except as noted.)*

• GERMAN-STYLE SPLIT PEA SOUP WITH KNOCKWURST OR FRANKS: Reduce water to 5 cups and add 3 cups (24 ounces) light or dark beer. Use yellow or green split peas. Omit ham. Cook soup with 8 ounces peeled rutabaga that has been cut into ³/₄-inch dice (about 2 cups) and foil-wrapped (see page 15). After cooking, stir in the diced rutabaga. Season soup with 1 to 2 teaspoons prepared mustard. (Any bitter taste from beer will quickly vanish.) Add 1 pound knockwurst or frankfurters, halved crosswise. Replace cover and simmer until they are hot, 3 to 5 minutes. Garnish individual portions with chopped fresh dill or parsley. Serve with black bread and butter.

• CURRIED COCONUT SPLIT PEA SOUP (Vegetarian): Reduce water to 6 cups and add one can (about 13.5 ounces) coconut milk. Omit ham. Cook soup with 2 tablespoons mild curry powder and 2 large whole carrots that have been peeled, trimmed, and foil-wrapped (see page 15). After cooking, slice carrots and stir into soup. Omit thyme and stir in more curry powder, if needed. Top each portion with a dollop of yogurt and a sprinkling of chopped fresh cilantro.

• FIVE-MINUTE RED LENTIL SOUP: Substitute red lentils for split peas. Reduce cooking time to 5 minutes and quick-release pressure under cold running water. (Fair warning: Red lentils turn olive green as they cook.)

PRESSURE POINTS

• If using a 4-quart cooker, divide recipe in half.

• Do not fill cooker more than halfway when cooking split peas.

Lentil Soup with Chickpeas and Mint-Feta Pesto

SERVES 6

My goal in creating this soup was to use lentils as the earthy backdrop for a range of exciting flavors. Inspiration came from the kitchens of the Middle East, where cinnamon, allspice, and mint frequently show up in savory dishes. Since chickpeas are at home with these seasonings, I tossed them in for some textural diversity and was pleased with the result.

5 minutes high pressure plus natural pressure release

1 tablespoon olive oil
$1^1/_2$ teaspoons whole cumin seeds
2 cups coarsely chopped onions
4 cups chicken or vegetable broth
4 cups water
1 pound ($2^1/_2$ cups) dried brown lentils, picked over and rinsed
$1^1/_2$ cups cooked chickpeas (see page 331) or 1 can (15 ounces), drained and rinsed
$1/_4$ to $1/_2$ teaspoon allspice
$1/_4$ to $1/_2$ teaspoon cinnamon
Salt
1 to 2 tablespoons freshly squeezed lemon juice (optional)

FOR THE MINT-FETA PESTO
$1^1/_2$ cups tightly packed fresh mint
$1/_2$ cup tightly packed parsley leaves and tender stems
Generous $1/_2$ cup toasted almonds (see page 19)
$1/_3$ cup feta cheese
3 to 5 tablespoons olive oil

Heat the oil in a 6-quart or larger pressure cooker. Add the cumin and toast until fragrant, about 20 seconds. Stir in the onions and cook a minute longer. Add the broth, water, and lentils.

Lock the lid in place. Over high heat bring to high pressure.

Reduce the heat just enough to maintain high pressure and cook for 5 minutes. Turn off the heat. Allow the pressure to come down naturally. Remove the lid, tilting it away from you to allow steam to escape.

Stir in the chickpeas, allspice, cinnamon, and salt to taste. Simmer uncovered while you prepare the Mint-Feta Pesto:

Chop the mint, parsley, and nuts in a food processor. Blend in the feta, 3 tablespoons of the oil, and salt to taste. Add more oil, if needed, to give the pesto a creamy, medium-thick consistency.

Add lemon juice to the soup, if needed, to pick up the flavors. Ladle the soup into bowls and top each serving with a generous dollop of Mint-Feta Pesto. Pass extra pesto at the table.

Variations

• Instead of brown lentils, use French green (du Puy), Spanish pardina, or black beluga lentils.
• After adding the spices, stir in 8 ounces chopped fresh spinach. Simmer until tender, about 1 minute.

Transformations *(Follow basic recipe except as noted.)*

• LENTIL SOUP WITH CHICKPEAS AND WINTER SQUASH: Reduce lentils to 1½ cups. Add 1½ pounds butternut squash, peeled, seeded, and quartered. After pressure release, stir to break down squash and thicken soup. Omit Mint-Feta Pesto.
• PROVENÇAL LENTIL AND CHICKPEA SOUP WITH BASIL PESTO: Substitute 1 teaspoon fennel seeds for cumin. Use French green (du Puy) lentils instead of brown lentils. Instead of allspice and cinnamon, add 1 to 2 teaspoons dried herbes de Provence. Instead of Mint-Feta Pesto, use Basil Pesto (page 42).
• LENTIL SOUP WITH CORN AND CILANTRO PESTO: Add 4 whole cloves peeled garlic and ¼ pound finely chopped chorizo (or other spicy cured sausage) with onions. After pressure release, omit chickpeas, allspice, and cinnamon. Stir in 1½ cups frozen corn, 1 large roasted red pepper, seeded and diced, and 1 jalapeño, seeded and diced (optional). Substitute lime juice for lemon juice. Instead of Mint-Feta Pesto, prepare Basil Pesto (page 42) but substitute cilantro for basil.

PRESSURE POINTS

• If using a 4-quart cooker, divide recipe in half. Alternatively, cook soup with just 5 cups water and stir in remaining 2 cups afterward.

• Lentils shed their skins and lose their shape if pressure is quick-released.

• Lentils taste best when cooked with a bit of salt (such as salt given off by sausage), but more than a modest amount can retard cooking and prevent them from softening completely. The inclusion of acidic ingredients such as tomatoes or balsamic vinegar during cooking also prevents lentils from becoming fully tender.

Black Bean Soup with Avocado Salsa

SERVES 4 TO 6

I love black beans, and this inky soup shows them off at their tooth-some best. A hillock of tomato-avocado salsa offers a lively finish. The soup is hearty enough to serve for lunch or a light dinner.

25 minutes high pressure plus natural pressure release

FOR THE SOUP
1 tablespoon olive oil
1 cup coarsely chopped onions
1^1/$_2$ teaspoons whole cumin seeds
7 cups water
1 pound (2^1/$_2$ cups) dried black beans, picked over and rinsed
1 meaty ham hock
4 to 6 cloves garlic, peeled
2 large bay leaves
Salt
1 to 2 tablespoons freshly squeezed lime juice

FOR THE AVOCADO SALSA
1 ripe Hass avocado, pitted and diced
2 large plum tomatoes, seeded and chopped
^{1}/$_3$ cup chopped red onion
^{1}/$_4$ cup chopped fresh cilantro
1 jalapeño, seeded and diced (optional)
2 to 3 tablespoons freshly squeezed lime juice
Salt

Heat the oil in a 6-quart or larger pressure cooker. Add the onions and cumin seeds and cook over medium-high heat, stir-ring frequently, until the onions begin to soften, about 2 minutes. Stir in the water, beans, ham hock, garlic, and bay leaves.

Lock the lid in place. Over high heat bring to high pressure. Reduce the heat just enough to maintain high pressure and cook for 25 minutes. Turn off the heat. Allow the pressure to come down naturally. Remove the lid, tilting it away from you to allow steam to escape.

If the beans are not tender, cover and simmer until done. Remove the bay leaves. Transfer the ham hock to a chopping board. Using an immersion or standard blender, puree enough of the beans to thicken the soup and provide a creamy base. (The soup will thicken further as it stands.) Stir in salt to taste. (The soup may need as much as 2 teaspoons.)

Set the soup over very low heat. Chop the meat from the ham hock (there won't be much) and finely dice, discarding any fat and gristle. Stir the ham into the soup.

Prepare the Avocado Salsa: In a bowl, gently toss the avocado, tomatoes, onion, cilantro, and jalapeño. Season to taste with lime juice and salt.

Just before serving, stir enough lime juice into the soup to enhance and sharpen the flavors. To serve, ladle the soup into bowls and top each portion with a few tablespoons of Avocado Salsa.

Variations

• VEGETARIAN VERSION: Use 4 cups water and 3 cups vegetable broth. Omit ham hock. After cooking, add a few drops of Liquid Smoke (available in most supermarkets).
• To add smoky heat, cook soup with 1 or 2 dried chipotle chiles or season with chipotle hot sauce after cooking.
• Add 2 to 3 tablespoons rum or dry sherry after pressure release.
• Omit the ham hock and substitute 4 ounces finely diced chorizo (or other spicy cured sausage).

Transformations *(Follow basic recipe except as noted.)*

• BLACK BEAN STEW WITH TOMATOES AND AVOCADO: Reduce water to 5½ cups. Do not make salsa. Instead, increase plum tomatoes to 4. Stir chopped, seeded tomatoes, onion, cilantro, and jalapeño directly into hot beans. Season with lime juice. Serve the beans over rice. Garnish with diced avocado and additional chopped fresh cilantro. Serve with lime wedges.

• BLACK BEAN SALSA SALAD: Omit ham hock and cook beans with 1 teaspoon salt. Reduce bean cooking time to 23 minutes high pressure plus natural release. Once beans are tender but still firm, drain in batches and gently spread out on a platter to cool. Double ingredients for Avocado Salsa and toss them with beans. Stir in enough olive oil to balance lime juice, usually 3 to 4 tablespoons. Serve on a bed of greens or shredded red cabbage accompanied by tortilla chips. Serves 8.

PRESSURE POINT

• If using a 4-quart cooker, divide recipe in half.

53

Elegant Bean Soup du Jour

Puree beans to silken smoothness in their cooking liquid to create a soup that is elegant in its simplicity. For a further touch of class, swirl a ribbon of good olive oil on top of each portion.

Make the soup with any bean. If I were pushed to name my favorite, it would be large dried limas because of their potatolike creaminess. Cannellini and black beans vie for second place.

This soup makes a lovely first course, or serve it as an entree with a salad or steamed vegetable and a hearty loaf of bread.

Check Bean Timing Chart (see page 331) and add 3 minutes to maximum suggested time.

---

1 tablespoon butter or oil
1 large onion, chopped
4 cups chicken broth
3 cups water
2 large bay leaves
1 pound (2^1/$_2$ cups) dried beans (see headnote), picked over and rinsed
^{1}/$_2$ teaspoon salt (omit if broth is salty)
Extra-virgin or herb-infused olive oil (such as Consorzio rosemary oil)

Heat 1 tablespoon of the butter in a 6-quart or larger pressure cooker. Add the onion and cook over medium-high heat, stirring frequently, for 1 minute. Stir in the broth, water, bay leaves, and beans. Add the salt (if using).

Lock the lid in place. Over high heat bring to high pressure. Reduce the heat just enough to maintain high pressure and cook for the time indicated for chosen bean plus 3 additional minutes.

Turn off the heat. Let the pressure come down naturally. Remove the lid, tilting it away from you to allow steam to escape. If the beans are not meltingly tender, cover and simmer until done.

Remove the bay leaves. Pass the soup through a food mill or puree using a standard or immersion blender. (Do not overprocess or the mixture could become gummy.) Add more salt to taste. Reheat, if necessary. Ladle the soup into bowls. Spoon 1 to 2 teaspoons olive oil over each serving and swirl into a ribbon.

Tip: The soup thickens dramatically when refrigerated, but loosens up when reheated. Stir in a few tablespoons broth or water, if needed, to return it to the desired consistency.

Variations

• VEGETARIAN VERSION: Use vegetable broth instead of chicken broth.
• Cook soup with a smoked ham hock or meaty pork bone. After cooking, remove meat (there won't be much), chop, and use for garnish.
• Garnish each portion with a mound of sliced mushrooms that have been browned in butter or oil.
• Top each portion with a small mound of goat cheese.

Transformations *(Follow basic recipe except as noted.)*
• RUSTIC BEAN SOUP WITH PESTO: Puree only 1 cup of beans. Stir into soup to thicken. Garnish each portion with a dollop of Basil Pesto (page 42 or storebought).
• PASTA E FAGIOLI: Increase water to 4 cups. Cook cannellini or Great Northern beans for 28 minutes high pressure plus natural pressure release. After beans are tender, do not puree. Stir in 1 can (15 ounces) diced tomatoes, including liquid, and 4 ounces butterfly (farfalle) or other short pasta, 1 tablespoon olive oil, 1 teaspoon dried Italian herb blend (page 18 or storebought), salt to taste, and 2 tablespoons chopped fresh parsley. Cook uncovered at a gentle boil, stirring occasionally, until pasta is ready, usually about 10 minutes. Add 1 to 2 teaspoons balsamic vinegar and a pinch of sugar, if needed, to enhance flavor.

55

PRESSURE POINTS

• If using a 4-quart cooker, divide recipe in half.

• Butter or oil is needed to prevent foaming beans from clogging an excess-pressure vent.

• Do not fill cooker more than halfway when cooking beans.

Meat, Chicken, or Turkey Broth

MAKES ABOUT 1¹/₂ QUARTS

The pressure cooker produces a full-bodied meat broth in one-third the usual time because it quickly draws the gelatin out of the bones. Carrots add a touch of sweetness, while celery and onions provide a vegetal backdrop, but nothing is essential to broth making except meaty bones and water.

30 to 60 minutes (depending on type of meat) plus optional natural pressure release

Choice of Meat or Poultry	Minutes High Pressure + Natural or Quick-Release
3 pounds beef neck bones or other meaty beef bones	60
OR 3 pounds veal neck bones or other meaty veal bones	45
OR 3 pounds turkey wings and necks (or 1 meaty turkey carcass, broken into pieces)	45
OR 3 pounds lamb neck bones or other meaty lamb bones	35
OR 3 pounds chicken wings, backs, and necks	30

6 cups water, plus more as needed
1 large onion, quartered (no need to peel)
A few leek greens (optional)
1 carrot, cut into chunks
1 rib celery, cut into chunks
2 large bay leaves
¹/₄ teaspoon whole black peppercorns

Select meat or poultry (choose from the chart). Pour the water into a 6-quart or larger cooker and bring to a boil over high heat as you add the onion, leek greens (if using), carrot, celery, bay leaves, peppercorns, and your choice of meat or poultry. Add more water, if needed, to just barely cover the ingredients.

Lock the lid in place. Over high heat bring to high pressure. (It will take longer than usual since the cooker is so full.) Reduce the heat just enough to maintain high pressure and cook for the recommended time. Turn off the heat. If time permits, allow the pressure to come down naturally. Otherwise, quick-release the pressure by setting the cooker under cold running water. Remove the lid, tilting it away from you to allow steam to escape.

Allow the broth to cool. Strain into one or more storage containers. Press the solids to release all the liquid into the containers. Discard the solid ingredients. Chill the broth, then remove congealed fat. For a more concentrated flavor, boil the broth vigorously until reduced. Refrigerate for up to 4 days or freeze for up to 4 months.

Variation
• Roast bones before pressure cooking. This extra step will darken broth and intensify flavor.

Transformations *(Follow basic recipe except as noted.)*
• AFTER-DINNER CHICKEN BROTH: Instead of choosing a meat from chart, use leftover bones from 3 to 4 pounds cooked chicken. Use a small onion and add just enough water to cover. Makes 2 to 3 cups.
• CHICKEN BROTH WITH POACHED WHOLE CHICKEN: Reduce water to 2 cups. Instead of choosing a meat from chart, set a whole 4-pound chicken in cooker, breast side up. Add neck, if available. Cook for 20 minutes high pressure. Allow pressure to come down naturally. Transfer chicken to a carving board. When cool enough to handle, carve off meat and reserve for another use (such as Quick Chicken Salads, see page 158). Return bones to

cooker and add 2 additional cups water. Cook for 20 minutes high pressure. Makes about 4 cups cooked chicken and about 1 quart broth.

• FISH BROTH: Instead of using a meat from chart, use 3 pounds thoroughly rinsed fish heads and bones. Omit carrots. Reduce cooking time to 8 minutes high pressure.

• SHRIMP BROTH: Instead of using a meat from chart, use peelings from 1 pound shrimp (about 2½ cups) and just enough water to cover. Omit carrots. Reduce cooking time to 5 minutes high pressure. Makes 2 to 3 cups.

PRESSURE POINTS
• If using a 4-quart cooker, use 2 pounds meaty bones and just enough water to cover.
• If using an 8-quart cooker, include up to 4 pounds meaty bones and add an extra carrot and celery rib.
• The flavors of parsley stems and dried herbs get lost under pressure, so there is no point in including them.

Quick Vegetable Broth

MAKES ABOUT 1¹/₂ QUARTS

Since you can prepare this broth in the amount of time it takes to clean up after dinner, consider making a weekly habit of tossing vegetables into the cooker, covering them with water, and letting the PC take care of the rest. If you keep a large plastic bag of vegetable trimmings in the refrigerator and add to it as the week goes by, you'll have a good head start. Consider this recipe a rough guide to quantities.

10 minutes high pressure plus optional natural pressure release

6 cups water, plus more if needed
2 medium onions, quartered (no need to peel)
3 large carrots, cut into chunks
3 large celery ribs, cut into chunks
3 to 4 cloves garlic (no need to peel)
2 large bay leaves
¹/₄ teaspoon whole black peppercorns
8 cups chopped vegetables, including:
   Asparagus and broccoli stalks
   Corn cobs (break in half)
   Leek greens
   Lettuce (can be wilted)
   Potatoes or potato peels
   Parsnips
   Zucchini
   Mushroom stems

Pour the water into a 6-quart or larger cooker and bring to a boil over high heat as you add the onions, carrots, celery, garlic, bay leaves, peppercorns, and your choice of additional chopped vegetables. Add more water, if needed, to just barely cover the ingredients.

Lock the lid in place. Over high heat bring to high pressure.

(It will take longer than usual since the cooker is so full.) Reduce the heat just enough to maintain high pressure and cook for 10 minutes. Turn off the heat. If time permits, allow the pressure to come down naturally. Otherwise, quick-release the pressure by setting the cooker under cold running water. Remove the lid, tilting it away from you to allow steam to escape.

Allow the broth to cool. Strain into one or more storage containers. Press the solids to release all the liquid into the containers. Discard the solid ingredients. Refrigerate the broth for up to 3 days or freeze for up to 4 months.

Variation
• To enhance flavor and deepen color, cook broth with one or more of the following: 1 tablespoon good-quality soy sauce (such as Japanese shoyu or tamari), 1 to 2 tablespoons tomato paste; 1/4 cup dried mushrooms.

Alternatives to Homemade Broth

Although the pressure cooker makes it easier than ever to prepare broths from scratch, there are always times when a storebought broth or bouillon comes in handy. There is a mind-boggling array to choose from, and the difference in taste among them is quite astounding. Even if you have a brand you enjoy, I encourage you to do a comparison tasting of 3 or more brands. You may be surprised to find one you like even better.

I've switched brands over the years as new choices have come on the market. My current preference is a paste called Better Than Bouillon. The beef, chicken, and vegetable versions are now available in many supermarkets. (For distribution information, call 800-300-4210 or visit www.superiortouch.com.) Typical of all pastes and bouillons, this brand is rather salty, so I generally use no more than a generous ½ teaspoon of the paste for every cup water. A good low-salt alternative is Pacific brand chicken broth, sold in aseptic packs.

Meat, Poultry, and Fish

For additional meat, poultry, and fish recipes, consult the Index.

MEAT

Tenderizing tough cuts of meat in record time is arguably the pressure cooker's most impressive feat. That's why this chapter is by far the longest.

Tough cuts come from the hardest working parts of the animal: the shoulder, neck, shank, rump, and ribs. Fine chefs who proudly list lamb shanks and beef short ribs on their menus know that these cuts offer maximum flavor for minimal cost. Trouble is, the tough cuts typically take 2 to 3 hours of slow braising to become meltingly tender. With the help of the pressure cooker and the detailed alphabetical guide called Meat Cuts and Making Them Pressure Perfect (see page 71), you'll soon be cooking four-star meals at home in well under an hour.

KEYS TO SUCCESS

In addition to saving time, pressure cooking differs from traditional meat cooking in other significant ways. Normally when meat is braised, the longer it cooks, the more tender it becomes. In the pressure cooker, something quite different happens: the meat becomes tender relatively quickly. If cooking continues, the meat passes through a stage of toughness before becoming tender again. However, by the time it reaches this second stage of tenderness, the meat has become dry and relatively tasteless. So the first key to success is to get the timing right.

Next it's important to recognize the role that fat plays in cooking. Fat carries flavor and contributes to the juiciness and tenderness we associate with properly cooked meat. The tough cuts that do best under pressure are either marbled or layered with fat. So, for example, a well-marbled chuck roast produces tastier, juicier results than a lean top round roast.

Since meat is about 30 percent leaner than it was a decade ago, it's a mistake to trim off every last speck of surface fat before cooking. For best results, pressure cook with some of the surface fat intact. Then allow a few minutes to degrease the sauce after cooking or, if your schedule permits, refrigerate the dish overnight and remove the congealed fat before reheating.

The third and final key to success is to understand the effect of the pressure release on texture and tenderness. When you use the quick-release and the pressure drops almost immediately from 15 pounds per square inch to zero, the meat fibers compress, toughen, and become stringy and dry. Though the meat relaxes somewhat after a resting period, it is never as tasty and tender as when the pressure comes down naturally.

As a result of my experiments, I have built a natural pressure release into the cooking time of most meats. So, for example, when the recipe for Classic Beef Stew calls for 16 minutes high pressure plus natural pressure release, allow about 15 minutes for the pressure to come down naturally and you will be rewarded with "fork-tender" meat. If you are in a rush and quick-release the pressure after the 16 minutes under pressure, the beef will be undercooked and tough.

LIBERATING OPTIONS

How many times have you stood in frustration before the meat case, searching for a certain cut and finding a dazzling assortment of options—but not the piece of meat you are looking for?

As a result of having this experience too often myself, I have built meat alternatives into many of the recipes. For example, if you are in the mood for a chuck pot roast but you can't find one, the same recipe for Pot Roast with Mushroom Gravy (page 96) offers the option of cooking a veal or pork roast—or a brisket, for that matter. Curry in a Hurry (page 124) can be made with chicken, pork, or lamb, and Classic Beef Stew (page 119) can be made with lamb or oxtails. You can also check the Meat Timing Chart on page 92 and use the recipe to cook whatever is in your freezer or on sale at the supermarket.

NO MORE BROWNING!

The shape of the pressure cooker—with its high sides and relatively small diameter—is not ideal for browning whole roasts or cubed meat efficiently. Indeed, it often takes longer to brown a batch of meat than to pressure cook it. To make matters worse, browned meat sometimes loses its color under pressure.

After a variety of experiments, I decided that browning is not in keeping with the fast-forward action of pressure cooking. I began skipping the step and came to the following conclusions.

Cubed meat and pot roasts cooked in a flavor-packed sauce look and taste sufficiently appealing without an initial browning.

Meat served on the bone—such as shanks and ribs—can look a bit neglected without a rich exterior color, but still taste pretty darn good. When company's coming, give these cuts a last-minute browning under the broiler.

Roasts and other large cuts that are lightly coated with soy sauce before cooking look as if they've been browned. Though you can't actually taste the soy, it deepens the flavor and color of the sauce.

WHERE HAVE ALL THE BUTCHERS GONE?

Most of the butcher shops in my Manhattan neighborhood have closed, so I've come to rely more on supermarkets for meat. Although I generally have to seek out the supermarket's butcher, I have usually found that he is quite willing to answer questions, bone a roast, or take a special order. Don't be shy. If you don't see what you're looking for in the case, ask.

If your supermarket doesn't carry some of the cuts you'd like to try, search out a market that serves a specific ethnic population. You're likely to find more pork cuts in a Hispanic market and more lamb cuts in a Middle Eastern neighborhood. If it's better sausages you're after, try an Italian or German deli. Excellent-quality meat is also available through mail-order (see page 317).

MEAT CUTS AND MAKING THEM PRESSURE PERFECT

This guide includes descriptions, alternate regional names, cooking tips, and timings for the various cuts of beef, lamb, pork, and veal that do well under pressure. You will find it particularly useful when cooking from recipes that offer meat options, but do not give details about each cut.

The Meat Timing Chart on page 92 distills this information down to the essentials.

BEEF

Beef is America's favorite meat, and it's also one of the best meats to cook under pressure. You will be delighted with the results if you remember one thing: for tender beef, always use a natural pressure release.

Brisket

Description: A flat, boneless portion of the breast. The front section, often called the point cut, is thicker and more compact than the rear section, which is called the first cut. (Yes, this is very confusing: who's on first?) Some people favor the point cut as it is fattier and therefore remains moister and more flavorful than the first cut.

Also Called: Point cut: brisket front cut, thick cut, second cut
First cut: flat cut, thin cut

Cooking Under Pressure: Both point and first cuts do exceedingly well. Opt for a piece of relatively even thickness and leave some surface fat intact for improved flavor and texture. Set the brisket, fatty side up, directly on the bottom of the cooker. (If using an electric stovetop, place it on a rack to prevent scorching.) If the piece of meat is long, let the ends run up the sides of the cooker. If your cooker loses liquid (see page 9), add enough extra to replace what will be lost during cooking. Always use the natural pressure release.

Be forewarned: brisket shrinks to about 50 percent of its original size during cooking. As a result, the cooked meat is very dense and portions tend to be smaller than with other cuts of beef.

Meat, Poultry, and Fish

Cooking Time: Calculate cooking time for maximum thickness as well as weight. Timings below are for briskets and corned beef about 1½ inches at the thickest part. Add 5 minutes high pressure for each additional ½-inch of thickness. Add 5 minutes per inch of thickness if the brisket is frozen.

Pounds	Minutes High Pressure + Natural Release	Serves
1½ to 2	45	2 to 3
2 to 3	45 to 55	3 to 4
3 to 4	55 to 60	4 to 6
4 to 5	60 to 70	6 to 8

Testing for Doneness: An instant-read thermometer should easily slide into the thickest portion of the brisket, and the temperature should read at least 150 degrees Fahrenheit. The meat on the ends should shred very easily. If so, cut deeply into thickest part and see if the inner meat also shreds easily. If not, return to high pressure for 5 minutes and again let the pressure come down naturally. Meat that is easy to shred but tastes dry and stringy has been accidentally overcooked. A good remedy is to return the slices to the gravy and simmer until they absorb some of the liquid and become juicy, usually about 3 minutes.

Serving: Scrape off and discard any fat on the surface of the brisket. Let the brisket rest for 10 minutes while you degrease the gravy. Slice across the grain. If the direction of the grain shifts midway, rotate the meat and continue slicing against the grain. Return slices to gravy to reheat and absorb some of the gravy.

Chuck Roast, Boneless

Description: A cut of meat from the neck, shoulder, and upper part of the front leg of the steer. In this guide, I distinguish between a chuck roast (more than 2 inches thick) and a chuck steak (less than 2 inches; see below). Often the label on the roast will tell you what part of the chuck the meat has been cut from, for example, "beef chuck arm pot roast" or "beef chuck shoulder roast." If you don't already have a favorite cut, rest assured, any roast with the word "chuck" on the label does very well under pressure.

Below is a mind-boggling list of alternative names and varieties of boneless chuck roast.

Beef Chuck Arm Pot Roast, boneless
Beef Chuck Shoulder Pot Roast, boneless
    Also Called: boneless English roast, cross rib roast, honey cut, boneless shoulder roast
Beef Chuck Cross Rib Pot Roast, boneless
    Also Called: boneless Boston cut, boneless English cut, boneless cross rib roast, English roll
Beef Chuck Under Blade Pot Roast, boneless
    Also Called: boneless roast bottom chuck, California roast, inside chuck roast
Beef Chuck Mock Tender
    Also Called: chuck eye, chuck fillet, chuck tender, fish muscle, medallion pot roast, Scotch tender
Beef Chuck Top Blade Roast, boneless
    Also Called: flat-iron roast, lifter roast, puff roast, shoulder roast thin end, triangle roast
Beef Chuck Eye Roast, boneless
    Also Called: boneless chuck roll, boneless chuck fillet, chuck eye roast, inside chuck roll

Cooking Under Pressure: Among all of the beef roasts available, chuck consistently yields the juiciest, tastiest meat. (Rump roast follows a close second; see below.) Select a well-marbled roast since the intramuscular fat will keep the meat moist as it cooks. Leave some of the surface fat intact for the same reason. Due to the size and shape of the cooker, a boneless roast is the most practical.

Tie large roasts or rolled roasts with kitchen twine so they will hold their shape. The roast can sit directly on the bottom of the cooker. (If cooking on an electric stove, set the meat on a rack to prevent scorching.) For cookers that lose liquid (see page 9), add enough extra to replace what will be lost during cooking.

Cooking Time: Calculate cooking time for maximum thickness as well as weight. Timings below are for chuck roasts between 2 inches and 4 inches thick. Add 5 minutes high pressure for each additional 1/2-inch of thickness beyond 4 inches. Add 5 minutes per inch of thickness if the roast is frozen. Cooking times are calculated for natural pressure release, which is essential for attaining juicy, tender meat.

Pounds	Minutes High Pressure + Natural Release	Serves
2 1/4 to 3	35 to 45	5 to 6
3 to 4	45 to 55	6 to 8
4 to 5	55 to 65	8 to 10

Testing for Doneness: An instant-read thermometer should easily slide into the thickest portion of the roast, and the temperature should read at least 150 degrees Fahrenheit. The meat on the surface should shred very easily. If so, cut deeply into thickest part and see if inner meat also shreds easily. If not, return to high pressure for 5 minutes and again let the pressure come down naturally. Meat that is easy to shred but tastes dry and stringy has been accidentally overcooked. A good remedy is to return the slices to the gravy and simmer until they become juicy, usually about 3 minutes.

Serving: Let the roast rest for 10 minutes while you degrease the gravy. Slice the meat against the grain. Return slices to the gravy to reheat.

Chuck Steaks (Cuts under 2 inches thick)

Description: Cut from the chuck into steaks from 1/2- to 2-inches thick. As with roasts, labels indicate the part of the chuck from which they are cut, such as "chuck arm steak" or "chuck under blade steak."

Here is a list of the various types of chuck steaks and their alternate names:

Chuck Arm Steak
   Also Called: boneless arm steak, boneless round bone steak, boneless Swiss steak
Beef Chuck Shoulder Steak
   Also Called: English steak, half cut shoulder steak
Beef Chuck Blade Steak
   Also Called: blade steak, chuck steak blade cut, first cut chuck steak
Beef Chuck 7-Bone Steak
   Also Called: center cut chuck steak, 7-bone steak
Beef Chuck Top Blade Steak
   Also Called: top chuck blade steak
Beef Chuck Under Blade Steak
   Also Called: bottom chuck steak, California steak, semi-boneless chuck steak, under cut steak
Beef Chuck Top Blade Steak
   Also Called: book steak, butler steak, lifter steak, petite steak, top chuck steak
Beef Chuck Eye Steak
   Also Called: boneless chuck fillet steak, boneless steak bottom chuck, chuck boneless slices, chuck eye steak, chuck fillet steak

Cooking Under Pressure: Steaks are convenient since they require less cooking time than roasts. Select a well-marbled steak since the intramuscular fat will keep the meat juicy as it cooks. Allow 6 to 8 ounces boneless meat per person. When the bone is intact, buy extra to account for its weight.

The steak can sit directly on the bottom of the cooker. (If cooking on an electric stove, set it on a rack to prevent scorching.) For cookers that lose liquid (see page 9), add enough extra to replace what will be lost during cooking.

Cooking Time: Thickness is more relevant than weight. For steaks thicker than 2 inches and heavier than 2 pounds, use CHUCK ROAST cooking times. For frozen steaks, allow 5 additional minutes per inch of thickness.

Thickness	Minutes High Pressure + Natural Release
1/2 to 1 inch	15 to 20
1 to 1 1/2 inches	20 to 25
1 1/2 to 2 inches	25 to 30

Testing for Doneness: Meat on the edges of the steak should shred very easily. An instant-read thermometer should slide into the thickest portion of the meat with little resistance, and the temperature should read at least 150 degrees Fahrenheit. If necessary, return to high pressure for a few more minutes and again allow the pressure to come down naturally.

Serving: Let the steak rest for 5 minutes before slicing or shredding.

Chuck for Stew Meat

It's ideal to buy a whole boneless chuck roast or steak and cube and trim it yourself. This way you know that all of the meat is from the same part of animal and will cook evenly. Buy about 30 percent more than the recipe calls for to allow for the weight of fat, gristle, and bone (likely in a steak). If buying already cubed meat, make sure it is labeled "chuck." See STEW MEAT.

Testing for Doneness: Meat should be fork-tender immediately after natural pressure release.

Corned Beef

Description: Brisket that has been cured with salt and sodium nitrate (which gives the meat its characteristic red color). Nitrate-free corned beef, known as "gray" beef, is less readily available. See BRISKET for other pertinent information and timing.

Flanken

See SHORT RIBS and FLANKEN

Neck Bones

Description: Slices from the neck with relatively little meat in proportion to bone.

Cooking Under Pressure: An economical choice for making broth or to flavor a pot of beans. The meat has a rich taste, with a texture similar to shank. Look for the meatiest ones you can find.

Cooking Time: For stewing, allow 30 minutes High Pressure + Natural Release. For making broth, allow 1 hour High Pressure + Natural Release.

Oxtails

Description: As the name suggests, oxtails are the sliced tail of beef cattle. The meat is rich, gelatinous, and full-flavored.

Cooking Under Pressure: Oxtails are one of the best cuts to prepare in the pressure cooker. The meat is rich, moist, and succulent, and the bones add depth and body to the sauce. Because they are so fatty, it is best to cook oxtails the day before and chill overnight so that you can discard the congealed fat. Look for the meatiest oxtails you can find, and allow 1 pound per person.

Cooking Time: Typically a package of oxtails contains pieces of various sizes and shapes ranging from 2 ounces to 7 ounces each. 30 minutes High Pressure + Natural Release works for all.

Testing for Doneness: Meat should be falling away from the bone and shred easily.

Round Roast, Boneless

See RUMP ROAST

Rump Roast, Boneless

Description: As the name suggests, this cut comes from the rump of the cow. It contains top round, eye of round, and bottom round.

Cooking Under Pressure: Bottom round rump roasts have enough marbled fat to work well in the pressure cooker. Top round and eye of round roasts are a lot leaner and the cooked meat is rather dry. I don't recommend pressure cooking them unless you are partial to their taste and texture. See **CHUCK ROAST** for cooking times and testing for doneness.

Shanks, Cross-Cut

Description: Cut from the hind shank or foreshank, perpendicular to the bone, so each steaklike slice contains a small, round bone. Most cross-cut shanks are 1 to 1½ inches thick, although they can be as thick as 2½ inches.

Also Called: center beef shanks, cross-cut shanks, fore shanks for soup meat (bone-in)

Cooking Under Pressure: A full-flavored meat with a fine texture, beef shanks are ideal for pressure cooking and make an economical alternative to veal shanks (osso bucco). Before cooking, score skin around exterior to prevent curling. For best texture, submerge meat in liquid. One or two shanks will flavor a whole potful of beans. Shanks don't easily get overcooked, so you can time them according to the needs of the other ingredients. If one shank (usually about 1 pound) per person seems too much, cube or shred the meat after cooking and divide into portions.

Thickness	Minutes High Pressure + Natural Release
1 to 1½ inches (¾ to 1 pound)	20 to 25
1½ to 2½ inches (1 to 1½ pounds)	25 to 35

Testing for Doneness: Meat should be falling away from the bone and shred easily.

Short Ribs and Flanken

Description: Short ribs are generally rectangular (length and thickness varies) with alternating layers of lean meat and fat. Flanken are cut lengthwise rather than between the ribs so they are longer and thinner than short ribs.

Also Called: barbecue ribs, braising ribs, English short ribs, breast flanken, flanken short ribs, kosher ribs

Cooking Under Pressure: These are absolutely delicious in the pressure cooker! Various lengths and thicknesses of short ribs and flanken cook in the same amount of time. Since these cuts are quite fatty, always allow time to degrease the gravy. Better yet, cook the ribs the day before, chill overnight, and discard the congealed fat. Allow 1 pound per person for bone-in short ribs and 6 to 8 ounces for boneless.

Cooking Time: 25 minutes High Pressure + Natural Release.

Testing for Doneness: Meat should be falling away from the bone and shred easily.

Stew Meat

Your best bet is to buy a chuck roast or a chuck steak and cube it yourself; see CHUCK FOR STEW MEAT. Alternatively, buy already cut-up meat labeled "chuck stew meat." If you buy generic stew meat, it may be a mixture cut from the chuck, round, brisket, rib, and plate, and the meat may not cook to uniform tenderness. If you have no choice but to buy generic stew meat, look for a batch that is marbled with fat. For 1- to 1½-inch cubes, try 16 minutes High Pressure + Natural Release. If the meat is not sufficiently tender, return it to high pressure for 5-minute intervals plus natural pressure release until done to your satisfaction.

LAMB

Lamb—especially shoulder—is an easy-going meat to cook under pressure. It cooks to fork-tenderness quickly and is difficult to overcook, so you can use the timing that works best for the accompanying ingredients.

As with other meats, the best lamb cuts for pressure cooking are the tough cuts that you would normally braise. For best texture and flavor, your best bet is to focus on cuts from the shoulder, including chops, shoulder neck slices, and cubed shoulder meat for stew. Some people favor leg for its milder taste and availability. Because it is much leaner than shoulder, pressure-cooked leg meat can end up slightly dry.

Breast/Riblets

Description: The breast is the part of the lamb's forequarters containing the ribs. It is an oblong cut with layers of fat and lean; fat covers one side. The long, narrow ribs (riblets) are cut from the breast and vary considerably in length.

Also Called: lamb riblets, lamb riblets breast

Cooking Under Pressure: For those who enjoy lamb, the riblets make a tasty alternative to pork ribs. You are likely to purchase a package of individual riblets or a section of the breast, usually about eight ribs of varying lengths. Trim off some of the surface fat covering one side. Cut into two-rib sections. Allow 1 to 1¼ pounds (five to six ribs) per person.

All ribs do not have to be submerged in liquid to cook properly. Ribs of different lengths and thicknesses cook evenly. Arrange slabs on their sides, if necessary, to fit into the cooker. Ribs are fairly fatty, so allow time to degrease broth or, better yet, cook the day before, chill, and remove congealed fat.

Cooking Time: 20 minutes High Pressure + Quick-Release.

Ground Lamb

Description: Lean meat and trimmings from all parts of animal.

Also Called: lamb patties

Cooking Under Pressure: Ground lamb cooks quickly and evenly, giving a rich lamb taste to sauces and stews. To avoid clumps of meat in the finished dish, brown the meat and break it up before adding the other ingredients.

Leg of Lamb, Boneless

Description: A boneless roast cut from the leg.

Also Called: butterflied leg of lamb, leg of lamb boneless for shish kebab

Cooking Under Pressure: This cut would not be my first choice for pressure cooking as it is quite lean and can easily be overcooked. However, I offer a timing since some people favor its mild taste, and in some parts of the country it is more readily available than lamb shoulder.

	Minutes High Pressure + Natural Release
1¹/₂-inch cubes	6

Neck Slices (for Stew)

Description: Cross cuts of neck containing a small round bone.

Also Called: lamb stew bone-in, lamb neck for stew, lamb neck pieces

Cooking Under Pressure: This cut is economical and an excellent choice when you want a rich lamb flavor but don't require a lot of meat—such as when making a broth or risotto. A few meaty bones will flavor a potful of beans or soup. But even the meatiest bones are over 50 percent bone and grizzle, so a pound will produce only a scant ¹/₂ cup meat. Allow at least 1 pound per person if making stew.

Slices of unequal size and shape cook evenly. The cut is quite fatty, so it's best to allow time to refrigerate overnight and remove congealed fat the next day. You may substitute lamb neck in recipes calling for oxtails, using the timing below or longer. This cut is difficult to overcook.

Thickness	Minutes High Pressure + Quick-Release
2 to 3 inches	23

Testing for Doneness: The meat should be falling away from the bone and shred easily.

Serving: Serve on the bone or remove from the bone and shred.

Riblets: see BREAST RIBLETS

Shanks

Description: Shanks can come from either the back legs (hind shanks) or front legs (foreshanks). The hind shank is smaller, but meatier. Look for the meatiest shanks you can find.

Also Called: lamb trotters

Cooking Under Pressure: For lamb lovers, lamb shanks are a very economical alternative to veal shanks and an elegant choice for company. The meat is very rich. Before cooking, trim off skin and surface fat. Always allow time to degrease the gravy. Better yet, refrigerate overnight and remove congealed fat. If you cannot get shanks of the same size, time the batch for the largest shank. All of the shanks do not have to be submerged in liquid to cook properly. A 1-pound shank is just about right for one person.

Pounds	Minutes High Pressure + Natural Release
½ to 1 each	25
1 to 1½ each	30

Testing for Doneness: The meat should be falling away from the bone and shred easily.

Shoulder Roast for Stew, Boneless

Description: The boneless cut is from the blade and arm section of the shoulder. It is usually sold rolled and tied and always has an outside covering of fat and skin.

Also Called: shoulder block, shoulder roast, square-cut shoulder, boneless shoulder netted, rolled shoulder roast

Cooking Under Pressure: Purchase a boned shoulder roast, trim off external fat and skin, and cube it yourself for stew meat. If unavailable, purchase SHOULDER CHOPS, NECK SLICES, or LEG instead.

Size	Minutes High Pressure + Natural Release
1 to 1½-inch cubes	12 to 16

Shoulder Chops

Description: There are two types of chops cut from the shoulder. Lamb shoulder blade chops are cut from the blade portion of the shoulder and contain part of the blade bone and backbone. Lamb shoulder arm chops are cut from the arm portion of the shoulder and contain a cross section of round arm bone and rib bones.

Also Called: blade cut chops, shoulder blocks, shoulder chops, shoulder blade chops, round bone chops, arm cut chops

Cooking Under Pressure: Both types of chops are well marbled and excellent for cooking whole or cubed for stew. (Include bones in stew for enhanced flavor.) Browning is not necessary. When rubbed with soy sauce, cooked in a dark sauce, or both, the meat develops rich color. Avoid loin and rib chops, which are lean, tender cuts that become very dry under pressure. Allow one chop per person. When cubing for stew, buy 30 percent extra to account for the weight of bone and fat.

Avoid placing one chop directly on top of another. If cooking more chops than fit in one layer, alternate direction of layers for even cooking. All of the chops do not have to be submerged in liquid to cook properly.

Thickness	Minutes High Pressure + Natural Release
1/2 to 3/4 inch	10
1 inch	11

Stew Meat

Description: Typically, stew meat will be cut from the LEG. If available, opt for SHOULDER ROAST or CHOPS and cube the meat yourself, or use NECK SLICES.

Size	Minutes High Pressure + Natural Release
Leg: 1 to 1¹/₂ inches, cubed	6
Shoulder: 1 to 1¹/₂ inches, cubed	12 to 16

PORK

The meat from the shoulder is juicy and full of flavor. It is an excellent choice for cooking under pressure. If you have trouble finding shoulder cuts, try a butcher or supermarket that caters to a Hispanic population. Your efforts are likely to be rewarded with terrific meat and favorable prices.

The pressure cooker also does an impessive job of cooking ribs in record time. One of my friends uses the cooker to tenderize ribs and melt away all their fat before setting them on the grill.

With the exception of ribs, cuts from the loin do not fare nearly as well. Because they are so lean, pressure cooked loin cuts tend to be dry and lacking in flavor. I particularly caution against pressure cooking loin, rib, and center-cut pork chops, which yield disappointing results.

Hocks (Smoked)

Description: Cured and smoked shank bones exposed at both ends.

Also Called: smoked hock, smoked ham hock

Cooking Under Pressure: Great for imparting smoky, salty flavor. Cooking time is flexible, from 15 minutes up depending upon the recipe.

If you wish, after cooking, shred the meat and return it to the dish. One hock yields less than ¹/₂ cup meat. For a higher meat yield, use a smoked shank, if you can find it.

Ribs

Country-Style (Bone-in)
Description: Made by splitting the blade end of the loin into halves lengthwise.

Also Called: country ribs, blade-end country spareribs

Pork Loin Back Ribs
Description: Cut from the blade and center section of the loin. The layer of meat covering the ribs comes from the loin eye muscle. These ribs have less meat than SPARERIBS and COUNTRY RIBS.

Also Called: pork backribs, loin backribs, country back bones, pork ribs for barbecue

Spareribs
Description: Cut from the belly of the pig, with substantial meat on the larger end.

Cooking Under Pressure: Everyone I know who loves ribs is pleased with the pressure cooker's ability to tenderize them quickly and render much of the fat. Look for the meatiest ribs you can find and allow 1 pound per person. Cut the racks into two- or three-rib portions or cook them in one piece. Arrange the slabs on their sides, if necessary to fit them into the cooker. All the ribs do not have to be submerged in liquid to cook properly.

Cooking Time: 15 minutes High Pressure + Quick-Release. (This timing works for all types of ribs, including boneless country ribs.)

Testing for Doneness: The meat should be falling away from the bone and fork-tender.

Roasts
Shoulder Arm Picnic (Bone-in or Boneless)
Description: A cut from the arm and foreleg that contains arm, shank, and blade bones, most commonly sold with bones intact. Contains more gristle than the SHOULDER BLADE ROAST.

Also Called: fresh picnic, picnic, whole (or half) fresh picnic, pork picnic shoulder

Cooking Under Pressure: In some parts of the country, this cut is much more readily available than blade roast (butt). Before cooking, remove the skin and trim off most of the surface fat. (Leave a thin layer of fat intact for improved flavor and texture.) When cooked with the bones intact, count on about 35 percent waste. The meat is very tasty but shreds rather than slices.

If you ask the butcher to remove the bones and tie the roast, use the timing for boneless SHOULDER BLADE ROAST below. If boneless, the roast may also be cubed for pork STEW MEAT.

Pounds	Minutes High Pressure + Natural Release	Serves
3¹/₂ to 4 (bone-in, trimmed weight)	50 to 55	3 to 4
4 to 5 (bone-in, trimmed weight)	55 to 65	4 to 5

Testing for Doneness: The exterior meat should shred very easily. An instant-read thermometer should easily slide into the thickest portion of the meat, and the temperature should read around 185 degrees Fahrenheit. If necessary, return to high pressure for a few more minutes and again allow the pressure to come down naturally.

Serving: Let the meat rest for 15 minutes before shredding.

Shoulder Arm Steak/Chop

Description: Same muscle and bone structure as SHOULDER ARM PICNIC, but cut thinner.

Also Called: pork arm chop, pork picnic steak.

Cooking Under Pressure: See SHOULDER BLADE STEAK.

Shoulder Blade Roast, Boneless

Description: The top portion of the whole shoulder with the blade bone removed. The meat is usually tied with string or wrapped in netting.

Also Called: boneless Boston butt, boneless pork butt, boneless pork Boston shoulder, boneless pork butt roast, boneless Boston roast, boneless rolled butt roast

Cooking Under Pressure: This roast produces moist and flavor-packed meat. Before cooking, remove the skin and trim off most of the surface fat. (Leave a thin layer of fat intact for improved flavor and texture.) The roast may also be cubed for pork STEW MEAT.

Pounds	Minutes High Pressure + Natural Release	Serves
3¹/₂ to 4 (trimmed weight)	45 to 50	6 to 8
4 to 5 (trimmed weight)	50 to 60	8 to 10

Testing for Doneness: Exterior meat should shred very easily. An instant-read thermometer should easily slide into the thickest portion of the meat, and the temperature should read around 185 degrees Fahrenheit. (The temperature will rise 5 to 10 degrees as the roast sits.) If necessary, return to high pressure for a few more minutes and again allow the pressure to come down naturally.

Serving: Let the meat rest for 15 minutes before slicing or shredding.

Shoulder Blade Steak/Chop

Description: Cut from the SHOULDER BLADE ROAST. Contains the blade bone and several muscles.

Also Called: blade pork steak, butt steak, pork loin seven-rib cut, pork seven-rib steak, pork steak, pork shoulder chop

Cooking Under Pressure: An excellent cut of pork to cook under pressure, either bone-in or boneless. Allow one 10-ounce bone-in steak (or 6- to 8-ounce boneless steak) per person.

Thickness	Minutes High Pressure + Natural Release
1/2 to 3/4 inches	4 to 5
3/4 to 1 inch	5 to 6
1 1/4 to 1 1/2 inches	7 to 8

Testing for Doneness: Meat at the edges should shred easily and the internal temperature should read 185 degrees Fahrenheit at the thickest portion.

Stew Meat

Description: Packaged stew meat comes from either the shoulder (darker, redder meat) or the loin (lighter, pale meat) and is likely to be a mixture of the two. Because meat from the shoulder remains juicier, your best bet is to opt for a SHOULDER ROAST or CHOPS and cube it yourself.

Cooking Under Pressure: Pork is considerably less fussy than beef. Although the natural pressure release produces the best texture, quick-release produces tasty meat, too. The optimum cooking time is given below, but if other ingredients require slightly longer cooking, pork shoulder will remain juicy.

Size	Minutes High Pressure + Natural Release
1-inch cubes (shoulder)	8

Testing for Doneness: After a 5-minute resting period, the meat should be fork-tender.

VEAL

Because veal is quite lean, there are only a few cuts that do well under pressure.

Breast/Riblets

Description: Rear portion of the foresaddle containing the lower ribs. It's quite lean with some fat layers. Individual ribs (called riblets) are long, narrow cuts. The bone is substantial and there is a thick layer of cartilage between the meat and the bone, so figure on at least 50 percent waste.

Cooking Under Pressure: Veal breast is much loved by the French but an acquired taste for most Americans. It is an excellent choice for pressure cooking as the meat remains moist and has more flavor than most other cuts of veal. Look for the meatiest breast or riblets you can find. Allow 1 pound or one meaty riblet per person. If cooking a 3- or 4-pound breast section, lean it against the side of the cooker if it doesn't fit flat. All the meat does not have to be submerged in liquid to cook properly.

Pounds	Minutes High Pressure + Natural Release
3 to 4 (bone-in, trimmed weight)	40 to 50

Testing for Doneness: The meat should be fork-tender and falling away from the bone.

Serving: Either serve on the bone or pop the bone out, carve away the layer of cartilage, and serve the strip of meat on its own.

Shank

Description: A thick slice cut from the hind shank or foreshank perpendicular to the bone. Most veal shanks are about 1½ inches thick and weigh approximately 1 pound.

Also Called: osso bucco

Cooking Under Pressure: This is the best cut of veal to make in the pressure cooker, but in some parts of the country the cost has put it in the special-occasion category. Because of the high level of collagen, the cooked meat tastes rich and juicy. Allow one shank per person. Look for the meatiest shanks you can find. The meat develops deep color when cooked in beef broth or dark sauces. If necessary, put the shanks under the broiler to brown after cooking. Many people savor the marrow spread on good bread.

Pounds	Minutes High Pressure + Natural Release
3/4 to 1 1/4 each (about 1 1/2 inches thick)	18 to 20

Testing for Doneness: The meat should be falling away from the bone. After resting for 5 minutes, it should shred easily.

Serving: If the bone falls out, just pop it back in.

Shoulder Roast, Boneless

Description: This is a roast cut from the shoulder, bones removed. It is usually rolled and tied to keep its shape. Boneless shoulder roast is a good source of veal STEW MEAT; see page 91.

Also Called: rolled veal shoulder, veal rolled roast.

Cooking Under Pressure: Use either the boneless shoulder clod, or even better, the chuck, which is a fattier section that more successfully withstands the high heat of the cooker. The roast can sit directly on the bottom of the cooker. (If using an electric stove, set it on a rack to prevent scorching.) Add enough extra liquid to replace what will be lost during cooking time (see page 9). Tie large roasts or rolled roasts with kitchen twine so they will hold their shape.

Pounds	Minutes High Pressure + Natural Release	Serves
2 1/2 to 3	45	4 to 6
3 1/2 to 4	50 to 55	7 to 8

Testing for Doneness: An instant-read thermometer should easily slide into the thickest portion of the meat, and the temperature should read 145 degrees Fahrenheit. The meat on the edges should shred very easily. If so, cut deeply into the thickest part and see if the inner meat also shreds easily. If not, return to high pressure for 5 minutes and again let the pressure come down naturally. Meat that is easy to shred but tastes dry and stringy has been accidentally overcooked. A good remedy is to return the slices to the gravy and simmer until they become juicy, usually about 3 minutes.

Shoulder Steak/Chop

Description: A bone-in slice of the shoulder between $1/2$- and 1-inch thick.

Also Called: veal shoulder blade steak, shoulder veal chop, shoulder arm steak, veal shoulder steak

Cooking Under Pressure: Avoid any veal steak or chop that does not have the word "shoulder" in the label, as it will be too lean to pressure cook. For best taste and texture, leave the surface fat intact and degrease the sauce after cooking. If you cook more than one chop at a time, avoid stacking one directly on top of the other by leaning them against the sides of the cooker. A $1 1/2$-pound chop serves two.

Thickness	Minutes High Pressure + Natural Release
$1/2$ inch	6
$3/4$ to 1 inch	8

Stew Meat

Description: The cubed veal sold in packages comes from various parts of the animal and may not cook evenly.

Cooking Under Pressure: Veal would not be my first choice of meat for a pressure cooked stew as it is relatively expensive and the taste is quite mild. It is also easily overcooked.

If you do want to make a veal stew, your best bet is to buy a boned veal shoulder roast or a chop and cube it yourself. If using a roast, there will be little to no waste. If using a chop, buy about 30 percent extra to account for the weight of the bones. Allow 6 ounces trimmed weight per person.

Cooking Time: 8 minutes High Pressure + Natural Release for $1 1/2$-inch cubes.

Testing for Doneness: The meat should be fork-tender.

Meat Timing Chart

All timings are calculated for natural pressure release except as noted. When cooking frozen meat, add 5 minutes high pressure for each inch of thickness. For detailed information on individual cuts and testing for doneness, refer to Meat Cuts and Making Them Pressure Perfect, pages 71 to 91.

Pounds or Thickness	Minutes High Pressure + Natural Release	Serves
BEEF		
Brisket		
1¹/₂ to 2 pounds	45	2 to 3
2 to 3 pounds	45 to 55	3 to 4
3 to 4 pounds	55 to 60	4 to 6
4 to 5 pounds	60 to 70	6 to 8
Chuck Roast (boneless, more than 2 inches thick)		
2¹/₄ to 3 pounds	35 to 45	5 to 6
3 to 4 pounds	45 to 55	6 to 8
4 to 5 pounds	55 to 65	8 to 10
Chuck Steak (less than 2 inches thick)		
¹/₂ to 1 inch	15 to 20	6 ounces/person
1 to 1¹/₂ inches	20 to 25	6 ounces/person
1¹/₂ to 2 inches	25 to 30	6 ounces/person
Corned Beef		
1¹/₂ to 2 pounds	45	2 to 3
2 to 3 pounds	45 to 55	3 to 4
3 to 4 pounds	55 to 60	4 to 6
4 to 5 pounds	60 to 70	6 to 8
Flanken	25	1 pound/person
Oxtails	30	1 pound/person

Round/Rump Roast		
2¼ to 3 pounds	35 to 45	5 to 6
3 to 4 pounds	45 to 55	6 to 8
4 to 5 pounds	55 to 65	8 to 10
Shanks, Cross-Cut		
1 to 1½ inches (¾ to 1 pound)	25	1 shank/person
1½ to 2½ inches	25 to 35	½ shank/person
Short Ribs/ Flanken	25	1 pound/person
Stew Meat (1- to 1½- inch cubes)	16	6 ounces/person
LAMB		
Breast/Riblets	20 + quick-release	1 pound/person
Chops: *see* **Shoulder Chops**		
Leg (boneless, 1½-inch cubes)	6	6 ounces/person
Neck Shoulder Slices (bone-in stew meat)		
1 inch	16 + quick-release	1 pound/person
2 to 3 inches	23 + quick-release	1 pound/person
Riblets: *see* **Breast**		
Shanks		
½ to 1 pound	25	1 shank/person
1 to 1½ pounds	30	1 shank/person
Shoulder (boneless, for stew)		
1- to 1½-inch cubes	12 to 16	6 ounces/person

Meat, Poultry, and Fish

Shoulder Chops		
$1/2$ to $3/4$ inch	10	1 chop/person
1 inch	11	
Stew Meat: *see* **Leg and Shoulder**		
PORK		
Ribs (bone-in and boneless)	15 + quick-release	1 pound/person
Shoulder Arm Picnic (bone-in)		
$3^1/2$ to 4 pounds (trimmed weight)	50 to 55	3 to 4
4 to 5 pounds (trimmed weight)	55 to 65	4 to 5
Shoulder Blade Roast or Picnic Shoulder (boneless)		
$3^1/2$ to 4 pounds (trimmed weight)	45 to 50	6 to 8
4 to 5 pounds (trimmed weight)	50 to 60	8 to 10
Shoulder Steaks/Chops		
$1/2$ to $3/4$ inch	4 to 5	6 ounces/person
$3/4$ to 1 inch	5 to 6	6 ounces/person
$1^1/4$ to $1^1/2$ inches	7 to 8	6 ounces/person
Stew Meat (1-inch cubes)	8	6 ounces/person
VEAL		
Breast **3 to 4 pounds**	40 to 50	1 pound/person
Shanks (osso bucco)		
$3/4$ to $1^1/4$ pounds	18 to 20	1 shank/person

Shoulder Roast (boneless)		
2$\frac{1}{4}$ to 3 pounds	45	4 to 6
3$\frac{1}{2}$ to 4 pounds	50 to 55	7 to 8
Shoulder Steak/ Chop (bone-in)		
$\frac{1}{2}$ inch	6	10 ounces/person
$\frac{3}{4}$ to 1 inch	8	10 ounces/person
Stew Meat (1$\frac{1}{2}$-inch cubes)	8	6 ounces/person

Meat, Poultry, and Fish

Pot Roast with Mushroom Gravy

SERVES 4 TO 8

(DEPENDING ON SIZE OF ROAST)

Here's a dependably delicious recipe for pot roast that celebrates comfort and tradition.

Instead of browning the roast—a messy and cumbersome task in the pressure cooker—coat it lightly with soy sauce to deepen the color and enhance flavor. You won't taste the soy, I promise, and you *will* discover a cook's secret alternative to browning.

---

20 to 65 minutes high pressure (depending on type and size of roast) plus natural pressure release

---

Choice of Meat	Minutes High Pressure* + Natural Release	Serves
Boneless Beef Chuck or Rump Roast		
2¹/₂ to 3 pounds	35 to 45	4
3 to 4 pounds	45 to 55	4 to 6
4 to 5 pounds	55 to 65	6 to 8
OR		
Boneless Veal Shoulder Roast		
3 pounds	45	5 to 6
4 pounds	55	7 to 8
OR		
Boneless Pork Shoulder Roast		
3¹/₂ to 4 pounds	40 to 50	4 to 6
OR		
Boneless Turkey Breast Roast		
2 to 2¹/₂ pounds	20	4 to 6

*Frozen roasts: Add 5 minutes high pressure per inch of thickness.

1 roast (select from chart)

1 to 2 tablespoons soy sauce (preferably Japanese tamari or shoyu)

2 tablespoons butter or oil

10 ounces button, cremini, or portobello mushrooms, trimmed and
    sliced

Salt

1 cup chopped onions

1 cup chopped carrots

1 cup chopped celery

2 tablespoons tomato paste

1/2 cup dry red wine or dry vermouth

1 1/2 cups beef or chicken broth or water (some cookers need more
    liquid; see Pressure Points)

2 large bay leaves

Freshly ground pepper

2 to 3 tablespoons cornstarch (optional thickener; use 1 tablespoon
    per cup of gravy)

Trim the roast, if necessary, leaving some fat intact for improved flavor and texture. Drizzle 1 tablespoon of the soy sauce onto a plate and roll the roast in it, adding the remaining soy sauce, if needed, to coat the roast thoroughly.

In a 4-quart or larger cooker, heat 1 tablespoon of the butter. Add half of the mushrooms and sprinkle lightly with salt. Cook over high heat, stirring frequently, until the mushrooms are browned, about 3 minutes. Set the browned mushrooms aside.

Heat the remaining tablespoon butter and stir in the onions, carrots, and celery. Blend in the tomato paste and wine. Boil until half the liquid has evaporated, about 1 minute. Stir in the broth, uncooked mushrooms, and bay leaves. Place the roast in the broth, along with any unabsorbed soy sauce. Season with pepper on top.

Lock the lid in place. Over high heat bring to high pressure. Reduce the heat just enough to maintain high pressure and cook for time indicated on the chart. Turn off the heat. Allow the pressure to come down naturally. Remove the lid, tilting it away from you to allow steam to escape.

Check the roast for doneness: Use an instant-read thermometer to check the internal temperature of the roast. It should read 145 degrees Fahrenheit (beef and veal), 185 degrees (pork), and 160 degrees (turkey). If the roast requires more cooking, return to high pressure for 5 to 10 more minutes and again let the pressure come down naturally. Transfer the roast to a carving board and let it rest for at least 10 minutes before slicing.

Prepare the gravy: Discard the bay leaves. Strain the broth and degrease it in a fat separator. Puree the broth with the solids and return to the cooker. To intensify the flavor, boil the gravy vigorously to reduce. Add the browned mushrooms and salt and pepper to taste.

If you wish to thicken the gravy: In a small bowl, blend the cornstarch into an equal amount of water. Bring the gravy to a boil, then lower the heat and stir in the cornstarch mixture. Cook at a gentle boil, stirring frequently, until the gravy reaches desired consistency.

Slice the roast against the grain. Return the slices to the cooker to reheat and absorb some of the gravy. To serve, arrange the meat on a platter, pour some gravy on top, and pass the remainder in a sauce boat.

Variations

• COOK-ALONG POTATOES (6-quart or larger cooker): Add as many scrubbed (unpeeled) potatoes as will fit around roast without exceeding maximum fill line. (Cook potatoes whole with roasts that cook 35 minutes or longer. Halve potatoes for shorter cooking recipes or to fit around roast.) Serve potatoes alongside roast or make them into Creamy Mashed Potatoes, page 287.
• COOK-ALONG CARROTS : Add large, whole carrots that have been peeled and foil-packed (see page 15). After cooking, mash them with butter and season with salt and pepper.

Transformations *(Follow basic recipe except as noted.)*
• GERMAN-STYLE POT ROAST: Omit tomato paste and wine, and substitute ¼ cup red wine vinegar. When you add bay leaves, also add 6 whole cloves and 5 crushed juniper berries. Instead of

using cornstarch, thicken pureed gravy with $1/3$ to $1/2$ cup crushed gingersnaps. Serve with buttered noodles or spaetzle.

• POT ROAST WITH LIGHT TOMATO SAUCE: Reduce broth to 1 cup (may need extra in some cookers; see Pressure Points, below). Add 2 teaspoons whole fennel seeds along with bay leaves. After setting roast in cooker, pour 1 can (15 ounces) diced tomatoes (with liquid) on top. After degreasing gravy, stir in 3 additional tablespoons tomato paste, 1 teaspoon dried oregano, and 1 or 2 cloves garlic, pushed through a press. Boil to reduce and thicken. Omit cornstarch. Stir in $1/4$ to $1/2$ cup grated romano or parmesan cheese. Serve with soft polenta.

• BRISKET WITH MUSHROOM GRAVY: Substitute a 3- to 4-pound brisket for one of the roasts listed above. Cook for 55 to 60 minutes plus natural pressure release.

PRESSURE POINTS

• If using a 4-quart cooker, choose a roast that weighs $3^1/2$ pounds or less to fit below manufacturer's recommended fill line.

• If using an electric stovetop, set roast on a rack to prevent scorching.

• Since some cookers lose significant liquid during cooking, it's necessary to add enough liquid at the beginning to prevent scorching and to ensure that you will have sufficient gravy. For roasts that cook longer than 20 minutes, add as much extra liquid as will be lost during required cooking time; see page 9 for details. If your cooker does not lose any liquid, you can reduce broth to 1 cup for a more concentrated gravy.

Beef in Beer and Mustard Gravy

It's not surprising that many cultures have a signature dish cooked in beer—a savory brew that has been inexpensive and readily available since time immemorial. In this recipe, beer imparts complex, lusty undertones that combine with the meat juices to create a robust gravy. After trying it, you may join me as a convert to using beer as a cooking medium.

To cook cuts with weights other than the ones listed below, check the Meat Timing Chart on page 92.

25 to 55 minutes high pressure (depending on type, size, and cut of meat) plus natural pressure release

Choice of Meat	Minutes High Pressure + Natural Release
3- to 4-pound brisket	55 to 60*
OR	
3- to 4-pound corned beef	55 to 60*
OR	
3- to 4-pound boneless beef chuck roast	45 to 55
OR	
4 pounds oxtails	30
OR	
4 pounds beef short ribs or flanken	25
OR	
4 beef shanks, about 1 inch thick	25

*For cuts thicker than 1¹/2 inches, cook an extra 5 minutes for each ¹/2-inch additional thickness.

3 to 4 pounds beef (select a cut from the chart above)

1 cup water (some cookers need more; see Pressure Points)

3 tablespoons Dijon mustard, preferably whole-grain, plus more if needed

2 large onions, peeled and cut into thick slices

1 cup diced carrots

2 large bay leaves

1 bottle (12 ounces) beer

Salt and freshly ground pepper

2 to 3 tablespoons cornstarch (optional thickener; use 1 tablespoon
    per cup of gravy)

Trim off some of the surface fat from the selected meat, leaving some fat intact for improved flavor and texture.

In a 6-quart or larger cooker, combine the water and mustard. Stir in the onions, carrots, and bay leaves. Add the meat and pour the beer on top. Do not stir.

Lock the lid in place. Over high heat bring to high pressure. Reduce the heat just enough to maintain high pressure and cook for the number of minutes indicated in the chart for your choice of meat. Turn off the heat. Allow the pressure to come down naturally. Remove the lid, tilting it away from you to allow steam to escape.

Test for doneness: Brisket, corned beef, and roast should register an internal temperature of around 150 degrees Fahrenheit on an instant-read thermometer. Oxtails, ribs, and shanks should be falling away from the bone and the meat should be fork tender. If the meat requires more cooking, return to high pressure for 3 to 5 more minutes and again let the pressure come down naturally. When the meat is done, transfer to a platter or carving board. Let the large cuts rest for at least 10 minutes before slicing.

Prepare the gravy: Strain the broth and degrease it in a fat separator. Remove the bay leaves. Puree the solids and return the puree and broth to the cooker. If the gravy isn't sufficiently full-flavored, boil it vigorously until the flavors become more concentrated. (Any bitterness you detect from the beer will soon dissipate.) Add 2 to 3 teaspoons more mustard, if needed, plus salt and pepper to taste.

If you wish to thicken the gravy: In a small bowl, blend the cornstarch into an equal amount of water. Bring the gravy to a boil, then lower the heat and stir in the cornstarch mixture. Cook at a gentle boil, stirring frequently, until the gravy reaches desired consistency.

Slice large cuts across the grain. Return the meat to the cooker to reheat and absorb some of the gravy. Arrange on a platter or individual plates. Pour some gravy on top and serve the remainder in a sauce boat.

Variations

• COOK-ALONG POTATOES (6-quart or larger cooker): Add as many scrubbed (unpeeled) potatoes as will fit around meat without exceeding maximum fill line. (Potatoes may be cooked whole with roasts that cook 30 minutes or longer. Halve potatoes for shorter cooking recipes or to fit around roast.) Consult Creamy Mashed Potatoes, pages 287, for ways to finish cooked potatoes.
• COOK-ALONG CARROTS: Add peeled, large whole carrots (or half carrots and half parsnips) that have been foil-packed (see page 15). After cooking, mash them with butter and season with salt and pepper.
• After flavor of gravy is sufficiently concentrated, stir in ½ pound frozen small whole onions. Cover and simmer for 2 minutes before thickening gravy with cornstarch. (If not using cornstarch, cook onions until tender.) Add meat and continue to simmer uncovered until onions are tender.

Transformations *(Follow basic recipe except as noted.)*

• BEEF IN HORSERADISH CREAM SAUCE: Use beef broth instead of beer and omit mustard. Just before returning meat to gravy, stir in enough heavy cream to give sauce a rich look and taste, usually 2 to 3 tablespoons. Stir in prepared horseradish to taste, generally 1 to 2 teaspoons. Return meat to cooker to reheat. Do not boil once horseradish and cream have been added.
• BRISKET IN BEER AND CHILI SAUCE: Use a 3- to 4-pound brisket. After adding beer, pour ½ cup bottled chili sauce (such as Heinz) on top. Sprinkle with 1 packet (about ⅓ cup) dried onion soup mix.

PRESSURE POINTS
• If using a 4-quart cooker, cook 3 pounds meat in the same amount of gravy.
• If using an electric stovetop, set brisket or roast on a rack and place cooker on a heat diffuser to prevent scorching.
• Sugars in beer can cause scorching on bottom of cooker, so it's best to pour beer on top.
• Since some cookers lose significant liquid during cooking, it's necessary to add enough liquid at beginning to prevent scorching. Add as much extra water as will be lost during required cooking time; see page 9 for details.

Meat, Poultry, and Fish

Corned Beef with Cabbage and Potatoes

No need to wait until St. Patrick's Day to enjoy this classic combination. With a pressure cooker, the dish is prepared in two simple steps. First the corned beef is cooked with potatoes. While the beef is resting, the cabbage gets a brief turn in the PC.

Be forewarned: corned beef shrinks as much as 50 percent. If you are serving four and want to have some leftovers for hash or sandwiches, buy a 5-pound brisket.

Cooking time for corned beef depends as much on thickness as on weight. For cuts thicker than $1\frac{1}{2}$ inches, cook an extra 5 minutes for each $\frac{1}{2}$-inch of additional thickness.

Accompany the meal with a variety of mustards or Horseradish Sour Cream (see Variations).

104

55 to 70 minutes high pressure (depending on weight of meat) plus natural pressure release

4 cups water

2 large bay leaves

3- to 5-pound flat-cut or point-cut corned beef brisket

4 pounds large potatoes, scrubbed

1 small green cabbage (about $2\frac{1}{2}$ pounds), quartered

Pour water into a 6-quart or larger cooker. Add the bay leaves. Set the beef in the water and pour in any brine and the contents of the enclosed flavor pack (if there is one). Arrange the potatoes on top.

Lock the lid in place. Over high heat bring to high pressure. Reduce the heat just enough to maintain high pressure and cook for 55 minutes (3 pounds), 60 minutes (4 pounds), or 70 minutes (5 pounds). Turn off the heat. Allow the pressure to come down naturally. Remove the lid, tilting it away from you to allow steam to escape.

Transfer the potatoes to a large platter and tent with aluminum foil to keep warm. Check the beef for doneness. It should measure around 150 degrees Fahrenheit on an instant-read thermometer inserted into the thickest part, and the meat on the ends should shred very easily. If necessary, return to high pressure for 5 to 10 more minutes. When done, transfer the beef to a carving board and let rest at least 10 minutes before slicing.

If there is less than 1 cup liquid remaining in the cooker, add enough water to equal 1 cup. Set over high heat as you add the quartered cabbage to the liquid.

Lock the lid in place. Over high heat bring to high pressure. (It may take longer than usual since the pot is so full.) Reduce the heat just enough to maintain high pressure and cook for 3 minutes. Turn off the heat. Quick-release the pressure. Remove the lid, tilting it away from you to allow steam to escape.

Remove the cabbage with tongs, drain it, and set on the platter. Scrape off and discard any surface fat on the corned beef. Slice the meat across the grain. If the direction of the grain shifts, turn the meat and continue slicing across the grain. If the meat seems dry or needs reheating, simmer for a few minutes in the broth. Arrange the slices on the platter and have a great feast!

Variations

• Use half beer and half water.

• COOK-ALONG BEETS: Use 4 scrubbed medium beets instead of or (if space permits) in addition to potatoes. First trim off root end and stems, taking care not to expose flesh. Arrange beets, stem side up, around potatoes. (Do not exceed maximum fill line recommended by manufacturer.) After cooking, peel and quarter beets and serve on the side—or use to make red flannel hash.

• Serve the corned beef with Horseradish Sour Cream: Blend 1 cup sour cream with 1/4 cup prepared horseradish and 1 teaspoon Dijon mustard. Add more horseradish and mustard to taste.

PRESSURE POINTS

• If using a 4-quart cooker, choose a 3-pound brisket and add only as many potatoes as will fit below manufacturer's recommended fill line.

• It's fine if ends of brisket run up the sides of cooker to fit.

Delectable Meats in
Gingered Plum Sauce

SERVES 4

Although simple to prepare, this complex, fruity sauce—made with prunes, soy sauce, and fresh ginger—cloaks meat with elegance. It is particularly suited to the rich, fatty cuts of beef, pork, and lamb suggested here.

It's also divine on chicken. The recipe creates ample sauce, enough to drizzle on top of potatoes, rice, or barley. Orzo Risotto with Wild Mushrooms (page 230) also makes a fine accompaniment.

8 to 65 minutes high pressure (depending upon choice of meat) plus natural pressure release

Choice of Meat	Minutes High Pressure + Release Method	Serves
4 pounds meaty spareribs or country-style ribs, divided into three-rib portions	15 + quick-release	4
OR 4 meaty lamb shanks (8 to 12 ounces each)	25 + natural release	4
OR 4 pounds meaty oxtails	30 + natural release	4
OR 4 pounds meaty beef short ribs or flanken	25 + natural release	4
OR 3½- to 4-pound beef brisket	55 to 60 + natural release	4 to 6

OR 3¹/₂- to 4-pound boned, rolled pork shoulder roast or picnic shoulder	45 to 50 + natural release	5 to 6
OR 4 veal shanks (12 to 16 ounces each), about 1 inch thick	18 to 20 + natural release	4
OR 4 to 6 bone-in shoulder (not loin or rib) lamb chops, about ³/₄ inch thick	10 + natural release	4 to 6
OR 4 pounds bone-in chicken breast halves and/ or thighs, skinned	8 + natural release	4

3¹/₂ to 4 pounds meat or chicken (select a variety and cut from the chart above)

1¹/₂ cups chicken or beef broth (some cookers need more; see Pressure Point)

2 cups coarsely chopped onions or leeks

1 tablespoon balsamic vinegar, plus more if needed

1 to 2 tablespoons soy sauce (preferably Japanese tamari or shoyu)

1¹/₄ cups tightly packed pitted prunes

1 to 2 teaspoons grated fresh ginger

Salt and freshly ground pepper

¹/₄ cup thinly sliced scallions, for garnish

Trim most of the surface fat off the meat, leaving some intact for improved flavor and texture.

In a 6-quart or larger cooker, combine the broth, onions, and vinegar.

Drizzle 1 tablespoon of the soy sauce on a large plate and turn the meat in it to coat thoroughly. Use the remaining soy sauce, if needed. Place the meat in the cooker along with any unabsorbed soy sauce. Scatter the prunes on top.

Lock the lid in place. Over high heat bring to high pressure.

Reduce the heat just enough to maintain high pressure. Cook for the number of minutes indicated on the chart. Turn off the heat. Use quick or natural pressure release, as directed. Remove the lid, tilting it away from you to allow steam to escape.

Test for doneness: The meat should be fork-tender. (For tips on judging doneness of individual meats, see pages 71 to 91.) If necessary, return to high pressure for another 1 to 5 minutes and release pressure as directed. Transfer the meat to a platter or cutting board. (Let brisket or pork roast rest for 10 minutes before slicing.)

Finish the sauce: If necessary, strain the broth and degrease it in a fat separator, or refrigerate overnight and discard the congealed fat. Return the degreased broth and solids to the cooker. (If you wish, use an immersion blender to puree the sauce, coarse or fairly smooth, as desired.) To thicken the sauce and intensify the taste, boil over high heat, stirring frequently, until reduced and slightly syrupy, usually 3 to 5 minutes. Add more vinegar, if needed, to balance the sweetness and sharpen the flavors. Stir in the ginger to taste. Season with salt and pepper.

Return the meat to the cooker to reheat and coat completely with the sauce. Transfer to a platter or individual plates and garnish with the sliced scallions.

Variations
• COOK-ALONG POTATOES: Add potatoes as space permits. Consult Vegetables A to Z (see page 263) for advice on cutting suitable to timing for your chosen meat.
• After sauce reaches the desired consistency, add 1/2 pound frozen small white onions. Cover and cook until tender, 2 to 3 minutes.
• Instead of fresh ginger and scallions, season with a pinch or two of cinnamon.
• Instead of vinegar, finish sauce with a tablespoon or two of freshly squeezed lemon juice and some lemon zest.
• Excess pureed sauce makes a terrific barbecue slather.

Transformation *(Follow basic recipe except as noted.)*

• DELECTABLE MEATS WITH AN ASIAN ACCENT: After sauce reaches desired consistency, season with soy sauce instead of salt. Along with ginger, add 1 to 3 teaspoons toasted sesame oil.

PRESSURE POINT

• Some cookers lose significant liquid during cooking so it's necessary to add enough extra liquid at the beginning to prevent scorching and to ensure that you will have sufficient sauce. For meats that cook 20 minutes or longer, add as much extra broth as will be lost during required cooking time; see page 9 for details.

Beer-Braised Ribs in Barbecue Sauce

SERVES 4

Calling all rib lovers—I have good news! The cooker tenderizes ribs and melts away fat in a flash. Beer makes a lively, gently sweet cooking medium.

After cooking the ribs, glaze them with barbecue sauce. Since I'm a city girl, I do this final step in the oven. If you are lucky enough to have a grill, finish them on the open fire.

Although most people think of pork spare ribs when the subject of barbecue comes up, beef and (very economical) lamb ribs are also delicious prepared this way. Figure on one pound of ribs per person for an entree portion. If you'd like to cook more than will safely fit in your cooker, you can use the same beer broth for a second batch.

Serve the ribs with cole slaw, Last-Minute Potato Salad (page 289), or both.

15 to 25 minutes high pressure (depending on type of ribs)

Choice of Ribs	Minutes High Pressure + Release Method
4 pounds pork spare ribs, country-style ribs, or baby back ribs	15 + quick-release
OR 4 pounds lamb ribs (often labeled "lamb breast" or riblets)	20 + quick-release
OR 4 pounds beef short ribs or flanken	25 + natural release

To Cook the Ribs

4 pounds ribs (select from the chart)
1 bottle beer (12 ounces)
1 cup water
2 tablespoons cider or red wine vinegar

For the Barbecue Sauce

1 cup bottled catsup or chili sauce
1/4 cup molasses
3 tablespoons Dijon mustard, preferably whole-grain
1 tablespoon chili powder
2 tablespoons cider or red wine vinegar
2 tablespoons soy or Worcestershire sauce
2 teaspoons Tabasco sauce or other hot sauce
1 teaspoon granulated or powdered garlic
A few drops of Liquid Smoke (optional)

To cook the ribs: Slice the pork and lamb ribs into three- or four-rib portions. If they are already divided into single ribs, that's fine, too.

Pour the beer and water into a 6-quart or larger cooker. Add the vinegar. Arrange the ribs in the cooker so that none are directly on top of each other. (You can lean some ribs against the side of the cooker, but do not fill the cooker more than two-thirds full.)

Lock the lid in place. Over high heat bring to high pressure. (It may take longer than usual since the cooker is so full.) Reduce the heat just enough to maintain high pressure and cook for the time indicated on the chart above, then release pressure as directed. Turn off the heat. Remove the lid, tilting it away from you to allow steam to escape.

Preheat the oven to 400 degrees Fahrenheit. Use tongs to transfer the ribs to a rack set over a foil-lined baking sheet. (If you wish, reserve the broth for another use.)

To prepare the Barbecue Sauce: Combine all of the ingredients in a bowl or storage container. Adjust balance of flavors to suit your taste. (The sauce may seem overly sweet, but that sweetness will diminish during cooking.)

Brush the Barbecue Sauce on both sides of the ribs. Roast until browned and crisp on top, 7 to 10 minutes. Turn ribs over and baste with additional Barbecue Sauce. Continue to roast until second side is deeply browned, about 5 minutes more. Brush a little extra sauce onto each rib and serve.

Refrigerate any extra Barbecue Sauce for up to 1 month. Refrigerate leftover broth for up to 3 days or freeze for up to 4 months.

Variation
• Use your favorite storebought barbecue sauce instead of home-made.

Transformations *(Follow basic recipe except as noted.)*
• RIBS WITH HONEY-MUSTARD SAUCE: Instead of Barbecue Sauce, use Honey-Mustard Sauce: Blend ¹/₂ cup whole-grain mustard, ¹/₂ cup honey, ¹/₄ cup balsamic vinegar, ¹/₄ cup soy sauce (preferably Japanese tamari or shoyu), and 1 teaspoon granulated garlic.
• RIBS WITH SESAME HONEY-MUSTARD SAUCE: Prepare Honey-Mustard Sauce, above. Blend in 2 to 3 teaspoons toasted sesame oil and 2 teaspoons sesame seeds (optional).

113

PRESSURE POINTS
• If using a 4-quart cooker, prepare only as many ribs as will fit beneath maximum fill line, usually no more than 3 pounds.
• If using an 8-quart cooker, prepare up to 6 pounds ribs.
• Ribs do not have to be completely submerged in liquid to cook properly.

Sauerkraut with Smoked Pork Chops, Sausage, Potatoes, and Dill–Sour Cream Sauce

SERVES 4

Toss potatoes into the cooker with sauerkraut and kielbasa to create a quick, one-pot meal inspired by the robust Alsatian dish *chacroute*. Add smoked pork chops and bratwurst after releasing the pressure since they require no more than thorough heating.

Mustard is the traditional condiment to serve, but I prefer a simple Dill–Sour Cream Sauce, which mellows out the assertive flavors in the dish.

---

3 minutes high pressure

---

2 pounds sauerkraut, drained

2 tablespoons butter

2 cups thinly sliced onions

1 cup beer (it can be flat)

$3/4$ to 1 pound kielbasa or other precooked sausage, cut into 2-inch chunks

2 large apples, quartered, and cored (no need to peel)

2 teaspoons caraway seeds

$1^1/2$ pounds waxy red-skinned potatoes, scrubbed and cut into 1-inch chunks

4 smoked pork chops

2 to 4 bratwurst, halved crosswise

One or more varieties of mustard, for serving

FOR THE DILL–SOUR CREAM SAUCE

$1/2$ cup sour cream

1 tablespoon water

$1/2$ teaspoon dried dill

Rinse the sauerkraut if it is too salty. Drain well.

Heat the butter in a 6-quart or larger cooker. Add the onions and cook over medium heat, stirring occasionally, until the onions are lightly browned, 3 to 5 minutes.

Add the beer and stir well to scrape up any browned bits stuck to the bottom of the cooker. Stir in the sauerkraut, kielbasa, apples, caraway seeds, and potatoes.

Lock the lid in place. Over high heat bring to high pressure. Reduce the heat just enough to maintain high pressure and cook for 3 minutes. Turn off the heat. Quick-release the pressure under cold running water. Remove the lid, tilting it away from you to allow steam to escape.

Stir the sauerkraut mixture well. Bury the pork chops and bratwurst under the sauerkraut. Set (but do not lock) the lid in place and simmer until the chops and bratwurst are heated and the potatoes are tender, 3 to 5 minutes.

Meanwhile, prepare the Dill–Sour Cream Sauce: blend the sour cream, water, and dill in a small bowl. Serve on the side.

Variations
• Before browning onions, brown 10 ounces sliced mushrooms in 1 tablespoon butter. Set aside to be added with bratwurst.
• Use 1 teaspoon crushed juniper berries instead of (or in addition to) caraway seeds.
• Substitute fully cooked chicken or turkey sausage for bratwurst.
• Increase kielbasa to 2 pounds and omit pork chops and bratwurst.

Transformation *(Follow basic recipe except as noted.)*
• SAUERKRAUT WITH BEANS AND KIELBASA: Use bean cooking liquid or unsalted chicken broth instead of beer. Cook sauerkraut with 1½ cups cooked white beans (or a 15-ounce can, rinsed and drained) and 1½ pounds kielbasa. Omit potatoes and bratwurst. Pork chops are optional.

Lamb Shanks with White Beans

For tenderizing beans and tough cuts like shanks, the pressure cooker can't be beat. When you prepare this classic combination together, the beans absorb the lamb's robust flavor and taste as if they've been simmering all day.

Lamb shanks vary in size from ½ to 1½ pounds. The size you buy will determine how many you can fit in your cooker (see Pressure Points). If you plan to serve the shanks on the bone, allow one per person. Otherwise, carve the meat from two large shanks and divide it among four portions. Look for the meatiest shanks you can find. A crisp green salad provides a refreshing contrast to the mellow textures of this dish.

---

28 minutes high pressure plus natural pressure release

---

1 tablespoon oil

1½ cups coarsely chopped onions or leeks

½ cup diced carrot

6 cups water

¾ teaspoon salt

2 large bay leaves

1¾ cups dried Great Northern or cannellini beans, picked over and rinsed

2 large (¾ to 1½ pounds each) or 4 small (about ½ pound each) lamb shanks, well trimmed

Freshly ground pepper

1 to 2 teaspoons balsamic vinegar

1 to 2 teaspoons fresh chopped rosemary

Sprigs of fresh rosemary, for garnish

Heat the oil in a 6-quart or larger cooker. Add the onions and carrot and cook over medium-high heat, stirring occasionally for a minute or two. Add the water, salt, bay leaves, beans, and shanks.

Lock the lid in place. Over high heat bring to high pressure.

Reduce the heat just enough to maintain high pressure and cook for 28 minutes. Turn off the heat. Allow the pressure to come down naturally. Remove the lid, tilting it away from you to allow steam to escape.

Discard any shriveled, uncooked beans that are floating on top or adhering to the shanks. Test the shanks and beans for doneness: the meat should be fork-tender and falling away from the bone. The beans should be uniformly soft. If the shanks and beans both require more cooking, return to high pressure for 3 to 5 more minutes and again let the pressure come down naturally. If only the beans require more cooking, remove the shanks and return the beans to high pressure. If only the shanks require more cooking, drain the beans and return the shanks to high pressure in the bean broth.

Transfer the shanks to a cutting board and season them well with salt and pepper. Remove the bay leaves. Drain the beans and degrease the broth in a fat separator. Return the beans and broth to the cooker. Season the beans with the vinegar, rosemary, salt and pepper. Reheat with the beans if necessary. Carve the shanks if dividing the meat among portions; otherwise leave them whole. Divide the beans among four large, shallow bowls and set the meat on top. Garnish each with a sprig of rosemary.

Variations

• COOK-ALONG GARLIC: Cook beans with a whole head of garlic (discard loose, papery skin). Remove garlic after cooking. To intensify garlic flavor, squeeze out some of the flesh and stir it into beans. Alternatively, reserve garlic for another use, such as spreading on bread.
• COOK-ALONG RUTABAGA (6-quart and larger cookers): Wrap 1 pound peeled rutabaga in heavy-duty aluminum foil. After cooking, dice rutabaga and stir into beans.
• Stir a few diced plum tomatoes into cooked beans.
• In addition to rosemary, season beans with lemon zest and 1/4 cup chopped fresh parsley.

Transformations *(Follow basic recipe except as noted.)*

• BEAN AND LAMB SHANK CASSEROLE: Pour beans and 1 to 2 cups broth into a large, heatproof casserole. Set shanks on top. If mixture is not already hot, heat in a microwave or a 425-degree Fahrenheit oven. Then set under broiler until beans are bubbly and shanks are lightly browned.

• OSSO BUCCO WITH WHITE BEANS: Instead of lamb shanks, use 4 veal shanks (about 1 pound each) tied with kitchen twine. Give beans a head start by cooking them for 8 minutes high pressure. Quick-release pressure and add shanks. Return to high pressure and cook for 20 minutes plus natural pressure release. Omit rosemary. Garnish with a sprinkle of Gremolata made by chopping together 1 cup tightly packed fresh parsley leaves, zest of 1 large lemon, and 1 clove garlic. Serves 4.

• SHRIMP WITH WHITE BEANS: Omit lamb shanks. Reduce water to 3 cups and add 3 cups chicken or vegetable broth. After cooking beans, stir in 1½ pounds peeled, medium shrimp that have been halved lengthwise. Simmer beans until shrimp are cooked, about 1 minute. Instead of vinegar, stir in 1 tablespoon freshly squeezed lemon juice. Instead of rosemary, stir in 2 tablespoons chopped fresh parsley, and 1 teaspoon each lemon zest and chopped fresh thyme. Garnish each portion with additional parsley. Serves 4.

PRESSURE POINTS

• If using a 4-quart cooker, prepare 2 lamb shanks with 1 cup leeks, ½ cup carrot, 1¼ cups beans, 4 cups water, and ¼ teaspoon salt.

• If using a 6-quart cooker, prepare 4 small or 2 large shanks, as per recipe.

• If using an 8-quart cooker, prepare up to 6 small or 4 large lamb shanks. Increase beans to 1 pound and water to 7 cups.

• Using a natural pressure release prevents bean skins from splitting. Though it is optional for lamb and veal shanks, a natural pressure release generally results in more tender meat.

Classic Beef Stew

Though I've been pressure cooking for more than fifteen years, it still amazes me that this magical appliance can transform tough cubes of meat into a fork-tender stew in under a half hour.

16 minutes high pressure plus natural pressure release

1 tablespoon olive oil
1 1/2 cups coarsely chopped onions
3/4 cup finely diced celery
3/4 cup finely diced carrot
1/2 cup red wine
2 tablespoons tomato paste
1 cup beef broth
2 large bay leaves
1/2 teaspoon salt (omit if broth is salty)
3 pounds beef chuck, cut into 1- or 1 1/2-inch chunks
1 to 2 teaspoons fresh thyme or 1/2 to 1 teaspoon dried
Freshly ground pepper
2 to 3 teaspoons balsamic or other red wine vinegar (optional)
2 tablespoons cornstarch (optional)
1 cup frozen peas
2 tablespoons chopped fresh parsley, for garnish

Heat the oil in a 4-quart or larger cooker. Stir in the onions, celery, and carrot. Cook over medium-high heat, stirring frequently, for 1 minute. Stir in the wine and tomato paste and cook until the liquid is reduced by half. Stir in the broth, bay leaves, and salt. Add the beef.

Lock the lid in place. Over high heat bring to high pressure. Reduce the heat just enough to maintain high pressure and cook for 16 minutes. Turn off heat. Allow the pressure to come down naturally, about 10 minutes. Remove the lid, tilting it away from you to allow steam to escape.

Skim off any fat that rises to the surface or degrease the broth in a fat separator. Discard the bay leaves. Stir in the thyme and salt and pepper to taste. Add a little vinegar to intensify the flavors.

If you wish to thicken the stew, blend the cornstarch into 2 tablespoons water. Bring the stew to a boil, then lower the heat and stir in the cornstarch mixture. Cook at a gentle boil, stirring frequently, until the stew reaches the desired consistency, usually 1 to 2 minutes. Stir in the peas. Let the stew rest for 3 to 5 minutes before serving.

Variations

• COOK-ALONG CARROTS: Wrap 3 large, peeled carrots in a foil-packet (see page 15) and add along with the beef. After cooking, cut into chunks and stir into stew.

• COOK-ALONG POTATOES: Set 4 to 6 medium potatoes, scrubbed or peeled, on top of stew. After cooking, serve potatoes either alongside stew or cube and stir in. (Potatoes will quickly absorb much of liquid and thicken stew, obviating need for cornstarch.)

• Instead of red wine, use ¼ cup balsamic or other red wine vinegar.

• Season stew with 1 to 2 teaspoons horseradish instead of balsamic vinegar.

• After degreasing broth, stir in 8 ounces frozen small whole onions or 12 ounces frozen cut string beans. Simmer until they are tender, 3 to 5 minutes.

Transformations *(Follow basic recipe except as noted.)*

• RUSTIC LAMB STEW: Use lamb broth or beer instead of beef broth. Instead of beef chuck, substitute 3 pounds boned, cubed lamb shoulder. Cook for 12 minutes high pressure plus natural release.

• HEARTY BEEF CHILI: Omit wine. Stir 3 tablespoons chili powder into broth. After adding beef, pour contents of 1 can (15 ounces) diced tomatoes with green chiles on top. Do not stir after adding tomatoes. Instead of thyme, add ¼ cup chopped fresh cilantro. Omit frozen peas and parsley garnish. If you wish, add 1 can (15 ounces) drained red kidney beans. Serve chili over rice and garnish with a dollop of sour cream or grated cheddar cheese.

• OXTAIL STEW (6-quart or larger cooker): Substitute 4 to 5 pounds oxtails for cubed beef. (For cookers that lose liquid, increase broth as needed to prevent scorching; see page 9). Cook for 30 minutes high pressure plus natural pressure release. Serves 4 to 6.

Goulash with Potatoes

SERVES 6

Goulash is stew with an Eastern European attitude supplied by abundant sweet, ruddy paprika and pungent, warming caraway seeds. Both seasonings are essential to a traditional goulash. You can make the goulash with beef, veal, or pork.

8 to 16 minutes high pressure (depending upon choice of meat) plus natural pressure release

3 slices bacon, finely chopped
2 cups coarsely chopped onions
2 tablespoons red wine vinegar
2 tablespoons tomato paste
1/4 cup sweet paprika
2 teaspoons caraway seeds
1 1/2 cups beer or broth
2 large bay leaves
1 teaspoon salt (omit if using salty broth)
3 pounds beef chuck, veal shoulder, or pork shoulder cut into 1-inch chunks
2 pounds medium red-skinned potatoes, peeled or scrubbed and halved
1/2 to 1 teaspoon dried thyme or marjoram
Salt and freshly ground pepper
1/2 cup sour cream, for garnish

Heat a 4-quart or larger cooker. Add the bacon and cook over medium-high heat, stirring occasionally, until it begins to render some of its fat. Stir in the onions and continue cooking until they begin to soften, about 1 minute.

Stir in the vinegar, tomato paste, paprika, and caraway seeds. Cook for 30 seconds, stirring constantly. Stir in the beer, taking care to scrape up any browned bits sticking to the bottom of the cooker. Add the bay leaves, salt, and meat. Set the potatoes on top.

Lock the lid in place. Over high heat bring to high pressure. Reduce the heat just enough to maintain high pressure and cook for 16 minutes (beef) or 8 minutes (veal or pork). Turn off the heat. Allow the pressure to come down naturally. Remove the lid, tilting it away from you to allow steam to escape.

Skim off the fat that rises to the surface or degrease the cooking liquid in a fat separator. Remove the bay leaves. Stir in the thyme or marjoram and season well with salt and pepper. Let the stew rest for about 5 minutes. (The potatoes will absorb some of the liquid and thicken the stew.) Spoon the goulash into lipped plates or large, shallow bowls. Top each portion with a dollop of sour cream.

Variations

• COOK-ALONG CARROTS: Wrap 3 peeled carrots, halved lengthwise, in a foil-packet (see page 15) and add along with meat. After cooking, cut into chunks and stir into stew.

• Cook stew with 1 pound drained sauerkraut. (Rinse sauerkraut if very salty.)

• Omit potatoes. Serve goulash over spaetzle or broad egg noodles.

• Add 1 tablespoon hot paprika in addition to sweet paprika.

• After pressure release, stir in a 10-ounce package frozen green beans. Simmer until beans are tender, about 5 minutes.

Transformation *(Follow basic recipe except as noted.)*

• CHICKEN PAPRIKASH WITH POTATOES: Use 1 cup chicken broth instead of beer. Add 6 ounces sliced mushrooms. Instead of meat, use 4 pounds bone-in, skinned chicken breast halves or thighs. Cook for 8 minutes high pressure plus 4-minute natural pressure release, then release any remaining pressure. Blend 1 cup cooking liquid with ½ cup sour cream. Stir mixture back into cooker. Add 1 or 2 tablespoons freshly squeezed lemon juice, if needed, to intensify flavors. Garnish with chopped fresh dill instead of sour cream.

Meat, Poultry, and Fish

Curry in a Hurry

SERVES 4 TO 6

"This recipe is too easy and too good to be true," said one of my pressure cooking cronies, who now makes a weekly batch of this curry for her family. By varying her choice of meat or chicken, she makes it seem like a new dish each time.

To get lots of flavor in a flash, the recipe relies upon Patak's Mild Curry Paste, an inexpensive and zesty blend of more than a dozen ingredients that has become a staple in my kitchen. Patak's is available in many supermarkets, and you can certainly find it in Indian and international groceries.

While you're shopping, pick up some of Patak's Mango Chutney and Eggplant (Brinjal) Pickle to serve alongside. Spoon the abundant curry-bright sauce over rice.

8 to 12 minutes high pressure (depending upon choice of meat) plus natural release

Choice of Chicken or Meat	Minutes High Pressure + Release Method
3 pounds bone-in chicken thighs and/or breast halves, skinned	8 + 4-minute natural release, then quick-release
OR 2 pounds boneless pork shoulder, trimmed and cut into 1-inch chunks	8 + natural release
OR 2 pounds boneless beef chuck, trimmed and cut into 1-inch chunks	8 + natural release
OR 2 pounds boneless lamb shoulder, trimmed and cut into 1-inch chunks	12 + natural release

1 cup water

4 tablespoons Patak's Mild Curry Paste (curry powder doesn't produce good results)

1 medium onion, coarsely chopped

3 pounds chicken or 2 pounds meat (select a cut from the chart)

1 cup plain yogurt (regular or low-fat)

$1^{1}/_2$ cups frozen peas (rinse away any ice crystals)

3 tablespoons chopped fresh cilantro

Salt

Pour the water into a 4-quart or larger cooker and blend in the curry paste. Set over high heat and add the onion and chicken or meat of your choice.

Lock the lid in place. Over high heat bring to high pressure. Reduce the heat just enough to maintain high pressure and cook for the time indicated in the chart. Turn off the heat. Allow the pressure to come down naturally. (If cooking chicken, release any pressure remaining after 4 minutes.) Remove the lid, tilting it away from you to allow steam to escape. If the chicken or meat is not tender, cover and simmer until done.

If necessary, skim off the fat that rises to the surface or degrease the broth in a fat separator. Blend the yogurt into 1 cup of the broth. Stir the peas into the curry and simmer until they are defrosted, about 1 minute. Turn off the heat and stir the yogurt mixture into the curry. Stir in the cilantro and salt to taste. Serve on lipped plates or in large, shallow bowls over rice.

Variations

• COOK-ALONG CASSEROLE WHITE RICE (6-quart or larger cooker): See page 183.

• Instead of Mild Curry Paste, substitute Patak's Hot Curry Paste. Start with 3 tablespoons and add more to taste.

• Use coconut milk instead of water.

• Stir in $^{1}/_3$ cup raisins after pressure release.

• Garnish with raw or roasted cashews.

• Toast one or more of the following spices (see page 19): 1 tablespoon black mustard seeds, 1 teaspoon whole fennel seeds, and 1 teaspoon whole cumin seeds. Stir them into curry along with yogurt. The extra bit of crunch and flavor makes this dish even more memorable.

Transformation *(Follow basic recipe except as noted.)*
• MEAT AND POTATO CURRY: Scrub or peel 1½ pounds potatoes and cut into 1½-inch chunks. Cook along with curry.

PRESSURE POINT
• Avoid cooking yogurt under pressure. It tends to sink to bottom of cooker and scorch.

126

Southwest Pork and Hominy Stew

SERVES 4

Hominy is an easy-to-love, chewy grain that is highly appreciated throughout the Southwest where it is known by its Spanish name, *posole*. Hominy is a large-kernel corn that has been processed to remove the tough hulls. Canned hominy is available in many supermarkets.

Tortilla chips provide the ideal crunchy contrast to the mellow textures of this stew. A crisp green salad is also a welcome accompaniment.

---

8 minutes high pressure plus natural pressure release

---

1 can (15 or 20 ounces) white or golden hominy
1 tablespoon olive oil
1^1/$_2$ cups chopped onions
1 teaspoon whole cumin seeds
2 tablespoons tomato paste, catsup, or chili sauce
1 cup chicken broth
1 tablespoon chili powder, plus more to taste
^{1}/$_2$ teaspoon salt, plus more to taste
1 large red bell pepper, seeded and finely chopped
2 pounds boneless pork shoulder (stew meat), trimmed and cut into
    1-inch chunks
1 medium zucchini, cut into ^{1}/$_2$-inch dice
1 to 2 cloves garlic, pushed through a press
1 teaspoon dried oregano
^{1}/$_2$ teaspoon dried sage
^{1}/$_4$ cup chopped fresh cilantro
Tortilla chips and lime wedges, for serving

Empty the can of hominy into a colander. Run water over the kernels to separate and rinse. Drain well.

Heat the oil in a 4-quart or larger cooker. Add the onions and cumin seeds and cook over medium-high heat, stirring frequently, until the onions begin to soften, about 1 minute. Blend in the tomato paste. Stir in the broth, chili powder, salt, bell pepper, and pork. Scatter the hominy on top.

Lock the lid in place. Over high heat bring to high pressure. Reduce the heat just enough to maintain high pressure and cook for 8 minutes. Turn off the heat. Allow the pressure to come down naturally. Remove the lid, tilting it away from you to allow steam to escape.

Stir in the zucchini, garlic, oregano, sage, cilantro, salt to taste, and more chili powder, if needed. Simmer uncovered until the zucchini becomes tender and the stew thickens slightly, about 5 minutes. Serve in large, shallow bowls, accompanied by a bowl of tortilla chips and lime wedges.

Variations
- Use 2 cans of hominy for a higher ratio of grain to meat.
- Cook stew with 1 or 2 chipotles. Remove them before serving. Alternatively, add a pinch of chipotle chile powder or 1 to 2 tablespoons diced, seeded jalapeño after cooking.
- Stir in 1 cup frozen corn shortly before serving and simmer until defrosted.
- Garnish each portion with sliced radishes, toasted pumpkin seeds, or a combination.
- Spoon stew over a bed of shredded green cabbage.

Transformation *(Follow basic recipe except as noted.)*
- TURKEY AND HOMINY STEW: Omit pork and substitute 2 pounds boneless, skinned turkey thighs (7 to 10 ounces each). After cooking, shred turkey and stir it back into stew.

Cabbage and Potatoes
with Kielbasa

SERVES 3 TO 4

This classic combination has lasted through the years because the intense flavor and chewiness of the kielbasa provide such a satisfying contrast to the soft, undemanding cabbage and potatoes. Be forewarned: it will look like you have a mountain of chopped cabbage, but it will shrink to a hillock after cooking.

Serve the stew with dark bread and butter for a fuss-free, casual supper.

---

3 minutes high pressure

---

1 cup chicken broth
2 tablespoons Dijon mustard, preferably whole-grain
1 cup coarsely chopped onions
1 to 1^1/$_2$ pounds kielbasa or other precooked sausage
1^1/$_2$ pounds red-skinned or other waxy potatoes, cut into ^{1}/$_2$-inch dice
1^3/$_4$ pounds green cabbage, quartered, cored, and thickly sliced crosswise (about 12 loosely packed cups)
1 teaspoon caraway seeds (optional)
^{1}/$_2$ teaspoon dried dill
Salt and freshly ground pepper

In a 6-quart or larger cooker, combine the broth, mustard, and onions.

Finely dice enough kielbasa to make 1 cup. Add the diced kielbasa to the cooker. Cut the remaining kielbasa into ¹/₂-inch slices and set aside.

Stir in the potatoes, cabbage, and caraway seeds, if using. (Don't be concerned if the cabbage reaches well beyond the maximum fill line; it will quickly shrink as the cooker comes up to pressure.)

Lock the lid in place. Over high heat bring to high pressure. Reduce the heat just enough to maintain high pressure and cook

Meat, Poultry, and Fish

for 3 minutes. Turn off the heat. Quick-release the pressure by setting the lid under cold running water. Remove the lid, tilting it away from you to allow steam to escape.

Stir in the sliced kielbasa, dill, and salt and pepper to taste. Simmer uncovered until the kielbasa is hot and the potatoes are thoroughly cooked, 3 to 5 minutes.

Variations

• While stew is cooking, pan-fry sliced kielbasa in a nonstick skillet.

• Cook stew with 1 cup diced kielbasa, but serve another kind of grilled or pan-fried whole sausage (such as bratwurst or frankfurters) with stew.

Transformations *(Follow basic recipe except as noted.)*

• KALE AND POTATOES WITH KIELBASA: Instead of cabbage, use 1 pound kale, stems thinly sliced and leaves coarsely chopped. Rinse kale thoroughly in a large bowl of water to release all sand. Drain well before adding.

• CABBAGE, POTATO, AND KIELBASA SOUP: After cooking, thin stew with chicken or vegetable broth. Adjust seasonings before serving.

PRESSURE POINT

• If using a 4-quart cooker, decrease broth to ³/₄ cup and divide remaining ingredients in half.

Moroccan Lamb and Lentil Stew with Minted Yogurt

SERVES 4

Cumin, cinnamon, and tart-sweet prunes give this exotic stew North African flavor.

Depending upon how much lamb you include, you can make either a lentil stew with lamb or a lamb stew with lentils. The eggplant dissolves into a puree that naps the lentils and thickens the sauce. Serve the stew on its own or accompanied by couscous or rice.

---

12 minutes high pressure plus natural pressure release

---

1 tablespoon olive oil
1^1/2 cups coarsely chopped onions
1^1/2 teaspoons whole cumin seeds
2 cups water

1 cup dried brown lentils, picked over and rinsed
12 pitted prunes
1 to 2 pounds boneless lamb shoulder, trimmed and cut into 1-inch chunks
1^1/2 pounds eggplant, peeled and cut into 2-inch chunks
1 teaspoon salt
^{1}/4 teaspoon ground cinnamon, plus more to taste
Grated zest of 1 lemon
1 to 2 tablespoons lemon juice

FOR THE MINTED YOGURT

^{1}/2 cup plain yogurt
2 tablespoons minced fresh mint or 1 teaspoon dried mint (you can empty a teabag.)

Heat the oil in a 6-quart or larger pressure cooker. Add the onions and cumin seeds and cook over medium-high heat, stirring frequently, for 1 minute. Stir in the water, lentils, prunes,

Meat, Poultry, and Fish

and lamb. Set the eggplant on top. Sprinkle with the salt and cinnamon.

Lock the lid in place. Over high heat bring to high pressure. Reduce the heat just enough to maintain high pressure and cook for 12 minutes. Turn off the heat. Allow the pressure to come down naturally, about 10 minutes. Remove the lid, tilting it away from you to allow steam to escape.

Skim off any fat that rises to the top. Stir well to blend in the eggplant. Add more cinnamon and salt, if needed. Stir in the lemon zest and enough of the lemon juice to balance the sweetness of the prunes.

To prepare the Minted Yogurt, stir the yogurt and mint together. Serve each portion of stew with a generous dollop of Minted Yogurt on top.

Variations
• VEGETARIAN VERSION: Decrease cumin to 1 teaspoon. Increase water to 3 cups and lentils to 1½ cups. Omit lamb.
• After cooking, stir in 1 teaspoon harissa (Moroccan chile paste) or a generous pinch of cayenne.
• Use fresh cilantro instead of mint in yogurt topping.

Transformation *(Follow basic recipe except as noted.)*
• MOROCCAN CHICKEN AND LENTIL STEW: Instead of lamb, use 3 to 4 pounds bone-in, skinned chicken parts. Cook for 8 minutes high pressure plus natural pressure release.

PRESSURE POINT
• If using a 4-quart cooker, limit lamb and eggplant to 1 pound each.

Meatloaf with Cheddar-Smashed Potatoes

SERVES 5

Meatloaf in a pressure cooker? I was as surprised as you probably are, but it turns out to be a quick-and-easy success. "Amazing," said the meatloaf maven who came to dinner. "It doesn't look or taste steamed."

But steamed it is, in the cooker's vegetable basket—or you can use a standard collapsible steaming basket instead. It's essential to cook the meatloaf in a container that has a perforated bottom.

Most supermarkets sell a combination of ground beef, pork, and veal labeled "meatloaf mix," which makes a particularly moist, flavorful loaf.

---

10 minutes high pressure

133

Cooking spray or oil, for preparing the steaming basket

2 large eggs

1 1/2 pounds meatloaf mix, or 8 ounces each ground beef, veal, and pork, or all ground chuck

1 cup finely chopped onions

1/2 cup finely chopped flat-leaf parsley

3/4 cup rolled oats (old-fashioned or quick-cooking)

1/2 cup catsup or chili sauce plus 1 to 2 tablespoons to coat the meatloaf

1 teaspoon salt

1/2 teaspoon granulated garlic or garlic powder

Freshly ground pepper

FOR THE CHEDDAR-SMASHED POTATOES

3 pounds russet (Idaho baking) potatoes, scrubbed or peeled, cut into 1-inch chunks

1 1/2 loosely packed cups (about 4 ounces) shredded sharp cheddar cheese

Meat, Poultry, and Fish

¹/₂ cup milk, plus more to taste
Salt and freshly ground pepper

Coat the bottom and sides of the steaming basket lightly with the cooking spray.

Beat the eggs in a large bowl. Add the ground meat, onions, parsley, oats, catsup, salt, garlic, and pepper to taste. Mix with your hands until blended. (The mixture may be fairly moist.) Transfer to the steaming basket and press into a disc of uniform thickness. (If your steaming basket has a central lifting pole, either remove it or shape the loaf around it.) Spread a very thin coating of catsup on top.

Pour 2 cups water into a 6-quart or larger cooker. Place the potatoes in the water. Set the steaming basket on top of the potatoes.

Lock the lid in place. Over high heat bring to high pressure. Reduce the heat just enough to maintain high pressure and cook for 10 minutes. Turn off the heat. Quick-release the pressure. Remove the lid, tilting it away from you to allow steam to escape.

Test for doneness: an instant-read thermometer inserted into the middle of the meatloaf should read at least 155 degrees Fahrenheit. If the meatloaf requires more cooking, remove the potatoes (set aside to keep warm), set the meatloaf on a trivet to raise it above the water, and steam it over high heat for another few minutes. When the meatloaf is done, let it rest in the basket for at least 5 minutes before slicing.

Meanwhile, prepare the Cheddar-Smashed Potatoes: Drain the potatoes and return them to the empty cooker. Set over very low heat and add the cheese and milk. Use a masher to coarsely smash the potatoes. For a moister mixture, stir in additional milk. Add salt and pepper to taste.

To serve, either unmold the meatloaf or slice it right in the basket. Serve the Cheddar-Smashed Potatoes alongside.

Variations
• Use all ground chuck instead of a meatloaf mix, but avoid very lean meat as it will produce a dry loaf.

• Substitute ground chicken or turkey for up to half of meat. (If you use all chicken or turkey, meatloaf may not be sufficiently moist or flavorful.)
• Instead of Cheddar-Smashed Potatoes, make Creamy Mashed Potatoes (page 287).
• Omit potatoes. Set meatloaf on a trivet to raise it above water.
• Reserve liquid drained from potatoes and use instead of milk to moisten mashed potatoes.

Transformations *(Follow basic recipe except as noted.)*
• "FROSTED" MEATLOAF: Unmold meatloaf and set on a plate. Top with Cheddar-Smashed Potatoes.
• STUFFED MEATLOAF: Press half of meatloaf mix into a steaming basket and smooth top. Scatter with 1 cup shredded Monterey Jack or cheddar cheese and ⅓ cup chopped, pimento-stuffed green olives. Press remaining meatloaf mix on top and proceed as directed.
• TEX-MEX MEATLOAF: Work 1 cup finely diced green or red bell pepper and 2 tablespoons chili powder into meatloaf mixture. Use Barbecue Sauce (page 112 or storebought) instead of catsup.
• ITALIAN MEATLOAF: Instead of oatmeal, use dry bread crumbs. Add 1 cup grated romano cheese and 1½ teaspoons Italian Herb Blend (page 18 or storebought). Substitute good-quality tomato sauce for catsup. Decrease salt to ½ teaspoon. Mix in ⅓ cup chopped, oil-packed dried tomatoes, Mediterranean olives, or a combination. (Mixture will be drier than basic recipe.) Increase cooking time to 12 minutes.
• MEATLOAF PARMIGIANA: Slather slices of meatloaf with good-quality tomato sauce and top with shredded mozzarella and grated parmesan cheese. Heat in oven until bubbly.

PRESSURE POINT
• If using a 4-quart cooker, you do not have sufficient room to make meatloaf.

Jiffy Meatballs with Tomato Sauce

SERVES 4

This recipe offers the time-saving convenience of cooking meatballs while you are making the tomato sauce. Serve the sauced meatballs on their own or over pasta, rice, or soft polenta.

---

5 minutes high pressure

FOR THE MEATBALLS
$1^1/_2$ pounds meatloaf mix (a prepackaged combination of ground beef, veal, and pork) or all beef chuck
1 large egg
$1/_2$ cup grated romano cheese
$1/_3$ cup seasoned dried bread crumbs
$1/_2$ teaspoon granulated garlic or garlic powder
2 tablespoons tomato paste
2 tablespoons milk or water
$1/_2$ teaspoon salt

FOR THE TOMATO SAUCE
1 to 2 tablespoons olive oil
1 cup coarsely chopped onions
1 medium green bell pepper, seeded and coarsely chopped
2 teaspoons whole fennel seeds
$1/_2$ cup red wine
$1/_2$ cup water
One can (28 ounces) crushed tomatoes in puree OR one can (28 ounces) plum tomatoes (with liquid), plus one can (6 ounces) tomato paste
$1/_2$ to 1 teaspoon granulated garlic or garlic powder
$1/_4$ cup grated romano or parmesan cheese, plus more for garnish and to pass at the table
Salt and freshly ground pepper
1 to 2 teaspoons sugar (optional)
$1/_4$ to $1/_2$ teaspoon crushed red pepper flakes (optional)
$1/_4$ cup chopped fresh basil or parsley (optional)

In a large bowl, use your hands to combine all the ingredients for the meatballs. Moisten your palms with water and shape the mixture into meatballs with a generous 1-inch diameter.

To prepare the Tomato Sauce, heat 1 tablespoon of the oil in a 4-quart or larger cooker. Add the onions, green pepper, and fennel seeds, and cook over medium-high heat, stirring frequently, until the onions begin to soften, about 1 minute. Stir in the wine, taking care to scrape up any browned bits sticking to the bottom of the cooker. Boil until the wine is reduced by half, about 1 minute.

Stir in the water, then add the meatballs. Pour the tomatoes and their puree over the meatballs. (If using whole plum tomatoes, crush them in your hand and distribute heaping tablespoonsful of the tomato paste on top.) Do not stir after adding the tomatoes. Sprinkle with the garlic.

Lock the lid in place. Over high heat bring to high pressure. (Since the cooker is fairly full, it may take longer than usual to come up to pressure.) Reduce the heat just enough to maintain high pressure and cook for 5 minutes. Turn off the heat. Quick-release the pressure by setting the cooker under cold running water.

Split a meatball in half to make sure it is thoroughly cooked. If the meatballs require more cooking, cover the cooker and simmer until they are done. Gently stir in the cheese and the remaining tablespoon of oil, if needed, to give the sauce a rich finish. Season to taste with sugar, red pepper flakes, and basil (if using). Serve in large shallow bowls. Garnish each portion with cheese and pass a bowl of extra cheese at the table.

Variation
- Add 6 ounces sliced mushrooms after adding the water.

Transformations (*Follow basic recipe except as noted.*)
- PORCUPINE MEATBALLS: Omit bread crumbs and mix 1 cup cooked white rice or ½ cup uncooked instant rice (such as Minute Rice™) into meatball mixture. Increase salt to ¾ teaspoon.

• GROUND LAMB MEATBALLS WITH GREEK-INSPIRED TOMATO SAUCE: Substitute ground lamb (sometimes sold as lamb patties) for meatloaf mix. Instead of romano, use crumbled feta in both meatballs and sauce. After cooking, season sauce with 1 teaspoon dried oregano, $1/8$ to $1/4$ teaspoon ground cinnamon, and fresh parsley. Serve over orzo.

• PASTA WITH MEATBALLS AND TOMATO SAUCE (6-quart or larger cooker): After reducing wine, add 2 cups water instead of $1/2$ cup. Set cooker over high heat and bring water to a boil. Add half the meatballs, then layer one-half of a 1-pound box of ziti, rigatoni, or other short pasta that normally cooks within 9 to 13 minutes. Add remaining meatballs and pasta. Pour tomatoes and their puree over top layer of pasta.

After pressure release, as you stir in cheese and final seasonings, break up any pasta that is stuck together. Let mixture rest, uncovered, for 5 minutes before serving. (If some of pasta is not quite tender or meatballs are not cooked through, set cover in place during this period and cook over low heat. Do not bring back up to pressure, which will cause scorching.)

• MOCK LASAGNE (a good use of leftovers from Pasta with Meatballs and Tomato Sauce, above): Layer pasta with crumbled or sliced meatballs, ricotta, extra sauce (if needed), and chopped fresh basil or Italian Herb Blend (page 18 or storebought). Top with sliced mozzarella. Heat until bubbly.

• MEATBALL STROGANOFF: When preparing meatballs, omit cheese. Increase the salt to 1 teaspoon, and blend in 2 teaspoons dried dill. Omit ingredients for tomato sauce. Pour 1 cup water into cooker and add meatballs. After pressure release, gently stir in contents of an undiluted can (10 ounces) cream of mushroom or golden mushroom soup, $1/4$ cup sour cream, 1 cup frozen peas, and $1/2$ to 1 teaspoon dried dill. Cover and simmer until meatballs are cooked through and dill flavor infuses sauce, 1 to 2 minutes. Add salt and freshly grated nutmeg to taste. Serve on its own or over wide egg noodles.

• MEATBALL STROGANOFF WITH BROAD NOODLES: Have available 12 ounces broad egg noodles that normally cook in 9 to 12 minutes—standard and no-yolk varieties both work fine. When preparing meatballs, omit cheese. Increase salt to 1 teaspoon and blend in 2 teaspoons dried dill. Omit ingredients for tomato sauce. Pour 3 cups beef or chicken broth into a 6-quart or larger cooker. Bring to a boil. Add half the noodles and distribute half the meatballs on top. Add remaining noodles and meatballs. After pressure release, gently stir in ¼ cup milk, ¼ cup sour cream, 1 undiluted can (10 ounces) cream of mushroom soup, 1 cup frozen peas, ½ to 1 teaspoon dried dill, and salt and pepper to taste. Take care to release any noodles clinging to bottom of cooker. Let mixture rest 3 to 5 minutes before serving. Cover mixture during this time if noodles or meatballs are not quite done.

PRESSURE POINTS

• If using a 4-quart cooker, halve quantities in Transformations that include pasta.

• When using an electric cooker, if bottom of cooker scorches, in the future use a slightly lower heat to bring up pressure and set a heat diffuser under cooker.

• The sugars in tomatoes can scorch bottom of cooker as it comes up to pressure. To prevent this, add tomatoes last and do not stir them in.

• Any pasta that is not submerged in liquid cooks by steam heat.

139

Un-Stuffed Cabbage in Sweet-and-Sour Tomato Sauce

I've made stuffed cabbage in the cooker in 7 minutes, but that doesn't take into account the preparation time involved in parboiling and stuffing the leaves. Making the traditional dish seems too time-consuming for the average pressured cook—delicious as it is.

My short-cut solution is to cook meatballs and chopped cabbage in a sweet-and-sour tomato sauce. The resulting stew offers all of the familiar tastes and textures of the time-honored dish without the stuff-and-roll fuss. Another advantage to this approach is that it offers a more generous ratio of cabbage to meat.

This dish tastes best after overnight refrigeration.

---

3 minutes high pressure

140

FOR THE MEATBALLS
2 large eggs

2 pounds meatloaf mix (a prepackaged combination of ground beef, veal, and pork) or all ground chuck

$1/3$ cup finely chopped onion

$1/3$ cup finely chopped flat-leaf parsley

1 cup cooked rice or $1/2$ cup uncooked instant rice (such as Minute Rice™)

1 teaspoon salt

$1/4$ teaspoon granulated garlic or garlic powder

Freshly ground pepper

FOR THE SWEET-AND-SOUR TOMATO SAUCE
$1/2$ cup water

2 tablespoons red wine vinegar

1 teaspoon salt

$1^1/2$ cups coarsely chopped onions

$1^3/4$ pounds green cabbage, quartered, cored, and sliced crosswise (about 12 cups, loosely packed)

One can (28 ounces) peeled plum tomatoes (with liquid)
$3/4$ teaspoon caraway seeds
$1/3$ cup raisins
1 teaspoon dried dill
1 to 2 tablespoons freshly squeezed lemon juice
1 to 3 teaspoons honey or sugar (optional)
Freshly ground pepper

Prepare the meatballs: Beat the eggs in a large bowl. Add the remaining ingredients and mix well with your hands. Shape into small meatballs about 1 inch in diameter.

In a 6-quart or larger cooker, blend the water, vinegar, and salt. Add the onions and half the cabbage. Distribute half the meatballs on top. Add remaining cabbage and meatballs. Pour the tomatoes over the meatballs, crushing them in your hand as you empty the can. Do not stir after adding the tomatoes. Sprinkle the caraway seeds and raisins on top.

Lock the lid in place. Over high heat bring to high pressure. (It will take longer than usual since the cooker is so full.) Reduce the heat just enough to maintain high pressure and cook for 3 minutes. Turn off the heat. Reduce the pressure by setting the cooker under cold running water. Remove the lid, tilting it away from you to allow steam to escape.

Cut a meatball in half to make sure it is thoroughly cooked. If the meatballs require more cooking, cover the pot and simmer until they are done. Season the mixture by gently stirring in the dill and just enough of the lemon juice and honey (if needed) to create a good sweet-sour balance. Add more salt and pepper to taste.

Variations
• Use $1/4$ cup fresh chopped dill instead of dried.
• Garnish each portion with a dollop of sour cream.

PRESSURE POINTS
• If using a 4-quart cooker, reduce cabbage to $1/2$ pound (about 4 cups chopped).

Meat, Poultry, and Fish

• Although there is less than the required minimum of 1 cup liquid in this recipe, onions, tomatoes, and cabbage release sufficient liquid to bring mixture up to pressure.

• Don't be concerned that ingredients exceed recommended maximum fill line; cabbage will shrink dramatically as cooker comes up to pressure.

Quarter-Hour Chili

Use ground meat instead of cubes and the cooking time of this flavor-packed chili is dramatically reduced. I've added diced sausage to enhance the texture and give the chili extra kick. Cocoa powder deepens the flavor.

Serve the chili accompanied by rice, polenta, or corn bread—or spoon it into taco shells and serve with one or more of the optional garnishes.

---

4 minutes high pressure

---

1 tablespoon olive oil

2 teaspoons whole cumin seeds

2 pounds lean ground beef, pork, turkey, or lamb (or a combination)

2 cups coarsely chopped onions

1/2 cup water

3 to 4 tablespoons chili powder

1 1/2 tablespoons unsweetened cocoa powder

1/2 pound chorizo or other spicy cured sausage, finely chopped (use a food processor)

1 large green bell pepper, seeded and finely chopped

One can (15 ounces) diced tomatoes or diced tomatoes with green chiles (with liquid)

1 or 2 cloves garlic, pushed through a press

1 teaspoon dried oregano

Salt and freshly ground pepper

FOR THE OPTIONAL GARNISHES

Sour cream and chopped cilantro

Grated cheddar cheese and shredded lettuce

Chopped red onion

Tortilla chips

143

Heat the oil in a 4-quart or larger cooker. Stir in the cumin seeds and toast for 20 seconds. Add the ground meat in small batches, stirring vigorously after you add each batch. Use a long-handled fork or spoon to break up and crumble the meat. Continue cooking over high heat until the meat is brown.

Stir in the onions and water. Take care to scrape up any browned bits sticking to bottom of cooker. Blend in 3 tablespoons of the chili powder and the cocoa. Add the chorizo and bell pepper. Pour the tomatoes on top. Do not stir after adding tomatoes.

Lock the lid in place. Over high heat bring to high pressure. Reduce the heat just enough to maintain high pressure and cook for 4 minutes. Turn off the heat. Quick-release the pressure. Remove the lid, tilting it away from you to allow steam to escape.

Stir in the garlic, oregano, and salt and pepper to taste, plus the additional chili powder if needed. Simmer the chili uncovered, stirring occasionally, until the flavors are integrated, 3 to 5 minutes. Serve in bowls or lift mixture with a slotted spoon and set into taco shells. Accompany with the garnishes of your choice.

Variations
• COOK-ALONG CASSEROLE WHITE RICE (6-quart or larger cooker). See page 183.
• For a hotter chili, add a pinch of ground chipotle or cayenne pepper after cooking—or stir in chopped fresh jalapeños.

Transformations *(Follow basic recipe except as noted.)*
• CHILI WITH BEANS: After pressure release, stir in 1 1/2 cups firm-cooked pinto, kidney, or black beans, or 1 can (15 ounces) drained and rinsed.
• CUBAN-STYLE CHILI (*Picadillo*): Reduce chili powder to 2 tablespoons and add 1/3 cup raisins. After pressure release, stir in 1/2 cup coarsely chopped pimento-stuffed olives along with garlic. Garnish with chopped fresh cilantro. Serve over rice.
• CURRIED LAMB OR BEEF WITH POTATOES (*Keema Alu*): Use ground lamb (sometimes sold as lamb patties) or beef. Omit chili powder, cocoa, chorizo, and green bell pepper. Add 2 pounds scrubbed or peeled Yukon Gold or red-skinned potatoes that

have been cut into ¾-inch chunks and 10 ounces fresh or frozen cut green beans. After adding tomatoes, sprinkle 1½ tablespoons curry powder and 1 teaspoon salt on top. After cooking, eliminate garlic and oregano and stir in 3 tablespoons chopped fresh cilantro, 2 teaspoons grated fresh ginger (optional), and more curry powder, if needed. If you wish, thicken stew by stirring in ½ to 1 cup yogurt. Serve over rice. Instead of optional garnishes, accompany with mango chutney or an Indian pickle, such as lime or eggplant. (I recommend Patak's brand for both.)

PRESSURE POINT

• The flavor of ground cumin doesn't survive the high heat of pressure cooking. Use whole seeds for authentic taste and texture.

Shredded Meat Tacos with Lime-Cilantro Cream

SERVES 3 TO 4

For a casual, fun lunch or dinner, use the pressure cooker to quickly cook your choice of meat. Then shred the meat and simmer it briefly in your favorite storebought salsa to make a zesty filling for warm tortillas. These stuffed tortillas, known as soft tacos, are not to be confused with crisp, deep-fried taco shells. Complement the meat filling with a dab of cooling Lime-Cilantro Cream and a choice of other garnishes.

Two pounds of boneless meat or 3 pounds bone-in yield 3 to 4 cups shredded meat. It's difficult to say precisely how many people this amount will serve: it depends on the size of the tortillas and how much meat and extras are stuffed into them. But you'll have enough to serve three hungry people for sure.

4 to 25 minutes high pressure (depending on type of meat) plus natural pressure release

Choice of Chicken or Meat	Minutes High Pressure + Release Method
2 pounds boneless chicken thighs (preferred for shredding) or split breasts, skinned	4 + 4-minute natural release, then quick-release
OR 3 pounds pork blade shoulder chops, 1/2 to 3/4 inch thick	4 to 5 + natural release
OR 2 pounds boneless turkey thighs, skinned	8 + natural release
OR 2 pounds boneless chuck steak, about 1 inch thick	20 + natural release
OR 3 to 4 cross-cut beef shanks (3 pounds total), about 1 inch thick	25 + natural release

1¹/₂ cups chicken or beef broth

2 or 3 pounds chicken or meat (select from the chart)

1 to 2 cups storebought salsa (mild or hot according to taste; Newman's Own Roasted Garlic Salsa is good)

Corn or flour (wheat) tortillas

FOR THE LIME-CILANTRO CREAM

¹/₂ cup sour cream (regular or low-fat)

1 tablespoon freshly squeezed lime juice

2 tablespoons chopped fresh cilantro

¹/₄ teaspoon salt (optional)

FOR THE OPTIONAL GARNISHES

Chopped red onion

Shredded lettuce or cabbage

Grated Monterey Jack cheese

Guacamole or sliced avocado

Chopped pimento-stuffed green olives

147

Pour the broth into a 4-quart or larger cooker and add your choice of poultry or meat.

Lock the lid in place. Over high heat bring to high pressure. Reduce the heat just enough to maintain high pressure and cook for the time indicated on the chart. Turn off the heat. Allow the pressure to come down naturally, either partially or completely, as directed. Remove the lid, tilting it away from you to allow steam to escape.

Transfer the meat to a cutting board and let it rest for a few minutes. Degrease the broth in a fat separator and reserve it for use in completing the dish or for one of the Transformations.

To shred the meat, hold it in place with a fork and pull small bits away with another fork. If the meat resists shredding, chop it finely. Place the shredded meat in the cooker and stir in just enough of the salsa to lightly coat. If the salsa is very thick, add about ¹/₄ cup of the broth. Cook over medium heat for a few minutes, stirring frequently, until the meat has absorbed the salsa's flavor and most of the liquid has evaporated.

Meat, Poultry, and Fish

Make the Lime-Cilantro Cream: Blend the ingredients together in a small bowl.

Warm the tortillas in a microwave or skillet. Wrap them in aluminum foil or a kitchen towel to keep warm. Serve the shredded meat in a bowl, accompanied by the Lime-Cilantro Cream and the garnishes of your choice in separate bowls or arrange the meat and garnishes on a large platter. Serve the warm tortillas and invite everyone to fill and roll their own.

Variations
• When simmering meat in salsa, stir in some frozen corn.
• Use filling for crisp taco shells instead of tortillas.

Transformations *(Follow basic recipe except as noted.)*
• PULLED CHILI-SEASONED MEATS FOR TACOS: After placing shredded meat in cooker, instead of adding salsa, sprinkle on 1½ tablespoons chili powder and ½ teaspoon ground cumin. Toss to coat. Cook over medium-high heat, stirring constantly, for a minute or two, just long enough to gently toast spices coating meat. Stir in 1 cup of reserved broth and 1 tablespoon red wine vinegar. Add salt to taste. Cook over medium heat until most of liquid has been absorbed, about 5 minutes. Stir in ¼ cup chopped fresh cilantro.

• CUBAN-INSPIRED SHREDDED MEAT OVER RICE: After placing shredded meat in cooker, stir in 2 cups salsa, ½ cup reserved broth, ½ cup chopped pimento-stuffed green olives, 1 to 2 tablespoons capers, and 1 tablespoon olive oil. Season with ¼ to ½ teaspoon each ground cumin and dried oregano. Cook over medium heat until meat becomes infused with flavor, about 5 minutes. Meanwhile, add more salsa, broth, or a combination to keep stew moist and flavorful. Omit tortillas, Lime-Cilantro Cream, and optional garnishes. Just before serving, stir in 2 tablespoons chopped fresh cilantro and 1 to 2 tablespoons freshly squeezed lime juice. Serve over rice.

• PULLED BARBECUE MEAT ON BUNS: Place shredded meat in cooker. Instead of salsa, stir in enough Barbecue Sauce (page 112 or storebought)—usually ¾ to 1 cup—to generously coat meat.

Stir in ½ cup reserved broth. Cook over medium heat until meat is infused with flavor and most of liquid has evaporated, 3 to 5 minutes. Omit tortillas, Lime-Cilantro Cream, and optional garnishes. Instead, pile meat onto soft buns and top with cole slaw.

• MOCK MOO SHU CHICKEN OR PORK WITH FLOUR TORTILLA "PANCAKES": Cook and shred either chicken or pork. Pour ¼ cup reserved broth into cooker. Add 6 cups shredded Napa or Chinese cabbage, 1 cup coarsely chopped onions, and 1 small red bell pepper that has been cut into matchsticks. Cover (but do not lock) and steam over high heat until cabbage is wilted, about 1 minute. Stir in shredded meat. Instead of salsa, stir in just enough storebought Hoisen Sauce to lightly coat mixture, usually ⅓ to ½ cup. Add 1 to 2 teaspoons toasted sesame oil and soy sauce to taste. Simmer, stirring occasionally, until meat is infused with flavor and most of liquid has evaporated, 3 to 5 minutes. Stir in ½ cup thinly sliced scallions and 2 teaspoons freshly grated ginger. Omit Lime-Cilantro Cream and optional garnishes. Instead serve spicy hot mustard to spread on warm tortillas before stuffing with moo shu mixture.

149

POULTRY

Does anyone ever have enough chicken recipes? Here are some delightful additions to your repertoire. And now that turkey parts have become so readily available, I've included some quick ways to enjoy the Thanksgiving bird all year round.

Poultry recipes are concentrated in the pages that follow, but they are also scattered throughout the book. Locate more of them by checking the Index under chicken and turkey.

Here are a few pointers to keep in mind when pressure cooking chicken:

Quick Versus Natural Release: While the quick release doesn't toughen chicken the way it does beef, allowing the pressure to come down naturally benefits the texture. The formula to use is 7 minutes for bone-in breast halves, or 8 minutes for bone-in thighs, plus a 4-minute natural release. After 4 minutes, release the pressure remaining in the cooker. If more convenient, you can cook the parts for 5 minutes high pressure and then let the pressure come down naturally for at least 15 minutes before removing the lid.

To Skin or Not to Skin: When cooking chicken parts, the skin shrivels in an unattractive way when you quick-release the pressure. For this reason, and from a health standpoint, it's best to remove all skin from chicken parts before cooking.

When cooking a whole chicken, it's difficult and usually not desirable to remove the skin. Brown the breast to give it some color (see page 70). Always allow the pressure to come down naturally to keep the skin intact. It's wise to cook and serve a whole pressure-cooked chicken with a colorful sauce to compensate for its paleness.

To Brown or Not to Brown: Skinned chicken is difficult to brown. As with the meat recipes in this book, I have found it unecessary to brown chicken to achieve good-tasting dishes.

Thighs Remain Moister: There, I've said it, but I know it won't make an iota of difference to devotees of white meat.

Testing for Doneness: Boneless parts are done when they are opaque in the thickest section and shred easily. For bone-in pieces, there should be no pink juices close to the bone.

A whole chicken is done when an instant-read thermometer inserted into the thigh joint reads at least 170 degrees Fahrenheit.

Here are a few tips for pressure cooking turkey:

Quick Versus Natural Release: The flavor and texture of turkey benefit from a natural pressure release.

To Skin or Not to Skin: Turkey is bred very lean, so from a health point of view, skinning is optional. Since natural release is recommended, the skin will remain fairly intact.

To Brown or Not to Brown: There is no need to brown turkey parts.

Thighs and Drumsticks Versus Breasts: Thighs are the most convenient turkey part to cook as they easily fit into the cooker, have rich-tasting meat, and shred easily. They also remain moister than turkey breast, which is extremely lean and can easily become dry if overcooked.

Drumsticks are also very tasty, but fall away from the bone in an unattractive way—so cook them when your intention is to chop the meat. Opt for small drumsticks (under 1½ pounds each). If necessary, lean them against the side of the cooker to fit.

Smoked Turkey Parts: These can be substituted for ham hocks but they impart less flavor.

Testing for Doneness: The meat should shred easily and an instant-read thermometer inserted into the thickest portion should read at least 160 degrees Fahrenheit for a breast roast and 170 degrees Fahrenheit for thigh meat.

Poultry Timing Chart

Note: When cooking frozen chicken parts, add 1 extra minute. When cooking a whole frozen chicken, add 1 extra minute per pound. When cooking frozen turkey parts, add 4 minutes for every 1 inch of thickness.

	Minutes High Pressure + Release Method	Serves
CHICKEN		
Whole		
3 pounds	18 + natural release*	3 to 4
4 pounds	20 + natural release*	4 to 5
Breast halves		
bone-in	7 + 4 natural release, then quick-release	1 pound serves 2
boneless	4 + 4 natural release, then quick-release	3/4 pound serves 2
Drumsticks	8 + 4 natural release, then quick-release	1 pound serves 2
Thighs		
bone-in	8 + 4 natural release, then quick-release	1 pound serves 2
boneless	4 + 4 natural release, then quick-release	3/4 pound serves 2
Thighs and Breast boneless, cut into 1-inch pieces	4 + quick-release	1 pound serves 2 to 3
CORNISH HEN		
Whole		
1 pound	6 + 6 natural release, then quick-release	1
1 1/2 pounds	8 + 6 natural release, then quick-release	2

TURKEY		
Breast Roast **boneless** 2 to 2^1/$_2$ pounds	20 + natural release†	4 to 6
Drumstick (small) 1 to 1^1/$_4$ pounds	12 + natural release	1
Thigh **bone-in** ^{1}/$_2$ to 1 pound 1 to 1^1/$_2$ pounds	 12 to 14 + natural release 14 to 16 + natural release	 1 2
boneless 7 to 10 ounces	8 + natural release	1 to 2
Tenderloin, **cut into 1-inch** **chunks**	4 + quick release	1 pound serves 2

*Temperature at thigh joint should read at least 170 degrees Fahrenheit.
†Temperature in thickest part should read at least 160 degrees Fahrenheit.

Meat, Poultry, and Fish

Whole Stuffed Chicken in Balsamic-Fig Sauce

SERVES 4

Balsamic vinegar, combined with dried figs and the rich juices of a whole chicken, produces a sophisticated wine-dark sauce. An invigorating finish of fresh rosemary and lemon zest brings the fruity sweetness into balance. Although this recipe has a "company's coming" appeal—take a look at the picture on the jacket of the book—it is easy enough to prepare on a weekday night.

Rice, barley, or a dainty pasta, such as orzo, tossed in a little butter makes a nice accompaniment, as does steamed green beans or a tossed salad.

20 minutes high pressure plus natural pressure release

FOR THE STUFFING
$^3/_4$ cup dry seasoned stuffing mix
$^1/_4$ cup finely diced celery
$^1/_4$ cup finely diced onion (use red onion for added color)
$^1/_4$ cup finely diced carrot

FOR THE CHICKEN AND SAUCE
One 4-pound whole chicken
Cooking spray or 1 to 2 teaspoons olive oil to coat the chicken
   breast
Salt and freshly ground pepper
1 tablespoon olive oil
$1^1/_2$ cups chopped leeks or onions
$^1/_4$ cup balsamic vinegar
2 tablespoons tomato paste
1 cup chicken or veal broth
12 dried figs, halved
$^1/_2$ to 1 teaspoon fresh chopped rosemary (dried rosemary does not
   work as a last-minute seasoning)
1 to 2 teaspoons freshly grated lemon zest

To prepare the stuffing, combine the stuffing mix; celery, onion, and carrot. (There is no need to moisten the stuffing.) Set aside.

Spray the chicken's breast with cooking spray or rub liberally with olive oil. Season with salt and pepper. Heat a 6-quart or larger cooker over high heat until a drop of water sizzles immediately. (Do not add any oil to the pot at this point.)

Place the chicken in the cooker, breast side down. Brown over high heat for 1½ minutes without moving. Peek underneath and, if the chicken hasn't developed enough color, continue to brown for another minute or two, taking care to avoid burning. Use two long-handled spoons or forks to transfer the chicken to a plate. (There is no need to brown the chicken's back.) Stuff the chicken and seal the opening with a toothpick or two. Truss the chicken, if you wish.

Add the 1 tablespoon of olive oil to the cooker and heat. Add the leeks and cook, stirring frequently, until they begin to soften, about 2 minutes. Stir in the vinegar and tomato paste and cook until the mixture becomes syrupy, about 20 seconds. Immediately add the broth, taking care to scrape up any browned bits sticking to the bottom of the cooker.

Set the chicken, breast side up, in the broth. Distribute the figs on top and around the chicken.

Lock the lid in place. Over high heat bring to high pressure. Reduce the heat just enough to maintain high pressure and cook for 20 minutes. Turn off the heat. Allow the pressure to come down naturally. Remove the lid, tilting it away from you to allow steam to escape.

Test for doneness: An instant-read thermometer inserted in the thigh joint should register at least 170 degrees Fahrenheit (or up to 180 degrees for very well-done dark meat). If necessary, cover and continue to cook over medium heat for a few more minutes.

Transfer the chicken to a platter, tent with aluminum foil, and let it rest for at least 5 minutes before carving. If necessary, strain and degrease the broth using a fat separator. Using a standard or immersion blender, puree some or all of the sauce. Boil the sauce over high heat, stirring occasionally, until it thickens and becomes syrupy. Season to taste with rosemary, lemon zest, and salt and pepper to taste. Spoon some of the sauce over the chicken and serve the remaining sauce in a gravy boat.

Variations
• COOK-ALONG POTATOES: Arrange 4 medium scrubbed (unpeeled) Yukon Gold or waxy potatoes around chicken. Serve whole or prepare Creamy Mashed Potatoes (page 287).
• Cook additional stuffing in a saucepan according to package directions.
• Omit stuffing. The timing will remain the same.

Transformations *(Follow basic recipe except as noted.)*
• CORNISH HENS IN BALSAMIC-FIG SAUCE: Instead of chicken, substitute 2 Cornish hens (about 1½ pounds each). Divide stuffing between them. Brown 1 hen at a time. After adding broth, squeeze them into cooker side by side. Cook for 8 minutes high pressure plus 6-minute natural pressure release. Quick-release any remaining pressure. Divide each hen in half to serve 4.
Note: If you can only get 1-pound hens, figure on 1 hen per person. Reduce cooking time to 6 minutes high pressure plus 6-minute natural pressure release.
• TURKEY THIGHS IN BALSAMIC-FIG SAUCE: Omit stuffing. Instead of chicken, use 4 bone-in, skinned turkey thighs. Do not brown. Cook for 14 minutes high pressure (for ³/₄- to 1-pound thighs) or 16 minutes high pressure (for 1- to 1½-pound thighs) plus natural pressure release.
• CHICKEN PARTS IN BALSAMIC-FIG SAUCE: Omit stuffing. Instead of a whole chicken, use 4 pounds skinned, bone-in chicken breast halves or thighs (or a combination). Do not brown. Cook for 8 minutes high pressure plus 4-minute natural pressure release, then release any remaining pressure.
• WHOLE CHICKEN IN BALSAMIC–DRIED TOMATO SAUCE: Add 1½ teaspoons whole fennel seeds when you add leeks. Instead of figs, use 4 ounces (1 cup tightly packed) dried tomato halves. Remove loose papery covering from 1 small head garlic and tuck

it in broth beside chicken. After cooking, remove garlic. For a more intense garlic taste, squeeze some cooked garlic into sauce. Instead of rosemary, stir in ¼ cup chopped fresh basil or 1 to 2 tablespoons Basil Pesto (page 42). Pass a bowl of grated parmesan at the table. Serve with Parmesan Mashed Potatoes (see page 288) made with Cook-Along Potatoes, page 156, the perfect accompaniment.

PRESSURE POINT
• If using a 4-quart cooker, substitute a 3-pound chicken and reduce stuffing mix to ½ cup. Cook for 18 minutes high pressure plus natural pressure release.

Meat, Poultry, and Fish

A Quartet of
Quick Chicken Salads

Quickly poach boneless chicken, and you'll be all set to make one of the four salads that follow. Prepare the dressing and chop the vegetables while the chicken is cooking, and you'll have any of these salads on the table in under 15 minutes.

Serve the salad on a bed of greens or accompanied by a steamed green vegetable.

---

4 minutes high pressure plus 4-minute natural pressure release

---

TO COOK CHICKEN
1 cup chicken broth or water
1/4 teaspoon salt (omit if using salty broth)
2 pounds boneless, skinned chicken breast halves or thighs

Pour the broth into a 4-quart or larger cooker. Add the salt (if using) and chicken.

Lock the lid in place. Over high heat bring to high pressure. Reduce the heat just enough to maintain high pressure and cook for 4 minutes. Turn off the heat. Allow the pressure to come down naturally for 4 minutes, then quick-release any remaining pressure. Remove the lid, tilting it away from you to allow steam to escape.

Transfer the chicken to a chopping board and let it rest for a few minutes. (Reserve the broth for another use.) Chop or shred the chicken into bite-sized pieces. You should have about 4 cups.

To make the chicken salad: Select one of the salads listed below. Toss the cooked chicken and other salad ingredients in a large bowl or storage container. Blend the ingredients for the dressing. Pour onto the chicken mixture and toss gently to coat. Adjust seasonings before serving.

Chicken Salad with Grapes and Tarragon-Mayonnaise Dressing

About 4 cups diced cooked chicken

1 cup diced celery

1 to 2 cups seedless red grapes, halved

1 cup toasted walnuts or pecans, coarsely chopped

FOR THE DRESSING

1/2 cup mayonnaise

1 tablespoon freshly squeezed lemon juice, plus more if needed

1 teaspoon dried tarragon

Salt and freshly ground pepper

Asian Chicken Salad with Sesame-Soy Dressing

About 4 cups shredded cooked chicken

1 cup diced red bell pepper or blanched chopped snow peas, cut on the diagonal

1/2 cup thinly sliced scallion greens

1/4 cup chopped roasted peanuts or 1 tablespoon toasted sesame seeds

1 can (11 ounces) mandarin oranges, drained (optional garnish)

FOR THE DRESSING

2 tablespoons peanut or canola oil

1 tablespoon toasted sesame oil

1 tablespoon rice wine vinegar

1 tablespoon soy sauce (preferably Japanese tamari or shoyu), plus more to taste

1 1/2 to 2 teaspoons freshly grated ginger

Indian-Inspired Chicken Salad with Mango-Yogurt Dressing

About 4 cups diced cooked chicken

1 cup diced celery

1/3 cup raisins (try yellow ones for added color)

1/2 cup pistachios or chopped roasted cashews

1 cup plain yogurt (whole milk or low-fat)
3 tablespoons sweet mango chutney, plus more to taste
1 teaspoon curry powder, plus more to taste
Salt and freshly ground pepper

Southwest Chicken Salad with Lime-Cilantro Vinaigrette

About 4 cups diced cooked chicken
1 firm but ripe Hass avocado, diced
$^1/_2$ cup diced red onion or $^1/_3$ cup thinly sliced scallion greens
$^1/_2$ cup diced roasted red pepper (see page 19)
3 tablespoons toasted pumpkin seeds
1 to 2 tablespoons seeded, diced jalapeño (optional)

For the Dressing
3 tablespoons olive oil
3 to 4 tablespoons freshly squeezed lime juice
$^1/_4$ cup chopped fresh cilantro
Salt and freshly ground pepper

Variations
• Add rice or another grain to salad. Increase dressing quantity as needed.
• Instead of chicken, use 2 pounds boneless, skinned turkey thighs (7 to 10 ounces each). Increase timing to 8 minutes high pressure plus natural pressure release.

Parmesan Chicken Packet

SERVES 1

If you've been on the lookout for a healthy version of fast food, consider this approach. Top a chicken breast cutlet with tomato sauce, mozzarella, and parmesan cheese, and wrap it in an aluminum foil packet. The cutlet steams in the confines of the packet, and remains juicy and flavorful.

I've written this recipe for a single chicken packet, but you can cook as many as will fit in your cooker (see Pressure Points). Use either heavy-duty aluminum foil or two layers of standard foil to avoid rips and leaks. Packets can be assembled in advance and frozen.

9 minutes high pressure (15 minutes if cutlets are frozen)

FOR EACH PACKET
4- to 6-ounce chicken breast cutlet
3 to 4 tablespoons good-quality tomato sauce
2 to 3 slices mozzarella cheese
1 tablespoon grated parmesan cheese

If any portion of the cutlet is thicker than ¹/₂ inch, place it on a flat surface and cover with plastic wrap. Use the flat side of a meat pounder or a heavy skillet to pound the cutlet to an even thickness of ¹/₂ inch or less.

Tear off a 1¹/₂-foot-long sheet of heavy-duty aluminum foil (or two layers of standard foil). Spoon 1 tablespoon of the tomato sauce in the center and position the cutlet on top of the sauce so that its length is parallel to the cut sides of the foil.

Use enough of the mozzarella slices to cover the top of the cutlet, spoon remaining sauce on top, then sprinkle with the parmesan.

To make the packet, bring together the two cut ends of the foil and fold them over a few times to seal, leaving some air space above the cutlet. Fold both ends of the packet several times to

Meat, Poultry, and Fish

seal. With the tip of a paring knife, poke a 1-inch steam vent in the top of the packet, just beneath the top fold. This is important!

Pour 1½ cups water into the cooker. Set the packet, folded side up, directly in the water. (If making more than one packet, see Pressure Points.)

Lock the lid in place. Over high heat bring to high pressure. Reduce the heat just enough to maintain high pressure and cook for 9 minutes (15 minutes if cutlets are frozen). Turn off the heat. Quick-release the pressure. Remove the lid, tilting it away from you to allow steam to escape.

Use tongs to remove the packet from the cooker. Carefully open the packet and check for doneness by poking the tip of a paring knife into the thickest part. If the chicken requires more cooking, reseal the packet and return to cooker. Set the lid in place (but do not lock it) and steam the chicken over high heat until done.

To serve, transfer contents of the packet to a plate.

Variations

• Use turkey breast cutlet instead of chicken. If they are cut very thin, stack two together to equal ½ inch.

• Add a layer of prosciutto under the mozzarella slices.

• COOK-ALONG SMASHED POTATOES (see Pressure Points): Scrub or peel potatoes and cut into 1-inch chunks (or 2-inch if cooking frozen cutlets). Set potatoes under chicken packet(s). After pressure release, drain potatoes and return to empty cooker. Smash with a potato masher and season with salt, pepper, olive oil, and grated romano cheese to taste (or see page 288 for other seasoning possibilities).

• COOK-ALONG CARROTS: Halve 1 medium carrot lengthwise and cut into ¼-inch slices. Set next to cutlet or wrap in its own foil packet.

• COOK-ALONG STRING BEANS: Add a portion of frozen string beans to packet. String beans will become quite soft and loose their sprightly color but will taste good.

Transformations *(Follow basic recipe except as noted.)*

• TEX-MEX CHICKEN PACKET: Substitute prepared salsa or barbecue sauce for tomato sauce. Use 3 to 4 tablespoons shredded sharp cheddar cheese instead of parmesan and mozzarella. Scatter chopped pimento-stuffed green olives over cheese.

• CHICKEN PACKET WITH HOISIN PEANUT SAUCE: Omit tomato sauce, mozzarella, and parmesan. In a small bowl, blend 2 tablespoons peanut butter (preferably chunky), 1 tablespoon hoisin sauce (storebought), 2 teaspoons rice wine or apple cider vinegar, and ½ teaspoon soy sauce (if needed). Smear both sides of cutlet liberally with mixture. Thinly slice 1 scallion and scatter on top.

• CHICKEN PACKET WITH ASIAN APRICOT SAUCE: Omit tomato sauce, mozzarella, and parmesan. In a small bowl, combine 1 tablespoon apricot preserves, 1 teaspoon soy sauce, 1 teaspoon whole-grain mustard, and ½ teaspoon white wine vinegar. Smear both sides of cutlet with mixture. Thinly slice one scallion and scatter on top.

• CHICKEN PACKET WITH YOGURT-CHUTNEY SAUCE: Omit tomato sauce, mozzarella, and parmesan. Instead blend together 2 tablespoons plain yogurt, 1 teaspoon mango chutney, 1 teaspoon Patak's Mild Curry Paste or curry powder, and a pinch of whole cumin seeds. Smear sauce liberally on both sides of cutlet. After cooking, sprinkle with chopped fresh cilantro.

163

PRESSURE POINTS

• If cooking cutlets of different thicknesses, place packets containing thicker cutlets on bottom of cooker where they will cook a bit faster.

• You can cook 2 packets in a 4-quart cooker, 4 in a 6-quart, and 6 in an 8-quart. Place second packet next to first, directly in water. (It may be necessary to squeeze them a little to fit.) Set additional layers at right angles to layer below. (Avoid stacking packets directly on top of each other.) Timing remains same no matter how many packets you are cooking at once.

• Cook-Along Potatoes: You can cook up to 2 packets and 2 potatoes in a 4-quart cooker; up to 3 packets and 3 potatoes in a 6-quart; and up to 5 packets and 5 potatoes in an 8-quart.

Meat, Poultry, and Fish

Chicken Cacciatore

SERVES 4

The rich and hearty taste of this dish belies the ease of preparation. Part of the secret is enhancing good-quality storebought tomato sauce with fresh green bell pepper and mushrooms. The rest of the secret is hidden under the lid of the pressure cooker.

I often serve the cacciatore with Parmesan Mashed Potatoes (page 288), but rice or polenta are also good choices. However, I suspect you'll forego these possibilities once you've tried the Pasta and Chicken Cacciatore (see Transformations).

---

8 minutes high pressure plus natural pressure release

---

1 tablespoon olive oil
2 cups chopped onions or leeks
1 medium green bell pepper, seeded and finely diced
$1/2$ cup red wine
10 ounces cremini or button mushrooms, sliced or quartered
3 pounds bone-in skinned chicken breast halves, thighs, or a combination
2 cups good-quality tomato sauce
2 tablespoons tomato paste
One can (6 ounces) pitted (black) olives, drained
2 tablespoons chopped fresh parsley or basil, plus more for garnish (optional)
$1/8$ to $1/4$ teaspoon crushed red pepper flakes (optional)
$1/2$ cup grated parmesan or romano cheese, plus more to pass at the table
Salt and freshly ground pepper

Heat the oil in a 4-quart or larger cooker. Add the onions and bell pepper and cook over medium-high heat, stirring frequently, until the onions soften slightly, about 2 minutes. Stir in the wine and boil until about half evaporates. Scrape up any browned bits sticking to the bottom of the cooker.

Stir in the mushrooms. Set the chicken on top. Cover the

chicken with tomato sauce. Do not stir. Plop the tomato paste on top.

Lock the lid in place. Over high heat bring to high pressure. Reduce the heat just enough to maintain high pressure and cook for 8 minutes. Turn off the heat. Allow the pressure to come down naturally. Remove the lid, tilting it away from you to allow steam to escape.

Stir in the olives, parsley, red pepper flakes (if using), cheese, and salt and pepper to taste. Let the cacciatore rest for 3 to 5 minutes.

To serve, lightly dust each portion with cheese and sprinkle with parsley. Pass extra cheese in a bowl.

Variations

• COOK-ALONG POTATOES (6-quart or larger cooker): Arrange 2 to 3 pounds medium potatoes, scrubbed or peeled and quartered, on top of the tomato sauce.
• COOK-ALONG CASSEROLE WHITE RICE (8-quart cooker): page 183.
• Instead of adding ripe black olives at the end, cook cacciatore with one or more varieties of Mediterranean olive, such as Cerignola, niçoise, or picholines.
• Stir in a bunch of chopped arugula along with olives.
• Vary flavor by using tomato sauce with sausage or roasted garlic.

Transformations *(Follow basic recipe except as noted.)*

• PASTA AND CHICKEN CACCIATORE (6-quart or larger cooker): After adding mushrooms, stir in 1½ cups chicken broth and 12 ounces short pasta (preferably a variety with crevices, such as spirals or campanelle) that normally cooks within 9 to 12 minutes. Instead of bone-in chicken, use 2 pounds boneless chicken, cut into 1-inch chunks. Cook under pressure for 5 minutes, then quick-release. Stir well as you add remaining ingredients. Separate any pasta that is stuck together, and release any that is clinging to bottom of cooker. If pasta is not uniformly cooked, cover and steam in residual heat during resting period.

Meat, Poultry, and Fish

- TURKEY CACCIATORE: Substitute skinned, boneless turkey thighs, 7 to 10 ounces each. Timing remains the same.

PRESSURE POINTS
- For electric and high-BTU stoves, set a heat diffuser (see page 17) under cooker before bringing up to pressure.
- The $1/2$ cup wine, supplemented by ample liquid given off by onions, mushrooms, and chicken, is sufficient to bring up the pressure and create plenty of sauce.

Three-Bean Turkey Chili

SERVES 6

Here is a low-fat, nutrition-packed, hearty chili that's quick to assemble and a feast for the eyes.

Serve the chili in bowls, over rice or polenta, or offer corn-bread on the side.

---

4 minutes high pressure

---

1 tablespoon olive oil
2 cups coarsely chopped onions
1 teaspoon whole cumin seeds
2 to 4 tablespoons chili powder
1/4 teaspoon ground cinnamon
1/2 cup beer or water
1 to 1 1/2 pounds turkey sausage (sweet or hot; casings removed)
1 pound boneless turkey breast, skinned and cut into 1-inch chunks
1 medium green bell pepper, seeded and finely chopped
1 can (15 to 20 ounces) kidney beans, rinsed and drained
1 can (15 to 20 ounces) black beans, rinsed and drained
1 can (15 to 20 ounces) chickpeas, rinsed and drained
1 can (15 ounces) diced tomatoes with green chiles
1/4 cup chopped fresh cilantro, plus more for garnish
Salt and freshly ground pepper
1/2 cup toasted pumpkin seeds, for garnish

Heat the oil in a 6-quart or larger pressure cooker. Stir in the onions, cumin seeds, 2 tablespoons of the chili powder, and the cinnamon and cook over medium-high heat, stirring frequently, for 1 minute. Stir in the beer. Taste the mixture, and if the chili flavor is not pronounced, add more chili powder to taste.

Stir in the turkey sausage, turkey, bell pepper, beans, and chickpeas. Break up any large pieces of sausage. Pour the tomatoes and their liquid on top. Do not stir after adding the tomatoes.

Lock the lid in place. Over high heat bring to high pressure. Reduce the heat just enough to maintain high pressure and cook

Meat, Poultry, and Fish

for 4 minutes. Turn off the heat. Quick-release the pressure. Remove the lid, tilting it away from you to allow steam to escape.

Add the cilantro plus salt and pepper to taste. Serve in bowls with a generous sprinkling of the pumpkin seeds and cilantro on top.

Variations
• Stir in 1 cup frozen corn after pressure release. Simmer until corn is defrosted, about 1 minute.
• After cooking, add 1 large roasted red pepper (see page 19) that's been seeded and chopped.

Transformation *(Follow basic recipe except as noted.)*
• CAJUN THREE-BEAN TURKEY STEW: Instead of turkey sausage, use andouille sausage. Instead of chili powder and cinnamon, use 2 tablespoons sweet paprika. After pressure release, stir in 1 teaspoon dried oregano and simmer until you can taste it, about 1 minute. Instead of cilantro, use 3 tablespoons parsley. Omit pumpkin seeds.

PRESSURE POINT
• If using a 4-quart cooker, stir in beans after cooking and simmer until they develop some flavor, 3 to 5 minutes.

FISH

Although fish cooks quickly using standard techniques, pressure cooking guarantees a moist result. The cooker also offers the option of simultaneously preparing potatoes or rice underneath the fish for a one-pot supper.

There are two foolproof ways to pressure-cook fish. The first is to steam it on a rack. This approach works well if you are making one or two fish steaks that can be arranged in a single layer. The second method is to enclose the fish in a foil packet. This is the best way to cook multiple portions and to infuse the fish with the flavors of a sauce.

Recipes using both of these approaches follow.

Fish Timing Chart

This chart works for firm-fleshed fish steaks or fillets, such as salmon, cod (scrod), or halibut.

Thickness*	Minutes High Pressure + Quick-Release
3/4 inch	4
1 inch	5
1 1/4 inches	6
1 1/2 inches	7

*Time for thickest portion.

Fish Packet Timing Chart

This chart works for any fish steak or fillet that flakes easily, such as scrod, salmon, pollack, tilapia, or orange roughy.

Thickness*	Minutes High Pressure + Quick-Release
1/4 inch	6
1/2 inch	8
3/4 inch	10
1 inch	13
1 1/4 inches	14
1 1/2 inches	15

*Time for thickest portion.

Fish with Sour Cream–Dill Smashed Potatoes

SERVES 2

Steamed fish served with dill-scented potatoes makes a simple, stylish meal. Set the potatoes on the bottom of the cooker to create a platform for the steaming basket. For best results, select fish steaks or fillets of relatively even thickness.

---

4 to 7 minutes under pressure (depending on thickness)

Cooking spray or oil, for preparing the steaming basket
2 firm-fleshed fish steaks or fillets (6 to 8 ounces each), such as salmon, cod (scrod), or halibut
2 teaspoons Dijon mustard (preferably whole-grain)
Salt and freshly ground pepper
1/4 cup sour cream (regular or fat-free)
1 tablespoon freshly squeezed lemon juice
1/4 teaspoon dried dill
1 pound russet (Idaho baking) or Yukon Gold potatoes, scrubbed or peeled, halved and cut into 1/2-inch slices
1 to 2 tablespoons butter (optional)
4 thin lemon slices, for garnish

Coat the inside of a steaming basket with the cooking spray.

Lightly smear both sides of the fish steaks or fillets with the mustard. Season well with salt and pepper. Arrange the fish on the steaming basket; avoid overlap. If cooking unskinned fillets, place skin side up.

In a small bowl, blend together the sour cream, lemon juice, and dill. Set aside for the flavor to develop.

Pour 1 cup water into a 4-quart or larger cooker. Add the potatoes and set the steaming basket on top.

Lock the lid in place. Over high heat bring to high pressure. Reduce the heat just enough to maintain high pressure and cook according to thickness for the time indicated on the Fish Timing

Chart on page 169. Turn off the heat. Quick-release the pressure. Remove the lid, tilting it away from you to allow steam to escape.

Test the fish for doneness by piercing the thickest part with the tip of a paring knife: the flesh should be opaque and flake easily. If the fish requires more cooking, set (but do not lock) the lid in place and steam over high heat until done. This should not take more than an additional minute or two; take care not to overcook.

Lift out the basket. Tip off most of the water. (Leave a few tablespoons to moisten the mash.) Add butter (if using) and 2 tablespoons of the sour cream–dill mixture and coarsely mash. Season with salt and pepper. Divide the potatoes and fish between two plates. Garnish each piece of fish with two lemon slices and spoon the remaining sour cream alongside.

Variations
• Cook 1 cup chopped onions or leeks with potatoes.
• Instead of smashing potatoes, leave them in chunks. Use dill sour cream as a sauce.
• Instead of Smashed Potatoes, follow directions for Last-Minute Potato Salad with Lemon-Dill Vinaigrette (page 289).

Transformation *(Follow basic recipe except as noted.)*
• FISH WITH SWISS CHARD–POTATO PUREE: Omit sour cream, lemon juice, and dill and reduce potatoes to ½ pound. Chop stalks of 1 pound Swiss Chard into ½-inch slices and leaves into 1-inch ribbons. Swish in several changes of water to rinse away all sand. Drain well. Place chard under potatoes. After pressure release, pass thoroughly drained potatoes and chard through a food mill. Return to cooker to reheat. Add 2 tablespoons butter. Season well with salt and freshly ground pepper. Divide puree between two plates and set fish on top.

Meat, Poultry, and Fish

Fish Packet with Puttanesca Sauce

SERVES 1 OR MORE

For a quick dinner, top fish with good-quality tomato sauce and wrap it in a foil-pack. As the fish steams, it releases a small pool of flavorful broth that is captured in the packet. Serve the fish on its own or over rice, surrounded by a "moat" of the broth.

This recipe works with any fish that flakes easily, including scrod, salmon, pollack, tilapia, or orange roughy. Do not use denser fish, such as swordfish or monkfish, since they take much longer to cook. For best results, select fish steaks or fillets of relatively even thickness. If that's unavailable, time for the thickest portion.

I've set up the recipe to make a single packet, but you can cook as many as will fit in your cooker (see Pressure Points). Prepare the number of packets you need in assembly line fashion. To avoid rips, use heavy-duty aluminum foil or two layers of standard foil.

---

6 to 15 minutes high pressure (time for thickest section)

---

3 tablespoons good-quality tomato sauce
1 fish steak or fillet (6 to 8 ounces), such as scrod, tilapia, orange roughy, grouper, or salmon
1 tablespoon chopped pitted black olives or 2 tablespoons whole olives
1 teaspoon chopped capers
Freshly ground pepper
Lemon wedges, for garnish

Tear off a 1¹/₂-foot-long sheet of heavy-duty aluminum foil. Spoon 1 tablespoon of the tomato sauce in the center of the foil and position the fish on top of the sauce so that its length is parallel to the cut sides of the foil. If fillet is thicker on one end, fold the thin end under. Spoon the remaining tomato sauce on top and scatter the olives and capers over the sauce.

To make the packet, bring together the two cut ends of the foil and fold them over a few times to seal, leaving some air space above the fish. Fold both ends of the packet several times to seal.

Pour 1½ cups water into the cooker. Set a footed collapsible steamer basket in place. Set the packet, folded side up, in the basket. (If making more than one packet, see Pressure Points).

Lock the lid in place. Over high heat bring to high pressure. Reduce the heat just enough to maintain high pressure and cook according to thickness (see Fish Packet Timing Chart, page 169). Turn off the heat. Quick-release the pressure. Remove the lid, tilting it away from you to allow steam to escape.

Use tongs to remove the packet from the cooker. Carefully open the packet and test for doneness by poking the tip of a paring knife into the center (or thickest part) of the fish. It should be opaque and flake easily. If the fish requires more cooking, reseal the packet, and return to the cooker. Set the lid in place (but do not lock it) and steam the fish over high heat until done. This should not take more than an additional minute or two; take care not to overcook.

Transfer the contents of the packet to a lipped plate or shallow bowl. Season with pepper and serve with lemon wedges.

Variations
• COOK-ALONG POTATOES (6-quart or larger cooker): Cook 1 potato per packet, scrubbed or peeled, and cut into 1-inch chunks. Set potatoes directly in water and place fish packet(s) on top. Drain cooked potatoes and smash with olive oil, grated parmesan, salt, and pepper to taste. Serve alongside fish.
• COOK-ALONG CASSEROLE WHITE RICE (6-quart or larger cooker): Cover Casserole White Rice (page 183) with foil. Make ten slashes with a paring knife to create steam vents. Set a roasting rack in bottom of cooker, and place casserole on rack. Arrange fish packets on top of casserole.
• Add ¼ cup frozen Fordhook limas to each packet.

Transformations *(Follow basic recipe except as noted.)*

• FISH PACKET WITH SALSA: Omit tomato sauce and substitute prepared salsa plus 1 teaspoon olive oil. Add ¼ cup frozen corn kernels to each packet. Garnish cooked fish with chopped fresh cilantro. Serve with lime wedges.

• FISH PACKET WITH LEMON-CAPER SAUCE: Omit tomato sauce and olives. Season fish with salt and pepper. Squeeze on about 1 tablespoon lemon juice. Top with a pat of butter. Sprinkle with capers, some grated lemon zest, and 2 teaspoons minced parsley.

• FISH PACKET WITH SESAME-SOY SAUCE: Omit tomato sauce, olives, and capers. In a small bowl, blend 1½ teaspoons Japanese soy sauce (tamari or shoyu) and ½ teaspoon toasted sesame oil. Brush onto both sides of fish. Chop 1 scallion and scatter on top. After cooking, sprinkle with 1 tablespoon chopped fresh cilantro and 1 teaspoon toasted sesame seeds.

PRESSURE POINTS

• You can cook 2 packets in a 4-quart cooker, 4 in a 6-quart, and 6 in an 8-quart. Avoid stacking packets directly on top of each other. Set the first two next to each other (squeeze them together if necessary) and place additional layers at right angles to the layer below.

• Cook-Along Potatoes: You won't have room for potatoes in a 4-quart cooker. In a 6-quart, you can cook up to 3 packets and 3 potatoes. In an 8-quart, up to 5 packets and 5 potatoes.

• Cook-Along Casserole White Rice: You'll have room for 2 packets in a 6-quart cooker and 4 packets in an 8-quart. Arrange them on top of casserole as described above.

174

Rice, Risotto, and Whole Grains

For additional recipes using rice and grains, consult the Index.

RICE

Although the time-saving for cooking white rice isn't dramatic, you'll enjoy the foolproof results. Try the festive and fun one-pot rice dinners such as jambalaya, paella, or biryani. These are short-cut versions of the traditional recipes, easy enough to prepare on a weekday night. And be sure to try a batch of risotto—the dish that makes as many converts to pressure cooking as short ribs and osso bucco.

Basic White Rice

MAKES 3 CUPS

When you use long-grain or basmati, the pressure cooker produces a moist and slightly sticky rice with a pleasant chewiness, similar to the rice you get in Chinese restaurants. When you use converted rice, the cooked grains remain more separate.

To cook larger quantities, use the proportions suggested in the White Rice Cooking Chart on page 181.

---

3 minutes high pressure plus 7-minute natural pressure release

---

1 tablespoon oil or butter
1 cup long-grain, basmati, or converted white rice
1¹/₂ cups water
¹/₂ teaspoon salt, or to taste

Heat the oil in a 4-quart or larger cooker over high heat. Add the rice and stir to coat it lightly with the oil. Stir in the water and salt.

Lock the lid in place. Over high heat bring to high pressure. Reduce the heat just enough to maintain high pressure and cook for 3 minutes. Turn off the heat. Allow the pressure to come down naturally for 7 minutes. Quick-release any remaining pressure. Remove the lid, tilting it away from you to allow steam to escape.

If the rice is not quite tender, replace the lid and steam in the residual heat for a few more minutes.

Mound the rice on plates. Alternatively, make timbales: Press hot, cooked rice into a small buttered ramekin or custard cup and unmold.

Tip: Extra rice may be refrigerated or frozen. For details, see Ready Rice and Grains on page 208.

Variations

• Use broth instead of water. Reduce salt if broth is salty.

• Cook rice with 2 to 3 teaspoons mild curry powder.

• Before adding rice, add 1 teaspoon whole cumin, anise, or fen-nel seeds, or a combination, and toast in oil until fragrant, about 20 seconds.

• For other ideas, see Dressing Up White Rice and Other Grains on page 184.

PRESSURE POINTS

• Do not fill cooker more than halfway when cooking rice. You can cook a maximum of 2 cups dry rice in a 4-quart cooker, 3 cups in a 6-quart, and 4 cups in an 8-quart.

• Timing remains the same no matter how much rice you are cooking.

• It is necessary to cook rice with a little butter or oil to control foaming.

• The amount of liquid and precise timing required for perfect rice varies slightly from one cooker to another. Experiment with succes-sive batches until you come up with the right formula, using the fol-lowing guidelines:

> If all liquid has been absorbed and rice is still not tender,
>   increase liquid in 2-tablespoon increments.
> If some liquid has not been absorbed and rice is still not tender,
>   increase natural pressure release time in 1-minute increments.

• Do not attempt to return an undercooked batch of rice to high pressure. There will be insufficient liquid, and rice is likely to scorch.

White Rice Cooking Chart

This chart works for long-grain, basmati, and converted white rice.

Do not fill cooker more than halfway when cooking rice. You can cook a maximum of 2 cups dry rice in a 4-quart cooker, 3 cups in a 6-quart, and 4 cups in an 8-quart.

Cups Rice	Cups Liquid*	Teaspoons Salt† (Optional)	Tablespoons Oil/Butter	Yield in Cups
1	1$^1/_2$	$^1/_2$	1	3
1$^1/_2$	2$^1/_4$	$^3/_4$	1	4 to 4$^1/_2$
2	3	1	2	5$^1/_2$ to 6
3	4$^1/_4$	1$^1/_2$	2	7$^1/_2$ to 8
4	5	2	2	11 to 12

*Water or broth.
†Omit if using salty broth.

Rice, Risotto, and Whole Grains

Casserole White Rice

MAKES 3 CUPS

Steam rice in a casserole over boiling water and serve it in the same dish. This convenient approach works best with long-grain white rice.

Use a heatproof, flat-bottomed, round casserole that fits easily into the cooker. A 5- to 7-cup Pyrex baking dish or a porcelain soufflé dish work well.

To cook larger quantities, use the proportions suggested in the Casserole White Rice Cooking Chart on page 183.

5 minutes high pressure plus natural pressure release

1 cup long-grain white rice
1½ cups water
½ teaspoon salt, or to taste

Set a rack or trivet in the bottom of a 6-quart or larger cooker.

Pour in 1 cup water. Cut a two-foot-long piece of standard-width aluminum foil and fold it twice lengthwise to create a long, wide strip for lowering the casserole into the cooker.

Combine the rice, water, and salt in the casserole. Center the dish on the strip and lower it onto the rack. Loosely fold the ends of the foil strip over the top of the dish.

Lock the lid in place. Over high heat bring to high pressure. Reduce the heat just enough to maintain high pressure and cook for 5 minutes. Turn off the heat. Allow the pressure to come down naturally, 7 to 10 minutes. Remove the lid, tilting it away from you to allow steam to escape.

Lift the casserole out of the cooker with the aid of the foil strip and serve immediately, or leave in the hot cooker, covered, until needed.

PRESSURE POINT

• If using a 4-quart cooker, you do not have sufficient room to make Casserole White Rice.

Casserole White Rice Cooking Chart

Cups Rice	Cups Water	Teaspoons Salt	Yield in Cups
1	$1^1/2$	$^1/2$	3
$1^1/2$	$2^1/4$	$^3/4$	4 to $4^1/2$
2	3	1	$5^1/2$ to 6

Casserole White Rice as Optional Cook-Along (6-quart or larger cooker)

For a one-pot meal, cook rice in a separate bowl on top of a stew that cooks for approximately 5 minutes under high pressure and uses a natural pressure release. Follow the instructions for Casserole White Rice on page 182. With the aid of the foil strip, lower the casserole into the cooker and set it directly on top of the stew. After pressure release, lift out the casserole and set it on a plate to catch drips.

If the rice requires more cooking, use one of the following approaches:

1) If slightly undercooked, immediately cover the casserole tightly with plastic wrap and continue steaming in the residual heat.
2) If significantly undercooked, cover with vented plastic wrap and finish cooking in the microwave. This usually takes only a few minutes.
3) Stir the rice into the stew and simmer until done.

Rice, Risotto, and Whole Grains

Dressing Up White Rice and Other Grains

Toss hot, cooked grains with one or more of the following:

A little olive oil or butter and chopped fresh
   herbs
Currants, chopped apricots, or other dried fruit
Toasted seeds or coarsely chopped nuts
Orange or lemon zest
Basil Pesto (page 42 or storebought)
Chopped pimento-stuffed green olives, olive
   oil, and lime juice
Capers, olive oil, chopped fresh parsley, and
   lemon juice

Dilled Rice with Carrot Specks

Flecks of coarsely grated carrot dress up a simple pilaf and add a touch of sweetness. This pilaf makes a festive accompaniment to pot roast, broiled chops, roast chicken, and grilled fish.

3 minutes high pressure plus 7-minute natural pressure release

1 tablespoon butter or oil
1 small onion, finely chopped
1 cup long-grain, basmati, or converted white rice
1^1/$_2$ cups chicken or vegetable broth
1 medium carrot, grated on the coarse side of a box grater
1 teaspoon salt (omit if broth is salty)
2 tablespoons chopped fresh dill

Heat the butter in a 4-quart or larger cooker. Add the onion and cook over medium-high heat, stirring frequently, for 1 minute. Stir in the rice, taking care to coat the grains with the butter. Stand back to avoid sputtering and add the broth, grated carrot, and salt.

Lock the lid in place. Over high heat bring to high pressure. Reduce the heat just enough to maintain high pressure and cook for 3 minutes. Turn off the heat. Allow the pressure to come down naturally for 7 minutes, then quick-release any remaining pressure. Remove the lid, tilting it away from you to allow steam to escape.

Stir in the dill and adjust for salt before serving.

Variation
• When you add dill, stir in 1 teaspoon grated lemon zest and/or ¼ cup dried currants.

185

Transformations *(Follow basic recipe except as noted.)*

• CUMIN-FLECKED PILAF WITH POTATOES AND PEAS: Along with onion, add 1 teaspoon whole cumin seeds, 2 teaspoons curry powder, and 1/4 teaspoon turmeric. Along with carrot, add 1/2 pound Yukon Gold or red-skinned, waxy potatoes, scrubbed and cut into 1-inch chunks. After pressure release, omit dill and stir in 1/2 cup frozen peas. Cover and steam until peas are tender, another minute. Garnish each portion with a tablespoon of plain yogurt. Serves 3 as a vegetarian entree or 5 to 6 as a side dish.

• CURRIED RICE AND POTATO SALAD: Prepare Cumin-Flecked Pilaf with Potatoes above. Transfer to a bowl and let cool slightly. Season with 1 to 2 tablespoons peanut or canola oil, 2 to 3 tablespoons freshly squeezed lime juice, and 2 to 3 tablespoons chopped fresh cilantro. Omit yogurt garnish.

Festive Rice with Fruits and Nuts

SERVES 6 TO 8 AS A SIDE DISH

This pilaf makes a fine side dish for roast chicken, turkey, or pork. Little rosy orbs of dried cranberries brighten the mix.

If the fruits are very dried out, plump them up in a little hot water before tossing them into the rice.

---

3 minutes high pressure plus 6-minute natural pressure release

---

1$^1/_2$ tablespoons butter or oil

1$^1/_2$ cups long-grain, basmati, or converted white rice

$^1/_4$ teaspoon ground allspice

$^1/_4$ teaspoon ground cinnamon

2$^1/_4$ cups water

1 teaspoon salt

$^1/_2$ cup mixed chopped dried fruits, such as figs, apples, dates, and apricots

$^1/_3$ cup dried cranberries or cherries

$^3/_4$ cup toasted hazelnuts, pecans, almonds, or walnuts (see page 19), whole or coarsely chopped

187

Heat the butter in a 4-quart or larger cooker over high heat. Stir in the rice, allspice, and cinnamon, taking care to coat the rice with the butter. Stir in the water and salt.

Lock the lid in place. Over high heat bring to high pressure. Reduce the heat just enough to maintain high pressure and cook for 3 minutes. Turn off the heat. Allow the pressure to come down naturally for 6 minutes, then quick-release any remaining pressure. Remove the lid, tilting it away from you to allow steam to escape.

Quickly stir in the dried fruits and adjust the seasonings. Immediately cover and let steam until the fruits are hot and the rice is tender, 1 to 2 minutes. Toss in the nuts and serve.

Rice, Risotto, and Whole Grains

Variations

• Use chicken broth instead of water. Omit salt if broth is salty.
• Use ⅓ cup toasted pumpkin or sunflower seeds instead of nuts.
• When you add nuts, toss in a few cups diced roasted squash or sweet potatoes.
• Use pilaf as a stuffing for baked squash.

Transformations *(Follow basic recipe except as noted.)*

• FESTIVE RICE SALAD: Prepare Orange Marmalade Dressing, page 212. Toss enough dressing into pilaf to lightly coat. Serve at room temperature.
• FESTIVE BROWN RICE: Instead of white rice, cook 1½ cups short-grain brown rice as directed on page 205. Drain. Heat butter in cooker and blend in allspice and cinnamon. Stir in cooked rice and dried fruits. Replace lid and steam for 5 minutes in residual heat. Meanwhile, grate 1 large unpeeled apple. Stir grated apple and nuts into rice and serve.

PRESSURE POINT

• If dried fruits were cooked under pressure with rice, they would become very soft. They maintain a pleasing chewiness when tossed in at the end.

Spanish Rice with Chicken and Sausage

SERVES 4 TO 6

Spicy chorizo sausage gives lots of character to this simplified version of Spanish arroz con pollo, while pimento-stuffed green olives and sweet paprika add Iberian charm. This is a very agreeable dish to serve to company.

---

3 minutes high pressure plus 6-minute natural pressure release

---

1 tablespoon olive oil
1 cup chopped onions
6 ounces diced chorizo or other spicy cured sausage (about 1¹/₂ cups)
2 cups long-grain white rice
1 tablespoon sweet paprika
1 cup chicken broth
2 large bay leaves
1 teaspoon salt
1¹/₂ pounds boneless, skinned chicken breasts, thighs or a combination, cut into 1-inch chunks
One can (15 ounces) diced tomatoes, including liquid
¹/₂ cup small pimento-stuffed green olives
1 roasted red bell pepper (page 19 or storebought), seeded and diced
1 teaspoon dried thyme
Freshly ground pepper
3 tablespoons chopped fresh parsley, for garnish

Heat the oil in a 4-quart or larger cooker. Add the onion and chorizo and cook over medium-high heat, stirring frequently, until the onion begins to soften, about 2 minutes.

Stir in the rice and paprika, taking care to coat the rice with the oil. Stir in the broth, bay leaves, and salt. Scrape up any browned bits stuck to the bottom of the cooker. Stir in the chicken. Pour the tomatoes and their liquid on top. Do not stir after adding the tomatoes.

Lock the lid in place. Over high heat bring to high pressure. Reduce the heat just enough to maintain high pressure and cook for 3 minutes. Turn off the heat. Allow the pressure to come down naturally for 6 minutes. Quick-release any pressure remaining in the cooker. Remove the lid, tilting it away from you to allow steam to escape.

Quickly stir in the olives, red pepper, and thyme. Immediately replace the lid and steam in the residual heat until rice is tender, usually no more than a minute or two.

Stir well to distribute the ingredients. Remove bay leaves. Add salt and pepper to taste. If there is any unabsorbed liquid, use a slotted spoon to serve. Garnish individual portions with parsley.

Variations

• Add 1 cup frozen peas or cooked black beans when you add olives.
• Add 1 to 2 teaspoons hot paprika or ¹/₂ teaspoon crushed red pepper flakes along with sweet paprika.

Transformations *(Follow basic recipe except as noted.)*

• CHICKEN JAMBALAYA: Omit chorizo. Add 1 medium green bell pepper, seeded and finely diced, along with chicken. While rice is cooking, slice and pan-fry 12 ounces andouille or other fully cooked smoked sausage. Stir into cooked rice (along with red pepper). Omit olives. Pass Tabasco sauce at the table.
• SEAFOOD AND CHICKEN JAMBALAYA: Prepare Chicken Jambalaya above and add ¹/₂ pound unpeeled medium or large shrimp along with chicken.
• SEAFOOD AND CHICKEN PAELLA: Soak ¹/₄ teaspoon saffron threads in 2 teaspoons warm water for 10 minutes. Add along with chicken broth. Add ³/₄ pound medium shrimp (shelling

optional), large scallops, or a combination, when you add chicken.

PRESSURE POINT

• If using an electric or high-BTU stove, set cooker on a heat diffuser before bringing up to pressure.

Rice, Risotto, and Whole Grains

Chicken Biryani

SERVES 4 TO 6

Here is a simple-to-prepare rice pilaf that celebrates the vivid flavors of the Indian kitchen. For a zesty, sweet topping to accompany the biryani, blend 1 heaping tablespoon sweet mango chutney into 1 cup plain yogurt. For a spicy-hot topping, blend 1 heaping tablespoon Patak's Eggplant (Brinjal) Relish into 1 cup plain yogurt.

3 minutes high pressure plus 7-minute natural pressure release

1 tablespoon butter
1¹/2 cups chopped onions
2 teaspoons anise seeds
2 teaspoons whole cumin seeds
2 tablespoons tomato paste
2 cups chicken broth
1 cup water
2 large bay leaves
1¹/2 teaspoons salt (¹/2 teaspoon if using salty broth)
4 teaspoons mild curry powder, plus more to taste
¹/4 teaspoon ground cinnamon
Pinch of cayenne (optional)
1¹/2 pounds boneless, skinned chicken, cut into 1-inch chunks
2 cups basmati or long-grain white rice
1 cup frozen peas
¹/2 cup toasted slivered almonds or chopped roasted cashews

Heat the butter in a 4-quart or larger cooker. Add the onions, anise seeds, and cumin seeds and cook over medium-high heat, stirring frequently, until the onions begin to soften, about 2 minutes. Blend in the tomato paste and cook for 20 seconds longer. Stir in the broth, water, bay leaves, salt, curry, cinnamon, and cayenne (if using). Taste the broth and, if there isn't a strong curry flavor, add more curry powder to taste. Stir in the chicken and rice.

Lock the lid in place. Over high heat bring to high pressure. Reduce the heat just enough to maintain high pressure and cook for 3 minutes. Turn off the heat. Allow the pressure to come down naturally for 7 minutes. Quick-release any remaining pressure. Remove the lid, tilting it away from you to allow steam to escape.

Quickly stir in the peas and almonds and additional salt, if needed. Replace the cover, and steam the mixture in the residual heat until the peas are defrosted, 1 to 2 minutes. Stir well to fluff up. Remove the bay leaves. Serve with bowls of yogurt toppings (see headnote) on the side.

Variation
• Add ⅓ cup raisins along with rice.

Transformations *(Follow basic recipe except as noted.)*
• LAMB BIRYANI: Omit chicken broth and increase water to 3 cups. Instead of chicken, use 1½ pounds boned lamb shoulder, cut into ¾-inch chunks and trimmed. (If boned shoulder is not available, buy 2½ pounds lamb shoulder chops; cut into cubes and trim yourself. Include bones for added flavor, then remove before serving.) Before adding rice, cook lamb for 8 minutes high pressure. Quick-release pressure and skim off any surface fat. Stir in rice and cook for 3 more minutes high pressure plus 7-minute natural pressure release.
• VEGETABLE BIRYANI (Vegetarian): Use vegetable broth instead of chicken broth. Instead of chicken, use 1½ cups cooked chickpeas (or a 15-ounce can, drained) and 1 pound peeled butternut squash cut into ¾-inch chunks. After cooking, stir in ¼ cup chopped fresh cilantro. Season with 1 to 2 tablespoons freshly squeezed lime juice.

Rice with Mussels

SERVES 3 TO 4

I was surprised to discover that mussels remain moist and succulent after cooking them under pressure. As the mussels open, their briny juices infuse the rice with flavor, creating a moist, risotto-like dish that makes elegant company fare.

3 minutes high pressure plus 7-minute natural pressure release

2 tablespoons butter or olive oil
$1/2$ cup chopped shallots or onions
$1/2$ cup chopped celery, plus a few minced celery leaves (if available)
$1^1/2$ cups long-grain white rice
$1/2$ cup dry white wine or dry vermouth
$2^1/4$ cups water
$3/4$ teaspoon salt
1 to 2 cloves garlic, peeled, or $1/2$ teaspoon garlic powder or granulated garlic
3 pounds mussels, rinsed and de-bearded
3 to 4 tablespoons minced fresh parsley
1 teaspoon grated lemon zest
Lemon wedges, for garnish

Heat the butter in a 6-quart or larger cooker. Stir in the shallots, celery, and rice and cook over high heat for 30 seconds. Add the wine and cook until it has almost evaporated. Stir in the water, salt, and garlic and bring to a boil. Add the mussels.

Lock the lid in place. Over high heat bring to high pressure. Reduce the heat just enough to maintain high pressure and cook for 3 minutes. Turn off the heat. Allow the pressure to come down naturally for 7 minutes. Quick-release any remaining pressure. Remove the lid, tilting it away from you to allow steam to escape.

Use a slotted spoon to transfer the mussels to a bowl. (Discard mussels that have not opened and any empty shells.) Drape the mussels with a kitchen towel to keep them warm. If the rice is not quite tender, set the lid in place (but do not lock it) and let it steam in the residual heat until done. Stir the parsley and lemon zest into the rice, and let the mixture sit for a few minutes before serving. Scoop the rice into large, shallow soup or pasta bowls and top with the mussels. Accompany with lemon wedges.

Variation

• Add 1 to 2 teaspoons fresh thyme—lemon thyme is especially tasty—when you add parsley.

Transformations *(Follow basic recipe except as noted.)*

• RICE WITH SMOKED FISH: Instead of mussels, use 2 fillets of smoked mackerel or trout (about ½ pound), skinned and boned. After cooking, transfer fish to a cutting board and replace cooker's lid to keep rice warm. Flake fish and stir into rice along with parsley. Add salt, if needed. Lemon zest is optional.

• THAI COCONUT RICE WITH SHRIMP: Omit wine. Use long-grain rice or substitute Thai jasmine or basmati rice. Reduce water to ¾ cup and add with a can (about 13.5 ounces) of coconut milk. Instead of salt, use 1 tablespoon Thai fish sauce. Omit garlic and substitute 1½ teaspoons Thai curry paste, or more, to taste. Add ½ cup diced red bell pepper. Instead of mussels, use 1½ pounds unpeeled medium or large shrimp. After cooking, substitute basil for parsley and lime wedges for lemon.

PRESSURE POINT

• If using a 4-quart cooker, use a maximum of 2 pounds mussels.

195

RISOTTO

The quick and easy preparation of risotto is one of the pressure cooker's greatest triumphs. Making risotto by the traditional method is a labor-intensive affair: at least 25 minutes of almost continuous stirring. The cooker does the job for you in 4 minutes, leaving you only 3 to 5 minutes of stirring at the very end. From start to finish, it takes about 15 minutes to prepare risotto, making it the ideal dish for a last-minute supper or casual-chic entertaining.

The formula for risotto is very simple. Toss some onions and Italian arborio rice in a little butter or oil, then add just enough wine to invite the rice to open its pores. Add some broth and any other cook-along ingredients, then let the pressure cooker go to work. After releasing the pressure, stir in any quick-cooking ingredients and garnish or final seasonings, such as seafood, grated parmesan cheese, or fresh herbs.

Basic Risotto

SERVES 4 AS AN ENTREE AND 6 AS A SIDE DISH

This basic risotto makes a good accompaniment to a broiled fish or chop. Add some shrimp or beans (see Transformations), and the risotto becomes a main dish.

Arborio is the most commonly available of the imported, plump, short-grain rices traditionally used to make risotto. If you use one of the other types of Italian risotto rice—Baldo, Vialone Nanno, or Carnaroli—cook for 5 minutes under pressure rather than 4.

---

4 minutes high pressure

---

1 tablespoon olive oil or butter
1/2 cup finely chopped onions or shallots
1 1/2 cups arborio rice
1/2 cup dry white wine or dry vermouth
3 1/2 to 4 cups chicken broth
1 teaspoon salt (omit if using salty broth)
1/2 cup grated parmesan cheese, plus more if needed
Freshly ground pepper
3 tablespoons chopped fresh parsley

Heat the oil in a 4-quart or larger cooker. Add the onions and cook over high heat for 1 minute, stirring frequently. Stir in the rice, taking care to coat it with the oil.

Stand back to avoid sputtering oil, and stir in the wine. Cook over high heat until the rice has absorbed the wine, usually about 30 seconds. Stir in 3 1/2 cups of the broth and salt (if using). Take care to scrape up any rice sticking to the bottom of the cooker.

Lock the lid in place. Over high heat bring to high pressure. Reduce the heat just enough to maintain high pressure and cook for 4 minutes. Turn off the heat. Quick-release the pressure by setting the cooker under cold running water. Remove the lid, tilting it away from you to allow steam to escape.

Set the cooker over medium-high heat and stir vigorously. (The risotto will look fairly soupy at this point.) Cook uncovered, stirring every minute or so, until the mixture thickens and the rice is tender but still chewy, usually 3 to 5 minutes. If the mixture becomes dry before the rice is done, stir in the remaining ½ cup broth. The finished risotto should be slightly runny; it will continue to thicken as it sits on the plate.

Turn off the heat. Stir in cheese, salt and pepper to taste, and the parsley.

Tip: Risotto tastes best when it's just made. However, the microwave does a nice job of reheating it.

Variations
- Use beef, veal, or vegetable broth instead of chicken broth.
- Use half grated parmesan and half grated romano.
- Use dry red wine instead of white.
- Add 1 teaspoon fennel seeds along with onions.
- Stir in a few ounces baby spinach shortly before rice is done.

Transformations *(Follow basic recipe except as noted.)*
- RISOTTO MILANESE: Steep ½ teaspoon saffron threads in 1 tablespoon warm water for 10 minutes or longer. After releasing pressure, stir in saffron and soaking water. Risotto Milanese is traditionally served with osso bucco (braised veal shanks; see page 94).
- RISOTTO DU JOUR: Stir in bite-sized pieces of roasted chicken, cooked meat, or vegetables shortly before rice is done.
- RISOTTO WITH BUTTERNUT SQUASH: After adding broth, stir in 1½ pounds butternut squash that's been peeled, seeded, and cut into 1-inch chunks (about 3 cups). After releasing pressure, stir well to dissolve squash into a thick sauce (with perhaps a few chunks remaining). Along with parmesan, add 2 teaspoons minced fresh sage or ½ to 1 teaspoon dried. (For a vegetarian version, substitute vegetable broth for chicken broth.)
- RISOTTO WITH HAM, GRUYÈRE, AND PEAS: Just before rice is tender, stir in 2 cups diced, cooked ham and 1 cup frozen peas. Reduce parmesan to ¼ cup and add 1 cup loosely packed shred-

ded Gruyère. (For a vegetarian version, use vegetable broth and omit ham.)

- Risotto with Sun-Dried Tomatoes and Smoked Mozzarella: After releasing pressure, stir in ⅓ cup chopped, oil-packed sun-dried tomatoes. When rice is cooked, turn off heat and stir in 6 ounces (1 cup tightly packed) shredded or diced smoked mozzarella. Omit parmesan. Instead of parsley, stir in ¼ cup chopped fresh basil, if you wish. (For a vegetarian version, use vegetable broth.)

- Risotto with Fresh Sausage, White Beans, and Tomato: After adding onions, stir in ½ pound fresh Italian sausage (sweet or hot; casings removed). Break up sausage meat and brown. Instead of broth, use 2½ cups water. After stirring in water and salt, pour a can (15 ounces) of diced tomatoes, including liquid, on top. Do not stir after adding tomatoes. After pressure release, stir in 1 cup cooked white beans. Increase parsley to ¼ cup.

- Shrimp Risotto: Add 6 oil-packed anchovies, finely chopped, when you add onion. (They will dissolve during cooking and give risotto a mildly briny flavor.) Add ½ tablespoon balsamic vinegar when you stir in wine. About 1 minute before rice is tender, stir in 1 pound medium peeled raw shrimp (or large shrimp, halved lengthwise), ¼ cup thinly sliced scallion greens, and 1 to 2 teaspoons grated lemon zest. Omit the parmesan.

- Risotto with Chickpeas, Spinach, and Raisins: After releasing pressure, stir in 1 clove garlic, pushed through a press, 3 tablespoons each raisins and pitted, chopped oil-cured black olives, and 1½ cups cooked chickpeas (or a 15-ounce can, rinsed and drained). Once mixture has returned to a boil, stir in a total of 4 tightly packed cups (about 8 ounces) finely chopped fresh spinach or watercress in 2 batches. Cook until spinach is wilted and the rice is tender. Substitute 2 to 3 tablespoons grated pecorino romano for the parmesan. (Adapted from Judith Barrett's *Risotto*.)

- Porcini Risotto: Soak 1 ounce (about 1 cup) dried porcini in 2 cups boiling water until soft, about 10 minutes. Reduce chicken broth to 1½ to 2 cups. After adding 1½ cups chicken broth, stir in soaked mushrooms. Pour in soaking liquid, taking care to leave behind any grit that has settled to bottom.

199

Barley Risotto with Lamb

Barley offers a fine alternative to arborio rice when you are in the mood for a hearty, main dish winter risotto. The lamb contributes such rich flavor that you can cook the rice in water rather than broth.

The best (and most economical) cut to use is bone-in lamb neck (sometimes labeled "lamb stew, bone-in"). The bones give the risotto a soothing gelatinous texture. For an informal presentation, serve the meat right on the bone. For a more refined entree, shred the meat and stir it back in.

23 minutes high pressure

4¹/₂ cups water

1 cup pearl barley, rinsed

1¹/₂ cups chopped onions

1 cup diced celery

1 tablespoon balsamic vinegar, plus more to taste

1 tablespoon tomato paste

1 tablespoon olive oil (needed to control foaming)

¹/₂ teaspoon salt

1¹/₂ to 2 pounds lamb neck, cut into 2-inch chunks and trimmed of
    surface fat

2 large whole carrots, peeled and wrapped in a foil packet
    (see page 15)

1 cup frozen peas

2 to 3 tablespoons grated romano or parmesan cheese, plus more
    to pass at the table

1 to 2 teaspoons chopped fresh rosemary

Freshly ground black pepper

Sprigs of fresh rosemary, for garnish

Combine the water, barley, onions, celery, vinegar, tomato paste, oil, salt, and lamb in a 4-quart or larger cooker. Float the carrot packet on top.

Lock the lid in place. Over high heat bring to high pressure. Reduce the heat just enough to maintain high pressure and cook for 23 minutes. Turn off the heat. Quick-release the pressure by setting the cooker under cold running water. Remove the lid, tilting it away from you to allow steam to escape.

Remove the foil-packet. Cut the carrots into bite-sized pieces. If not serving on the bone, remove the lamb to a cutting board and shred or chop the meat.

Skim off any fat that rises to the top of the risotto. Bring to a boil over high heat. Cook uncovered, stirring frequently, until the mixture has the consistency of a loose porridge. Stir in the carrots, shredded lamb, peas, cheese, and rosemary. Add salt and pepper to taste, plus an additional teaspoon or two of vinegar if the flavors need sharpening. The barley will continue to absorb liquid, so the risotto should be somewhat soupy when you ladle it into large, shallow bowls. Garnish each serving with a sprig of rosemary. Pass additional cheese at the table.

Variations

• For added textural and visual interest, cook barley with 2 tablespoons of a dark specialty rice such as calusari red or black japonica.
• Instead of carrots, use 1 pound rutabaga, peeled, cut into 1-inch chunks, and wrapped in foil.
• Season with 1 teaspoon dried sage instead of rosemary.
• Use 1/4 to 1/2 cup crumbled feta instead of romano cheese.
• Substitute a 10-ounce package of fresh baby spinach for the frozen peas.

Transformations *(Follow basic recipe except as noted.)*
• BARLEY AND WINTER VEGETABLE RISOTTO: Use chicken broth or vegetable broth instead of water. Omit lamb. Add 1 pound butternut or other winter squash that's been peeled, seeded, and quartered and 1 large (about 8 ounces) Yukon Gold or red-skinned waxy potato, scrubbed and left whole. Use 4 foil-packed carrots instead of 2. Reduce cooking time to 18 minutes high pressure. After cooking, dice potato and stir it into risotto

Rice, Risotto, and Whole Grains

along with frozen peas. (As you stir, most of squash will dissolve and thicken risotto.) Serves 4 as a main dish and 6 to 8 as a side dish.

• SCOTCH BROTH (6-quart and larger cookers): Increase water to 8 cups and reduce barley to ½ cup. Instead of onions, use 3 cups chopped leeks (including dark greens). Increase lamb neck to 2½ pounds. Omit romano cheese. Serves 6 to 8 soup portions.

PRESSURE POINT

• If using a 4-quart cooker, cut recipe in half.

WHOLE GRAINS

Whole grains like brown rice and wheat berries are high in fiber, low in fat, and rich in nutrients—good reasons to include them in any healthy diet. Using standard cooking techniques, they take an hour or two to prepare, so many cooks have never gotten into the habit of making them. Using the PC, you can count on making perfectly cooked whole grains in a half hour or less.

Nowadays most supermarkets carry brown rice and pearl barley. For other whole grains, you may need to go to a health food store or order by mail. (My favorite source of organic grains is Gold Mine Natural Food Company; see page 317.) Since their oil-rich germ is intact, whole grains can go rancid quickly if not properly stored. Freeze them in heavy zipper-topped bags and the grains will remain fresh for at least 6 months. There is no need to defrost them before cooking.

Grain Blends

It's easy and fun to cook a variety of grains together. Whole grains are more forgiving than white rice and remain pleasantly chewy even when cooked slightly longer than required. As a result, grains with approximately the same cooking time can be cooked together, using the time recommended for the longer-cooking grain (see Whole Grains Timing Chart, page 207). For example, cook short-grain brown rice with pearl barley for 18 minutes, although the brown rice requires only 15.

When you wish to combine grains with vastly different cooking times, use one of these approaches:

1) Give the longer cooking grain a head start, then release the pressure and add the shorter-cooking grain. For example, cook wild rice for 10 minutes under pressure, quick-release the pressure, and add the brown rice. Continue cooking for an additional 15 minutes. This may sound like a nuisance, but it's really a snap: the cooker comes right back up to pressure after adding the second grain.

2) Soak longer-cooking grains overnight to reduce their cooking time by about 50 percent. Then they'll be ready to cook with shorter-cooking grains. For example, soak wheat berries or kamut overnight and then cook them with brown rice for 15 minutes.

Basic Whole Grains

MAKES 3 CUPS

Cook brown rice and other whole grains in an abundance of water—the way you cook pasta. Using this foolproof method, the grains cook quickly and evenly, and there's no concern that they will absorb all of the liquid and scorch the bottom of the pot. Use this recipe for all of the grains listed in the Whole Grains Timing Chart.

For timing, see the Whole Grains Timing Chart on page 207

1¹/₂ cups brown rice or other whole grains, rinsed
5¹/₂ cups water
1 tablespoon oil
³/₄ teaspoon salt (optional)

Combine the grains, water, oil, and salt (if using) in the cooker.

Lock the lid in place. Over high heat bring to high pressure. Reduce the heat just enough to maintain high pressure and cook for the time indicated in the Whole Grains Timing Chart on page 207. Turn off the heat. Quick-release the pressure by setting the cooker under cold running water. Remove the lid, tilting it away from you to allow steam to escape.

If the grains are not sufficiently tender (keep in mind that whole grains are always a bit chewy) simmer uncovered until done. Stir from time to time to prevent grains from sticking to the bottom of the cooker.

Pour the contents of the cooker through a large strainer. (Reserve the broth for making soup.) Rinse briefly under warm water to wash away surface starch. Bounce up and down vigorously to release all surface liquid. For drier, fluffier grains, return the grains to the hot cooker, set the lid in place, and let them steam in the residual heat for 5 minutes. Stir to fluff up the grains before serving. For suggestions on dressing up cooked grains, see page 184.

Tips: Grains dry out and become hard when refrigerated. To rejuve-nate: Set in a bowl, cover lightly with a paper towel, and heat briefly in the microwave.

PRESSURE POINTS

• Do not fill cooker more than halfway when preparing grains. You can cook a maximum of $1^1/2$ cups dry grains in a 4-quart cooker, 3 cups dry grains in a 6-quart cooker, and 4 cups dry grains in an 8-quart cooker.

• Be sure to add oil as instructed. Oil subdues foam that develops as grains cook. Excess foam can cause spitting or clogging at excess-pressure vents.

• When cooking grains, quick-release pressure by setting cooker under cold running water. Using a stovetop quick-release method usually causes foaming and sputtering at vent.

• After cooking grains, always thoroughly clean cooker's lid, pres-sure mechanism, and vents to remove any starchy residue.

Whole Grains Cooking Chart

Do not fill cooker more than halfway when preparing grains. You can cook a maximum of $1^1/2$ cups dry grains in a 4-quart cooker, 3 cups dry grains in a 6-quart cooker, and 4 cups dry grains in an 8-quart cooker.

Cups Grain	Cups Water	Tablespoons Oil	Teaspoons Salt (Optional)	Approximate Yield in Cups
1	4	1	$1/2$	2
$1^1/2$	$5^1/2$	1	$3/4$	$3^1/4$
2	7	$1^1/2$	$3/4$	$4^1/2$
3	9	$1^1/2$	1	7
4	11	2	$1^1/2$	9

Whole Grains Timing Chart

All timings are based on quick-releasing pressure by setting the cooker under cold running water. If using an electric cooker, subtract 5 minutes from cooking time and allow the pressure to come down naturally for 10 minutes, then quick-release any remaining pressure.

15 Minutes*	18 Minutes	25 Minutes	35 Minutes
brown rice (short- and long-grain; basmati)	pearl barley	wild rice	kamut
calusari red rice (Christmas rice)	black barley	rye berries	oat groats
black japonica rice			spelt
wehani rice			wheat berries

*This timing also works for packaged brown rice blends that usually call for 45 minutes cooking time.

Ready Rice and Grains

Because it's so convenient to have ready-to-eat grains on hand, cook more than you need and freeze the extra in zipper-topped plastic freezer bags for up to 3 months. I know it's hard to believe, but cooked whole grains that have been stored in the freezer and then defrosted in the microwave taste just about as good as a freshly made batch.

The grains usually freeze in a block. If you don't need the whole bagful, bang the bag against the kitchen counter to loosen up the amount you need. Set the grains in a strainer and rinse away any ice crystals. You can stir frozen grains directly into soups and stews and simmer until they are defrosted, usually a minute or two.

If serving the grains on their own, place them in a bowl, drape a paper towel on top, and microwave on high, stirring once or twice, until the grains are hot and rehydrated, usually 1 to 3 minutes. (You can also steam the grains in a little water in a covered saucepan.) Use the same technique to rehydrate grains that have dried out in the refrigerator.

Cranberry-Nut and Brown Rice Pilaf

SERVES 6 TO 8 AS A SIDE DISH

This pilaf is made in two easy steps. First cook the rice in a tasty broth. Then steam the grains briefly with dried cranberries, pecans, and sage.

You can use all brown rice, but it's pleasant to speckle the pilaf with a dark grain like wehani or calusari red rice.

---

15 minutes high pressure

TO COOK THE BROWN RICE
1 tablespoon oil
2 cups coarsely chopped onions
1 cup diced celery
4 cups chicken or vegetable broth
2 cups water
1½ cups short-grain brown rice, rinsed
½ cup specialty rice, such as black japonica, wehani, or calusari red (or use additional brown rice), rinsed

FOR THE PILAF
1 tablespoon butter or oil
¾ cup pecans, whole or coarsely chopped
½ teaspoon dried sage
½ to 1 cup dried cranberries (depending on how fruity you'd like it)
1 cup thinly sliced scallion greens
Salt and freshly ground pepper
2 teaspoons grated orange zest

Heat the oil in a 6-quart or larger cooker. Add the onions and celery and cook over medium-high heat, stirring frequently, for a minute or two. Add the broth, water, and grains.

Lock the lid in place. Over high heat bring to high pressure. Reduce the heat just enough to maintain high pressure and cook for 15 minutes. Turn off the heat. Quick-release the pressure by setting the cooker under cold running water. Remove the lid, tilting it away from you to allow steam to escape.

Pour the contents of the cooker through a large strainer. (Reserve the broth for another use.) Bounce up and down vigorously to release all surface liquid.

Heat the butter in the empty cooker. Stir in the pecans and sage and cook over medium-high heat, stirring occasionally, until the pecans are lightly toasted, 1 to 2 minutes. Stir in the cooked grains, cranberries to taste, and scallion greens. Cover, turn off the heat, and let steam for about 5 minutes. Add salt and pepper to taste. Transfer to a large bowl, stir in the orange zest, and serve.

Tip: Grains dry out and become hard when refrigerated. To rejuvenate, set in a bowl, cover lightly with a paper towel, and heat briefly in the microwave.

Variations

• Use any combination of whole grains. Check Grain Blends on page 204 for suggestions, and consult Whole Grains Timing Chart for timing; see page 207.

• Toss cubed, roasted squash into finished pilaf.

Transformations *(Follow basic recipe except as noted.)*

• CRANBERRY-NUT AND BROWN RICE STUFFING: Toss ¼ cup chopped fresh parsley into finished pilaf and use as a stuffing for chicken or baked squash.

• BROWN RICE PILAF WITH RAISINS, CHICKPEAS, AND SPINACH: Omit pecans. Instead of sage, use ¼ teaspoon ground cinnamon. After returning cooked grains to cooker, stir in 1½ cups cooked chickpeas (or a 15-ounce can, drained and rinsed), and 1 package (12 ounces) frozen spinach that's been thawed. Instead of dried cranberries, use ⅓ cup raisins. Cover and cook over very low heat for 5 minutes, stirring occasionally. Serves 8 as a side dish or 4 as a vegetarian entree.

PRESSURE POINTS

• If using a 4-quart cooker, divide recipe in half.

• If using an electric cooker, subtract 5 minutes from grain cooking time and allow the pressure to come down naturally for 10 minutes, then quick-release any remaining pressure.

• If you cooked sage and cranberries with brown rice from the start, their flavors would dissipate during the relatively long time under pressure.

Brown Rice Waldorf Salad with Orange Marmalade Dressing

SERVES 6 TO 8

To make this fetching salad, toss brown rice with the ingredients traditionally used in a Waldorf salad. Coat the mixture with an orange marmalade dressing for an intriguing finish.

With a wedge of Brie, the salad makes a nice light-lunch entree. Alternatively, serve it for dinner with roast chicken. It's also a terrific dish to bring to a potluck.

Be sure to use an apple variety that doesn't brown when sliced. Granny Smith is a good choice.

---

15 minutes high pressure

TO COOK THE BROWN RICE

5 cups water

1 cup short-grain brown rice, rinsed

2 tablespoons specialty rice, such as calusari red, wehani, black japonica (or use additional brown rice), rinsed

1 tablespoon oil (needed to control foaming)

$1/2$ teaspoon salt

FOR THE SALAD

1 Granny Smith apple, peeled and diced (about 2 cups)

1 cup diced celery (preferably from the tender inner ribs)

$1^1/2$ cups seedless red grapes, halved

$3/4$ cup toasted pecans or walnuts (see page 19), halved

$1/3$ cup dried cranberries

FOR THE ORANGE MARMALADE DRESSING

$1/4$ cup canola oil

2 tablespoons orange marmalade

3 tablespoons freshly squeezed lemon juice, plus more if needed

$1/4$ teaspoon salt

Pour the water into a 4-quart or larger cooker and bring to a boil over high heat as you measure and add the rices, oil, and salt.

Lock the lid in place. Over high heat bring to high pressure. Reduce the heat just enough to maintain high pressure and cook for 15 minutes. Turn off the heat. Quick-release the pressure by setting the cooker under cold running water. Remove the lid, tilting it away from you to allow steam to escape.

If the rice is not sufficiently tender (remember that whole grains are always a bit chewy), simmer uncovered until done. Drain thoroughly, bouncing the strainer up and down a few times to release excess liquid. Immediately return the rice to the hot cooker, set the lid in place, and let the rice steam in the residual heat for 5 minutes.

Transfer the rice to a large bowl. When cool, add the apple, celery, grapes, pecans, and cranberries.

To prepare the dressing: In a jar, combine the oil, marmalade, lemon juice, and salt. Shake until well blended. Pour the dressing into the salad and toss. Add more lemon juice and salt, if needed.

213

Tip: Once refrigerated, the grains in the salad harden. To rejuvenate, set in a bowl, cover lightly with a paper towel, and heat briefly in the microwave. This won't do any damage to the crisp ingredients.

Variations
• Stir in 2 tablespoons mayonnaise after adding Orange Marmalade Dressing. Mayonnaise gives mixture a creaminess characteristic of a traditional Waldorf salad.
• Substitute 1/3 cup toasted sunflower seeds for nuts.
• Use raisins or snipped dried apricots instead of dried cranberries.
• Make salad with wheat berries instead of brown and specialty rices. Cook wheat berries for 35 minutes high pressure.

Brown Rice Tabbouleh

SERVES 4 TO 6

For an interesting twist, use chewy brown rice instead of bulgur wheat to make this refreshing grain salad. For variegated color, add one of the many specialty rices now available—such as wehani or black japonica.

This tabbouleh tastes best when freshly made. Serve it with a small mound of Hummus (page 240) on the side for a cooling summer lunch.

15 minutes high pressure

TO COOK THE BROWN RICE
6 cups water
$1^1/2$ cups short-grain brown rice, rinsed
$1/2$ cup specialty rice, such as calusari red, wehani, black japonica
    (or use additional brown rice), rinsed
$1^1/2$ tablespoons oil (needed to control foaming)
1 teaspoon salt

FOR THE TABBOULEH
$1/4$ cup fruity olive oil
2 cups finely chopped fresh parsley leaves and tender stems (from
    2 good-sized bunches)
$1/2$ cup finely chopped fresh mint
4 to 5 tablespoons freshly squeezed lemon juice
Salt

Pour the water into a 4-quart or larger cooker and bring to a boil over high heat as you measure and add the rices, oil, and salt.

Lock the lid in place. Over high heat bring to high pressure. Reduce the heat just enough to maintain high pressure and cook for 15 minutes. Turn off the heat. Quick-release the pressure by setting the cooker under cold running water. Remove the lid, tilting it away from you to allow excess steam to escape.

If the rice is not sufficiently tender (remember that whole

grains are always a bit chewy), simmer uncovered until done. Drain thoroughly, bouncing the colander up and down a few times to release excess liquid. Immediately return the rice to the hot cooker, set the lid in place (but do not lock it), and let steam in the residual heat for 5 minutes.

Transfer to a large bowl and immediately stir in the olive oil. When the rice has cooled, stir in the parsley, mint, and enough lemon juice to give the salad a distinct citrus edge. Add salt to taste. Serve at room temperature.

Tip: To rejuvenate salad, set in a bowl, cover lightly with a paper towel, and heat briefly in the microwave. To give the flavor a lift, toss in more fresh parsley and lemon juice.

Variations
• Instead of two types of rice, use 2 cups wheat berries or kamut (or a combination). Increase cooking time to 35 minutes.
• Add 1 to 2 cups seeded, diced plum tomatoes or quartered cherry tomatoes.
• Add 1 to 2 cups peeled, seeded, diced cucumber.
• If fresh mint is not available, add 1 teaspoon dried—you can empty it out of a mint teabag.
• Add 1 or 2 chopped scallions or ½ cup finely chopped red onion.

Transformations *(Follow basic recipe except as noted.)*
• FRUIT AND NUT TABBOULEH: Add ½ cup raisins, ¼ cup toasted pine nuts (see page 19), and 1 teaspoon grated lemon zest.
• TABBOULEH WITH GREEK FLAVORS: Add ½ to 1 cup crumbled feta, 1 to 2 cups diced tomatoes, and ½ cup chopped calamata olives. Use dill instead of mint.
• LENTIL TABBOULEH: Instead of rice or other grains, cook 1½ cups French green (du Puy) lentils for 1 minute high pressure plus 8-minute natural pressure release. Release any remaining pressure. If lentils are not tender, simmer until done. Place drained lentils in a bowl and toss with tabbouleh ingredients plus

2 cups seeded, diced tomatoes and ½ cup finely diced red onion. **Note:** French green lentils hold their shape better than brown lentils, so they're more suitable for a salad.

• TABBOULEH SOUP: Add small portions of tabbouleh to good-quality chicken or vegetable broth.

Pasta

For additional pasta recipes, consult the Index.

The first time I unlocked the lid of a pressure cooker containing rigatoni and homemade tomato sauce, I was amazed that the pasta hadn't turned to mush. On the contrary, the rigatoni has a pleasing texture and tasted absolutely delicious, having absorbed the flavor of the sauce as it cooked. This success opened up the world of one-pot pasta dinners and emboldened me to experiment further.

Cooking pasta suppers under pressure turns out to be easy and fun, as you will soon discover. Here are a few general guidelines to keep in mind if you'd like to try adapting your own favorite recipes:

Use short, cut pasta like ziti or elbows—or shapes like shells or spirals. Long, thin pasta like spaghetti, linguine, and fettuccine tends to clump.

For pasta that normally cooks within 9 to 13 minutes, cooking time is generally 5 minutes under pressure.

Pasta that is not submerged in liquid will cook by steam pressure.

When adding pasta to a recipe, include $1/2$ cup additional water or broth for every 4 ounces dry pasta. In other words, for 8 ounces of pasta add 1 cup additional liquid; for 12 ounces add $1^1/2$ cups; and for 1 pound add 2 cups. Knowing this formula, you can increase or decrease the amount of pasta and liquid in the recipes that follow.

When making pasta in a tomato sauce, since hardly any liquid is lost by evaporation, it's important to use a thick canned tomato product like crushed tomatoes in puree. If unavailable, substitute a 28-ounce can of plum tomatoes (coarsely chopped, including liquid) plus a 6-ounce can of tomato paste.

After pressure release, stir well to break up any pasta that is stuck together or clinging to the bottom of the cooker.

Pasta dishes benefit from a resting period of 3 to 5 minutes after pressure release. During this time, the sauce becomes more concentrated as the pasta continues to absorb liquid and flavor.

If the pasta is quite undercooked or has not cooked to uniform tenderness under pressure, replace the lid during the resting period, set the cooker over very low heat, and continue cooking until done.

Pasta with Meat Sauce

SERVES 3 TO 4

This one-pot pasta dish is quick, easy, and very good. It is especially satisfying when made with spirals or shells, which catch bits of meat in their crevices.

5 minutes high pressure

1 to 2 tablespoons olive oil
$3/4$ to 1 pound ground beef, pork, or lamb
$1^1/2$ cups coarsely chopped onions
1 teaspoon whole fennel seeds
$1/2$ cup dry red wine or dry vermouth
$1^1/2$ cups water
$3/4$ teaspoon salt
$1/2$ to 1 teaspoon granulated garlic or garlic powder
12 ounces spirals or other short, cut pasta that normally cooks in
    9 to 13 minutes
One can (28 ounces) crushed tomatoes in puree OR
    one can (28 ounces) plum tomatoes (with liquid), plus
    one can (6 ounces) tomato paste
$1/4$ cup chopped fresh parsley
$1/4$ cup grated parmesan or romano cheese, plus more to pass at
    the table
$1/4$ to $1/2$ teaspoon crushed red pepper flakes
    (optional)
Pinch of sugar (optional)

Heat 1 tablespoon of the oil in a 4-quart or larger cooker. Add the ground meat and brown over high heat, stirring frequently to break up any clumps. Stir in the onions and fennel seeds, and continue cooking for 1 minute.

Stir in the wine, taking care to scrape up any browned bits sticking to the bottom of the cooker. Boil over high heat until some of the liquid has evaporated, about 1 minute. Stir in the water, salt, and garlic. Bring to a boil. Add the pasta and pour the tomatoes on top. (If using whole plum tomatoes, crush them in your hand and distribute heaping tablespoonsful of the tomato paste on top.) Do not stir after adding the tomatoes.

Lock the lid in place. Over high heat bring to high pressure. Reduce the heat just enough to maintain high pressure and cook for 5 minutes. Turn off the heat. Quick-release the pressure by setting the cooker under cold running water. Remove the lid, tilting it away from you to allow steam to escape.

Stir in the parsley, cheese, and crushed red pepper flakes (if using). Add the remaining tablespoon of oil and sugar, if needed, to round out the flavors. Break up any pasta that is stuck together and release any that is clinging to the bottom of the cooker.

Let the dish rest uncovered in the cooker for 3 to 5 minutes. If the pasta is not uniformly tender, replace the lid during this period and set the cooker over very low heat, stirring occasionally, until the pasta is done.

Serve in large shallow bowls. Sprinkle cheese on top of each portion and serve additional cheese in a small bowl.

Variations

• Instead of beef, use fresh Italian sausages (sweet or hot; casings removed). After browning, pour off any excess fat before adding onions.
• Use meatloaf mix (a prepackaged combination of ground beef, veal, and pork) instead of one type of meat.
• Stir in 1 cup ricotta when you add parsley.

Transformations *(Follow basic recipe except as noted.)*

• PASTA WITH MUSHROOM SAUCE (Vegetarian): Omit ground meat. Reduce water to $1\frac{1}{4}$ cups. Add 8 ounces sliced portobellos or other mushrooms along with pasta.
• PASTA WITH SEAFOOD AND TOMATO SAUCE: Omit ground meat. After adding pasta, add 1 pound medium or large shrimp (peeling optional) or $\frac{1}{2}$ pound shrimp and 1 pound mussels. Parmesan is optional.
• NORTH AFRICAN LAMB WITH PASTA: Use ground lamb (sometimes sold as lamb patties). After adding tomatoes, sprinkle $\frac{1}{2}$

teaspoon ground cinnamon and $\frac{1}{3}$ cup raisins on top. After cooking, omit parmesan.

Note: This dish is especially pretty when made with bowtie pasta.

PRESSURE POINT

• If cooking on an electric or high-BTU stove, set the cooker on a heat diffuser before bringing up the pressure.

Ziti with Three Cheeses

This homey dish brings to mind all the goodness of traditional baked ziti, but it's ready in minutes rather than hours. And only one pot to clean!

5 minutes high pressure

1 cup water
1 cup coarsely chopped onions
$1/2$ teaspoon salt
8 ounces ziti or other short pasta that normally cooks in 9 to 13 minutes
One can (28 ounces) peeled plum tomatoes (with liquid)
2 to 4 cloves garlic, peeled, or 1 teaspoon garlic powder
1 to $1^1/2$ teaspoons Italian Herb Blend (page 18 or storebought)
1 cup ricotta (whole milk or low-fat)
$1/4$ cup grated parmesan or romano, plus more for garnish
1 cup (about 6 ounces) shredded or finely chopped mozzarella cheese
Freshly ground pepper

223

Combine the water, onions, and salt in a 4-quart or larger cooker.

Bring to a boil. Stir in the ziti. Pour the tomatoes on top of the ziti, crushing the tomatoes in your hand as you empty the can. Do not stir after adding the tomatoes. Add the garlic.

Lock the lid in place. Over high heat bring to high pressure. Reduce the heat just enough to maintain high pressure and cook for 5 minutes. Turn off the heat. Quick-release the pressure under cold running water. Remove the lid, tilting it away from you to allow steam to escape.

Stir in the Italian Herb Blend, ricotta, and parmesan. Separate any ziti that are stuck together and release any that are clinging to the bottom of the cooker. Distribute half of the mozzarella on top. Use a rubber spatula or large spoon to scoop ziti from the bottom and set it on top of the mozzarella. Repeat with remaining mozzarella. Season with salt and pepper to taste.

Let the dish rest in the cooker for 3 to 5 minutes, giving the mixture time to thicken. If the pasta is not uniformly tender, cover the cooker during this period and cook over very low heat, stirring occasionally, until the pasta is done.

Serve in pasta bowls with a generous dusting of parmesan on top of each portion.

Variations
• Use smoked mozzarella instead of plain.
• Add ½ to 1 cup finely diced soppressata, chorizo, or other cured sausage when you add the cheeses.
• For a lighter version, leave out the ricotta.
• Stir in ¼ cup chopped fresh basil or parsley along with the cheeses.

Transformations *(Follow basic recipe except as noted.)*
• ZITI WITH MEAT OR FRESH SAUSAGE: Before adding water and onions, brown ½ pound ground meat (beef, pork, veal, or lamb) or fresh Italian sausage (sweet or hot; casings removed) in 1 tablespoon olive oil. Pour off any excess fat. When you add water, be sure to scrape up any browned bits sticking to bottom of cooker.
• ZITI WITH MUSHROOMS: Reduce water to ¾ cup and add 6 ounces sliced mushrooms along with onions.
• ZITI CASSEROLE: Preheat oven to 350 degrees Fahrenheit. Transfer hot, cooked mixture to an oiled shallow heatproof dish. Top with additional shredded mozzarella. Set under broiler until lightly browned and bubbly. (Note: If using cold leftovers for casserole, heat them in microwave or oven before popping them under broiler.)

PRESSURE POINTS
• If cooking on an electric or high-BTU stove, set cooker on a heat diffuser before bringing up pressure.

• It's not wise to cook dairy products in cooker. They tend to sink to bottom and scorch.

• It's risky to double this recipe, even in an 8-quart cooker. The increased time it would take for cooker to come up to pressure may cause ingredients on bottom to scorch.

Chicken Noodle "Casserole" with Mushroom Sauce

SERVES 3 TO 4

Here's an easy way to get a homespun dinner on the table in about 20 minutes. Cook the noodles and chicken together, then stir in an undiluted can of cream of mushroom soup to create an instant, creamy sauce.

---

4 minutes high pressure

2$^{1}/_{2}$ cups chicken broth
1 cup chopped onions
10 ounces mushrooms (cremini or portobello are nice), sliced
8 ounces wide egg noodles that normally cook in 8 to 11 minutes
2 pounds boneless, skinned chicken, cut into 1-inch chunks
    (thighs remain moister)
One can (10 ounces) cream of mushroom soup
$^{1}/_{2}$ teaspoon dried thyme
1 cup frozen peas
Salt and freshly ground pepper
1 tablespoon lemon juice (optional)
2 tablespoons chopped fresh dill or parsley, for garnish

Combine the broth, onions, and mushrooms in a 4-quart or larger cooker. Add the noodles and scatter the chicken on top.

Lock the lid in place. Over high heat bring to high pressure. Reduce the heat just enough to maintain high pressure and cook for 4 minutes. Turn off the heat. Quick-release the pressure. Remove the lid, tilting it away from you to allow steam to escape.

Stir in the condensed soup, thyme, peas, and salt and pepper to taste. Gently break up any noodles that are sticking together and release any clinging to the bottom of the cooker. Cover and simmer until the peas are defrosted and the noodles are uniformly cooked, usually about 1 minute.

Just before serving, stir in the lemon juice, if needed, to

brighten the flavors. Transfer to a large bowl or individual plates and garnish with the dill or parsley.

Variation
• Instead of wide egg noodles, use short cut pasta like spirals or bowties that normally cooks in 9 to 13 minutes. Increase cooking time to 5 minutes under pressure.

Transformation *(Follow basic recipe except as noted.)*
• TURKEY NOODLE "CASSEROLE": Instead of chicken, use boneless, skinned turkey.

227

Penne with Winter Squash and Ricotta

SERVES 3 TO 4

The idea of combining pasta and squash comes from the kitchens of northern Italy. I've added ricotta to make the dish more substantial. A generous quantity of toasted hazelnuts provides agreeable crunch to this otherwise mellow dish.

The squash is cut into two sizes. The smaller pieces "melt down" and blend with the ricotta to create a pale orange sauce that coats the penne. The larger pieces break up into small chunks and offer dots of bright color. Serve as an entree accompanied by a crisp salad.

---

5 minutes high pressure

2¹/2 pounds butternut squash, peeled, halved, and seeded

1 tablespoon butter or olive oil

1 cup coarsely chopped onions

3 cups chicken broth

1 teaspoon salt (omit if using salty broth)

12 ounces penne or other short, cut pasta that normally cooks in 9 to 13 minutes

1 cup ricotta (whole-fat or low-fat)

1/2 to 3/4 teaspoon ground sage

2 to 4 tablespoons chopped fresh parsley

1/4 cup grated parmesan, plus more to pass at the table

1 cup toasted hazelnuts or walnuts (see page 19), coarsely chopped

Cut half the squash into 3/4-inch chunks and the remaining squash into 2-inch pieces. Set aside.

Heat the butter in a 6-quart or larger cooker. Stir in the onions, chicken broth, salt (if using), and smaller pieces of squash. Bring to a boil and add the pasta. (It's okay if all of the pasta is not covered with liquid.) Set the remaining squash on top.

Lock the lid in place. Over high heat bring to high pressure. Reduce the heat just enough to maintain high pressure and cook for 5 minutes. Turn off the heat. Quick-release the pressure. Remove the lid, tilting it away from you to allow steam to escape.

Add the ricotta, sage and parsley to taste, and the parmesan. Stir gently until some of the squash dissolves. Break apart any pasta that is stuck together.

Let the dish rest in the cooker for 3 to 5 minutes so that the flavors can meld. If the pasta is not uniformly tender, replace the lid during this period and set the cooker over very low heat, stirring occasionally, until the pasta is done.

Stir in the toasted nuts. Serve in large, shallow bowls. Pass additional parmesan at the table.

Variations

• VEGETARIAN VERSION: Use vegetable broth instead of chicken.
• Brown ½ pound ground pork or veal in oil before adding onions.
• Instead of sage, use dried oregano or freshly grated nutmeg to taste.
• Use a kabocha squash instead of butternut. Kabocha (also called Hokkaido pumpkin) is available in some supermarkets and many health food stores. It is not necessary to peel kabocha; just scrub well and trim off any blemishes.

Orzo Risotto with Wild Mushrooms

SERVES 4

For an elegant side dish, cook the tiny tear-shaped pasta called orzo in an intense mushroom broth.

This risotto goes well with hearty meats like lamb and veal shanks, short ribs, or oxtails.

---

4 minutes high pressure

---

1 ounce dried porcini or other wild mushrooms
1 tablespoon olive oil
$1/2$ cup chopped shallots or onions
1 cup chicken broth
$1^1/4$ cups orzo (also called riso)
$1/2$ teaspoon salt
1 to 2 teaspoons balsamic vinegar
$1/4$ cup grated parmesan cheese, plus more for for serving

Place the mushrooms in a large Pyrex measuring cup and pour 2 cups hot water over them. Cover and let sit until the mushrooms are soft, about 10 minutes. Lift out the mushrooms with a slotted spoon and squeeze to release all liquid. If the mushrooms feel gritty, rinse them. Chop any large pieces. Set aside mushrooms and soaking liquid.

Heat the oil in a 4-quart or larger cooker. Add the shallots and cook for 1 minute. Stir in the mushroom soaking liquid, taking care to leave behind any grit that has settled in the bottom of the cup. Add the broth, orzo, mushrooms, salt, and 1 teaspoon of the vinegar.

Lock the lid in place. Over high heat bring to high pressure. Reduce the heat just enough to maintain high pressure and cook for 4 minutes. Turn off the heat. Quick-release the pressure by setting the cooker under cold running water. Remove the lid, tilting it away from you to allow steam to escape.

The risotto will be soupy at this point. Add more salt to taste and the remaining teaspoon vinegar, if needed to sharpen the flavors. Boil over medium-high heat, stirring frequently, until the mixture thickens and the orzo is tender but still a bit chewy, 3 to 4 minutes. Add a little water during this time if the mixture becomes dry. While the risotto is still slightly soupy, dish onto plates or serve in small bowls. Top with a light dusting of parmesan.

Variations
• Stir in 2 tablespoons chopped parsley or 1 to 2 teaspoons chopped fresh rosemary just before serving.
• Stir in 1 cup frozen peas during last minute of cooking.

Transformation *(Follow basic recipe except as noted.)*
• ASIAN ORZO RISOTTO WITH SHIITAKE: Instead of porcini, use 1¹/₂ ounces dried shiitake. After soaking, discard stems (or reserve for making broth) and cut caps into ¹/₄-inch slices. Use 2 teaspoons toasted sesame oil instead of olive oil and 1¹/₂ tablespoons soy sauce instead of salt. After pressure release, stir in 1 to 2 teaspoons grated fresh ginger and 2 tablespoons each chopped fresh cilantro and thinly sliced scallion greens. Season with more soy sauce and toasted sesame oil, if needed. Omit balsamic vinegar and parmesan.

Beans

For additional recipes using beans, consult the Index.

With a pressure cooker at arm's reach, you can spontaneously decide to have home-cooked bean soups or stews for dinner. There is no need for presoaking, and the cooker hydrates and tenderizes beans in one-third the standard cooking time.

When selecting beans, look for batches with bright color and skins intact. Faded color means faded flavor, and broken or chipped beans turn to mush. Before cooking, pick over the beans and discard any that are damaged.

Cooking times inevitably vary from one batch of beans to the next—and even within batches. As a general rule, the older and drier the beans, the longer they'll take to cook. But, since there's usually no way to know a bean's age or condition, there's a bit of guesswork involved in determining cooking time.

When preparing a soup or stew, it's not a problem if the beans are very soft, but if you need firm specimens for a salad, it's best to bring the beans close to tenderness under pressure, then simmer them under a watchful eye to complete cooking. I've offered a range of times in the Bean Timing Chart (see page 238); select the best time to suit your purpose.

Here are a few other guidelines to keep in mind when pressure cooking beans:

• Beans foam when they cook. To prevent foam from spouting out of the vent, and to prevent a loose bean skin from blocking the vent, always add 1 tablespoon oil. Add 2 tablespoons when cooking limas and soybeans, which foam more than other beans.

• Do not fill the cooker more than halfway when cooking beans.

• Adding too much salt retards cooking time and can prevent the beans from becoming fully tender, so don't add more than suggested in the Basic Beans in Aromatic Broth recipe on page 236. Don't add any salt when cooking beans with salty ingredients like ham hocks.

• Always allow time for natural pressure release. Quick-release causes the beans to split, lose their shape, and become mushy.

• If beans are to be cooked with tomatoes or other acidic ingredients, soak them overnight and cut the cooking time in half. Unsoaked beans don't become fully tender when cooked in an acidic broth. Even when using presoaked beans, it's best to keep acidic ingredients to a minimum.

Basic Beans in Aromatic Broth

MAKES 5 TO 7 CUPS COOKED BEANS

When cooking beans from scratch, its practical to prepare more than you need and store extra for future use. Beans cook most evenly in an abundance of liquid, providing the perfect excuse to simultaneously prepare an aromatic broth for another use.

Most cookbooks warn you to avoid adding salt until the beans are nearly cooked. When cooking under pressure, adding a little salt right from the start enhances the beans' flavor and— more importantly—helps them hold onto their delicate skins and beautiful shape.

For timing, see the Bean Timing Chart on page 238.

---

1 pound (about 2¹/₂ cups) dried beans, picked over and rinsed
9 cups water
³/₄ teaspoon salt
1 tablespoon oil (needed to control foaming)
2 to 4 unpeeled cloves garlic
2 large bay leaves
1 large carrot, halved
1 celery rib, halved
A few leek greens (optional)

In a 6-quart or larger cooker, combine the beans, water, salt, and oil. Add the garlic, bay leaves, carrot, celery, and leek greens (if using).

Lock the lid in place. Over high heat bring to high pressure. Reduce the heat just enough to maintain high pressure and cook for the length of time indicated on the Bean Timing Chart on page 238. Turn off the heat. Allow the pressure to come down naturally, 15 to 20 minutes. Remove the lid, tilting it away from you to allow steam to escape.

Test the beans for doneness. They should mash easily and have a creamy texture. If just short of tender, replace (but do not lock) the lid and simmer until done. If still quite hard, return to high pressure for another minute (if they have just a bit of crunch) to 5 minutes (if they are quite hard) and again allow the pressure to come down naturally.

If time permits, allow the beans to cool in the cooking liquid, uncovered. (During this time, the beans will firm up and any slightly underdone beans will complete cooking.) Drain in batches in a large colander. Avoid crushing the beans by piling them in a big heap. Reserve the broth for making soup or stew. Discard the bay leaves and vegetables. Refrigerate beans for up to 5 days or freeze for up to 4 months.

Tips: Although dried beans keep well, they'll taste best if you cook them within 6 months of purchase. It's convenient to freeze cooked beans in 1¹/₂ cup quantities for use in recipes that call for a 15-ounce can.

Variations
• Reduce water to 8 cups. Add a small, meaty pork bone.
• Omit salt and add a ham hock.

Transformations *(Follow basic recipe except as noted.)*
• SMASHED BEANS: Drain beans while they are still hot. Return beans to cooker and mash with olive oil, roasted garlic, chopped fresh herbs, and lots of salt and pepper. Smashed Beans make a nice alternative to mashed potatoes.
• MULTI-BEAN SOUP: Instead of one type of bean, use a variety. (This is a good way to use up leftover dried beans in your pantry—or use a storebought bean soup mixture.) Reduce water to 4 cups and use 4 cups chicken broth. (If broth is salty, do not add more salt until beans are cooked.) Peel garlic cloves and chop carrots, celery, and leek greens. Use timing for longest cooking bean. After pressure release, season with salt, pepper, and chopped fresh herbs.

PRESSURE POINT
• If using a 4-quart cooker, divide recipe in half but use a full table-spoon of oil.

Bean Timing Chart

For firm beans, to be served on their own or in salads, cook for the minimum suggested time. For bean soups, stews, or purees, cook for the maximum suggested time. Allow 15 to 20 minutes for the natural pressure release, which is essential to completing the job properly. Allow extra time for any additional cooking that may be needed.

Always add 1 tablespoon oil to control foaming; 2 tablespoons oil for limas and soybeans. Do not fill the cooker more than halfway when cooking beans.

1 Cup Dried Beans	Minutes High Pressure* + Natural Release	Yield in Cups
Adzuki (Azuki)	16 to 21	2
Black (Turtle)	22 to 25	2
Black-Eyed Peas	6 to 8	2$\frac{1}{4}$
Cannellini	28 to 32	2
Chickpeas (Garbanzos)	32 to 35	2$\frac{1}{2}$
Cranberry (Borlotti)	28 to 34	2$\frac{1}{4}$
Flageolet	28 to 34	2
Great Northern	25 to 30	2$\frac{1}{4}$
Lentils (brown or French green)	1[†] to 5	2
Lentils (red)	5[‡]	2
Lima (large)[§]	9 to 10	2$\frac{1}{2}$
Lima (baby)	13 to 15	2$\frac{1}{2}$
Navy (pea)	22 to 25	2
Peas (split, green or yellow)	10 to 12	2

Pinto	19 to 22	$2^1/_4$
Red Kidney	25 to 30	2
Romano (Roman)	25 to 30	2
Small Red Beans	26 to 30	2
Soybeans (beige)§	28 to 35	$2^1/_4$
Soybeans (black)§	32 to 37	$2^1/_2$

*For soaked beans, cut cooking time in half.
†After 1 minute high pressure, allow pressure to come down naturally for 8 minutes, then quick-release any remaining pressure.
‡Red lentils do not hold their shape when cooked, so you can use the quick-release method.
§Use 2 tablespoons oil per 1 cup beans to control foaming.

Beans

Hummus

MAKES 2¹/₂ CUPS

Chickpeas are notoriously difficult to cook properly using standard techniques. The pressure cooker can be counted on to make every batch melt-in-your-mouth tender. Hummus made from freshly cooked chickpeas is absolutely delicious.

Serve hummus as a dip for raw vegetables or offer a mound of it to accompany Brown Rice Tabbouleh (page 214). For a light lunch, stuff hummus into pita bread with shredded lettuce and chopped tomatoes.

While you're at it, why not cook a whole pound of chickpeas (see Basic Beans in Aromatic Broth, page 236)? Set aside 3 cups of the cooked chickpeas to prepare the hummus. Refrigerate or freeze the extra chickpeas until needed.

35 minutes high pressure plus natural pressure release

FOR THE CHICKPEAS
1¹/₄ cups dried chickpeas, picked over and rinsed
7 cups water
1 tablespoon oil (needed to control foaming)
¹/₂ teaspoon salt

FOR THE HUMMUS
1 clove garlic (optional)
3 to 4 tablespoons tahini (sesame seed paste)
5 tablespoons freshly squeezed lemon juice, plus more to taste
1 teaspoon salt
¹/₃ to ³/₄ cup chickpea cooking liquid

FOR THE GARNISHES
1 tablespoon olive oil
Paprika
Oil-cured olives

In a 4-quart or larger cooker, combine the chickpeas, water, oil, and salt.

Lock the lid in place. Over high heat bring to high pressure. Reduce the heat just enough to maintain high pressure and cook for 35 minutes. Turn off the heat. Allow the pressure to come down naturally, 15 to 20 minutes. Remove the lid, tilting it away from you to allow steam to escape. If the chickpeas are not uniformly tender, replace (but do not lock) the lid and simmer until done.

Drain the chickpeas, reserving the cooking liquid. Discard any loose bean skins. Allow the chickpeas to cool to room temperature. (Run cold water over them if you're in a hurry.)

To make the hummus: If using garlic, pass the clove through the feed tube of a food processor while the motor is running. Add the chickpeas, tahini, lemon juice, and salt. With the motor running, add enough of the cooking liquid—usually ⅓ to ¾ cup—to make a smooth, thick paste. Add more lemon juice and salt, if needed. Use immediately or refrigerate for up to 1 week.

To serve, transfer to a bowl and surround with a ring of olive oil. Garnish with a light sprinkle of paprika and some olives.

241

Variation
• Instead of raw garlic, add a few cloves roasted garlic (see page 18).

Transformations *(Follow basic recipe except as noted.)*
• PARSLEY HUMMUS: Roughly chop 2 cups loosely packed parsley leaves and tender stems in food processor before adding chickpeas.
• RED PEPPER HUMMUS WITH TOASTED CUMIN SEEDS: Puree 1 roasted, seeded red bell pepper before adding chickpeas. Add 1 teaspoon toasted cumin seeds with chickpeas.
• JALAPEÑO HUMMUS: Add 1 or 2 seeded, quartered jalapeños to food processor along with chickpeas.
• CHICKPEA TAHINI SOUP WITH ROASTED RED PEPPER: For every ½ cup of Red Pepper Hummus (see above), blend in ½ cup chickpea cooking liquid. Add more salt, if needed. Heat thoroughly. (This soup is rich; allow about ¾ cup per serving.)

Sub-limey Refried Beans

SERVES 4 TO 6

For a fresh take on traditional refried beans, mash the beans with lightly browned onions, then add some grated jalapeño Jack cheese, lime juice, and a little lime zest.

Use the beans as a filling for tacos or enchiladas along with shredded crisp lettuce and guacamole or sliced avocado. Alternatively, serve the beans as an accompaniment to grilled steak or eggs scrambled with a tablespoon or two of salsa.

Consider cooking a whole pound of beans (see Basic Beans in Aromatic Broth, page 236), then freeze the extra for later use. You'll need about 3½ cups cooked beans for this recipe.

---

22 to 25 minutes high pressure (depending on type of beans)

1½ cups dried pinto, black, or red kidney beans, picked over and
    rinsed
6 cups water
½ teaspoon salt, plus more to taste
2 tablespoons olive oil
1 cup finely chopped onions
1 teaspoon whole cumin seeds or ½ teaspoon ground cumin
1 large clove garlic, minced
½ teaspoon dried oregano
½ cup grated jalapeño Jack cheese, plus more for garnish
½ to 3 tablespoons freshly squeezed lime juice, plus ¼ to
    ½ teaspoon grated zest
¼ cup toasted pumpkin seeds, for garnish (optional)

In a 4-quart or larger cooker, combine the beans, water, ½ teaspoon salt, and 1 tablespoon of oil (needed to control foaming).

Lock the lid in place. Over high heat bring to high pressure. Reduce the heat just enough to maintain high pressure and cook for the maximum minutes suggested on the Bean Timing Chart, page 238. Turn off the heat. Allow the pressure to come down naturally. If the beans are not very soft, replace (but do not lock) the lid and simmer until done. Drain the beans. Reserve the cooking liquid to thin the refried beans.

In the cooker or a large skillet (easier to maneuver), heat the remaining tablespoon oil. Add the onions and cumin seeds and cook over medium-high heat, stirring occasionally, until the onions are limp, about 3 minutes. Add the garlic and oregano and cook, stirring frequently, until the onions are lightly browned, 2 to 3 minutes more.

Stir in 1 cup of the bean cooking liquid. Lower the heat to medium and add half the beans. Use a potato masher or fork to mash them. Add the remaining beans and mash. You can leave the mixture quite coarse, with some beans intact, or continue mashing until fairly smooth. Stir well and make sure the beans are thoroughly heated.

When most of the liquid has been absorbed, turn off the heat. Stir in the cheese, 2 tablespoons lime juice, lime zest, and salt to taste. (You may need as much as 1 teaspoon.) Add more lime juice, if needed to create a delicate citrus edge. Serve hot, with a sprinkling of grated cheese and pumpkin seeds (if using).

Variations
• Add 1 teaspoon chili powder when you add garlic and oregano.
• Use sharp cheddar or feta instead of jalapeño Jack.
• Stir in ⅓ cup thinly sliced scallion greens when you add cheese.
• Do as the Mexicans do and garnish refried beans with chopped radish.

Transformations *(Follow basic recipe except as noted.)*
• BEANS WITH BARBECUE SAUCE: Add 2 tablespoons Barbecue Sauce (page 112 or storebought) when you add bean cooking liquid. Omit lime juice and zest. Add more Barbecue Sauce, if needed, after you stir in cheese.

• BEAN TOSTADAS: Spread a generous layer of refried beans on a corn tortilla. Set tortilla in a skillet over medium heat. Sprinkle diced tomato and grated cheese on tortilla. Cover and heat until cheese is melted and beans are hot, about 4 minutes. Either fold in half or serve flat like a pizza.

Garlicky Lima Beans
with Tomatoes

SERVES 4 TO 6

Large lima beans are a real treat to eat. They have a hint of sweetness and the texture and appearance of creamy, miniature potatoes. In fact, they make a delightful alternative to spuds.

Limas are in the "limalight" in this soupy bean stew. Serve it in small bowls as a side dish, or in larger bowls as a vegetarian entree accompanied by a salad. Be sure to cook large (not small) limas beans for this recipe.

10 minutes high pressure plus natural pressure release

TO COOK THE BEANS
6 cups water

1¹/₂ cups coarsely chopped onions

1 pound (about 2¹/₂ cups) large dried lima beans, picked over and rinsed

8 cloves peeled garlic

2 tablespoons olive oil (needed to control foaming)

1 teaspoon salt

TO FINISH THE BEANS
3 large plum tomatoes, seeded and diced (about 3 cups)

1 tablespoon, chopped fresh oregano or 1 teaspoon dried

Salt

1 to 3 teaspoons balsamic vinegar

In a 6-quart or larger cooker, combine the water, onions, beans, garlic, oil, and salt.

Lock the lid in place. Over high heat bring to high pressure. Reduce the heat just enough to maintain high pressure and cook for 10 minutes. Turn off the heat. Allow the pressure to come down naturally, usually 15 to 20 minutes. Remove the lid, tilting it away from you to allow steam to escape. If the limas are not uniformly tender, replace (but do not lock) the lid and and simmer until done.

Stir in the tomatoes and oregano. Add salt to taste and enough vinegar to sharpen the flavors. Simmer uncovered, stirring occasionally, until the mixture thickens slightly and the flavors meld, 3 to 5 minutes. Serve in bowls.

Variations

• Use black beans instead of limas. Cook for 25 minutes high pressure plus natural pressure release.

• Instead of fresh plum tomatoes, use Pomi brand aseptic-packed chopped tomatoes.

• Use 1 to 2 teaspoons chopped fresh rosemary instead of oregano.

• Use lemon juice and zest instead of vinegar.

Transformations *(Follow basic recipe except as noted.)*

• LIMA BEANS WITH BUTTER AND FINES HERBES: Omit chopped onions. Drain cooked limas, reserving broth. Omit tomatoes and oregano. Heat 3 tablespoons butter in cooker. Turn off heat and stir in 1½ teaspoons fines herbes (a gourmet blend available in many supermarkets) or use 1 teaspoon dried tarragon instead. Let herb butter sit for a few minutes. Gently stir in limas and ½ cup broth. Reheat over low heat. (Reserve remaining broth for another use.)

• LIMA BEAN SALAD WITH ZUCCHINI, CORN, AND LEMON-OREGANO VINAIGRETTE: Decrease dried limas to 2 cups and omit chopped onions and garlic. Reduce cooking time to 9 minutes high pressure plus natural pressure release. When limas are tender but still firm, drain and gently transfer to a large bowl. Discard any loose bean skins. Instead of tomatoes, add 3 cups diced zucchini and 2 cups cooked corn. Prepare a vinaigrette by combining ¼ cup each olive oil, lemon juice, and finely chopped shallots or red onion, 2 tablespoons chopped capers, 1 teaspoon Dijon mustard, ½ teaspoon dried oregano, and ½ teaspoon salt. While beans are still warm, pour on vinaigrette and gently toss. Add extra salt and lemon juice to taste. Serve in small bowls as a side dish.

• GARLICKY LIMA BEAN SOUP WITH TOMATOES: Add 2 cups chicken or vegetable broth along with water. Reduce salt to ½ teaspoon if broth is salty. To thicken cooked soup, puree 1 cup limas with 1 cup broth and stir back in. Instead of fresh tomatoes, add 1 can (15 ounces) diced tomatoes.

PRESSURE POINTS
• If using a 4-quart cooker, divide recipe in half.
• Lima beans foam like crazy when they cook. Be sure to add 2 tablespoons oil to control foaming.
• If you own a jiggle-top cooker, avoid this recipe as foaming limas could clog an excess-pressure vent.
• Take special care to clean lid and pressure regulator after cooking lima beans.

Bean Salad Niçoise

This pretty salad—a hearty version of the traditional *Salade Niçoise*—is full of interesting tastes and textures. Instead of serving the tuna in a chunk, flake the fish and toss it with the beans. Serve the salad with the suggested accompaniments for a refreshing warm-weather entree.

22 to 28 minutes high pressure (depending on type of beans)

TO COOK THE BEANS
1 cup dried cannellini, navy, or Great Northern beans, picked over and rinsed
5 cups water
$1/2$ teaspoon salt
1 tablespoon oil (needed to control foaming)

FOR THE SALAD
$1/2$ cup diced red onion
1 can (6 ounces) tuna
1 cup diced plum tomatoes or halved cherry tomatoes
$1/4$ to $1/3$ cup niçoise or other small Mediterranean olives
1 to 3 tablespoons olive oil
2 tablespoons freshly squeezed lemon juice, plus more to taste
1 tablespoon balsamic or other red wine vinegar
10 large fresh basil leaves (or the equivalent)
Salt

FOR THE SUGGESTED ACCOMPANIMENTS
Bed of mixed greens
Sliced hard-boiled eggs
Steamed green beans
Cornichons
Wedge of Brie or other cheese

To make the beans: In a 4-quart or larger cooker, combine the beans, water, salt, and oil.

Lock the lid in place. Over high heat bring to high pressure. Reduce the heat just enough to maintain high pressure and cook for the minimum length of time indicated on the Bean Timing Chart, page 238. Turn off the heat. Allow the pressure to come down naturally, 10 to 15 minutes. Remove the lid, tilting it away from you to allow steam to escape. If the beans are not uniformly tender, replace (but do not lock) the lid and simmer until done.

If time permits, allow the beans to cool in the cooking liquid, uncovered. (During this time, the beans will firm up and any slightly underdone beans will complete cooking.) Drain in batches and transfer to a large bowl. Avoid crushing the beans by piling them in a big heap. Reserve the cooking liquid for making soup or stew.

To make the salad: Soak the diced onion in cold water to tame its "bite"—at least 10 minutes. Drain well.

If the tuna is packed in olive oil, empty the whole can into the bowl containing the beans; otherwise drain first. Flake the tuna with a fork. Stir in the onion, tomatoes, olives, and enough oil to generously coat the mixture. Add the lemon juice and vinegar.

Stack the basil leaves, roll them into a cigar shape, and cut across into very fine strips. Stir the basil into the salad. Add salt to taste—you are likely to need a generous amount—plus more olive oil and lemon juice, if needed.

Serve from the bowl or arrange on a large platter with your choice of accompaniments. The salad may be refrigerated for up to 4 days.

Variations
• Skip soaking red onions if you enjoy their strong bite.
• Add 1 to 2 tablespoons capers.

Transformations *(Follow basic recipe except as noted.)*
• SOUTHWEST BEAN AND TUNA SALAD: Instead of white beans, niçoise olives, lemon juice, and basil, use black beans, chopped pimento-stuffed green olives, lime juice, and 1/4 cup tightly packed chopped cilantro. If you wish, add 1 cup cooked corn and

Beans

1 jalapeño pepper that's been seeded and diced. Accompany salad with slices of avocado lightly sprinkled with salt.

• BEAN AND FETA SALAD: Omit tuna and substitute 1 cup crumbled feta. Let salad sit for 30 minutes before serving.

• WHITE BEAN BRUSCHETTA: Coarsely mash drained beans with $1/2$ teaspoon finely minced garlic. Omit tuna, tomatoes, and olives. Stir in remaining salad ingredients in the following amounts: $1/4$ cup finely chopped red onion, 2 tablespoons each olive oil and lemon juice, 1 teaspoon balsamic vinegar, 2 tablespoons minced fresh basil, and salt to taste. Spread mashed bean mixture on thinly sliced toasted Italian bread. Serve as an hors d'oeuvre.

Beefed-Up Beans

SERVES 4

This rustic bean stew requires very little preparation and is ideal for a last-minute Sunday supper. White turnips, cooked whole and then cut into chunks, add their gentle sweetness and lighten the dish. (I humbly implore any turnip haters out there to give them another try in this context.)

"So where's the beef?" you ask. It comes in the form of a beef shank—a lean but rich-tasting cut that deserves to be better known. The shredded meat from one cooked shank adds just the right amount of flavor and texture to make the dish work as a casual supper entree.

Choose a bean that takes at least 25 minutes to cook—the amount of time required for the shank. Then allow time for the natural pressure release to keep the beef tender and the bean skins intact.

25 to 32 minutes (depending on type of bean)

1 1/2 cups dried beans, such as cannellini, Great Northern, red kidney, or black, picked over and rinsed

6 cups water

1/2 teaspoon salt

1 large bay leaf

1 cup coarsely chopped onions

1 tablespoon olive oil (needed to control foaming)

3/4 to 1 pound white turnips (1 large or 2 medium), peeled and left whole

1 pound bone-in, cross-cut beef shank (shin), about 1 inch thick

1 to 2 teaspoons dried dill or 2 tablespoons chopped fresh

2 to 3 teaspoons balsamic or cider vinegar (optional)

In a 6-quart or larger cooker, combine the beans, water, salt, bay leaf, onions, and oil. Add the turnips and shank.

Lock the lid in place. Over high heat bring to high pressure. Reduce the heat just enough to maintain high pressure and cook for the maximum time indicated for the type of bean; see Bean Timing Chart, page 238. Turn off the heat. Allow the pressure to come down naturally, about 15 minutes. Remove the lid, tilting it away from you to allow steam to escape.

Transfer the shank and turnips to a cutting board. If the beans are not uniformly tender, either replace (but do not lock) the lid and simmer until done or return to high pressure for a few minutes and again let the pressure come down naturally. Add more salt and the dill to taste. The mixture will thicken after standing about 20 minutes, but if you wish to thicken it immediately, puree a cupful of beans, then stir them back into the stew.

When the shank is cool enough to handle, cut the meat from the bone and chop or shred. Dice the turnip. Stir the meat and turnip into the beans. Adjust seasonings, adding vinegar, if needed to bring up the flavors. Simmer until the dill infuses the stew, 2 to 3 minutes.

Variations

• Cook beans with 3 to 6 whole peeled cloves of garlic.
• Use 2 or 3 beef shanks (but do not fill cooker more than halfway).
• Instead of turnips, cook 3 large peeled carrots wrapped in a foil-pack (see page 15). Slice and add to stew after cooking.
• Substitute 1 large whole Yukon Gold potato for turnip.
• Use 2 tablespoons chopped fresh parsley instead of dill.
• Garnish each portion with a dollop of Dill–Sour Cream Sauce (page 114).

Transformations *(Follow basic recipe except as noted.)*

• BEAN STEW WITH SHORT RIBS: Instead of beef shank, add 1 pound trimmed, meaty beef short ribs. After pressure release, skim off fat that rises to surface or degrease broth in a fat separator. Season with oregano instead of dill.
• BEEFED-UP BEAN SOUP: Thin stew with a few cups beef broth.

PRESSURE POINT

• If using a 4-quart cooker, cut recipe in half.

Beans with Sausage and Greens

SERVES 4 TO 6

The triumvirate of beans, sausage, and greens shows up in many kitchens around the world because it's inexpensive and tastes so good. Select a fully cooked, juicy sausage—the kind that's stored under refrigeration and requires no more than a last-minute heating.

Using this recipe as a loose guide, you can create whatever combination suits your mood. Here are some possibilities:

Great Northern Beans with Kielbasa and Kale
Cannellini Beans with Garlic Sausage and Swiss Chard
Black Beans with Linguica and Kale
Red Kidney Beans with Andouille and Collards
Baby Limas with Smoked Chicken Sausage and Swiss Chard

---

22 to 32 minutes (depending on type of bean)

---

1 pound kale, collards, or Swiss chard
1 to 1¹/₂ pounds fully cooked sausage
7 cups water
1 pound (about 2¹/₂ cups) dried beans, picked over and rinsed
1¹/₂ cups coarsely chopped onions
2 to 4 whole cloves garlic, peeled
1 tablespoon olive oil (needed to control foaming)
Salt and freshly ground pepper
2 to 3 teaspoons cider or red wine vinegar
Hot sauce, to pass at the table

Prepare the greens: Trim off and discard tough stems about 1 inch from the root end. Rip or slice the leaves from the ribs. Set the leaves aside. Thinly slice the ribs and stems. Rinse well.

Dice one-fourth of the sausage. Set aside remaining sausage.

Pour the water into a 6-quart or larger cooker and set over high heat. Stir in the beans, sliced ribs and stems, diced sausage, onions, garlic, and oil.

Lock the lid in place. Over high heat bring to high pressure. Reduce the heat just enough to maintain high pressure and cook for the maximum time indicated on the Bean Timing Chart, page 238. Turn off the heat. Allow the pressure to come down naturally. Remove the lid, tilting it away from you to allow steam to escape. If the beans are not uniformly tender, either return to high pressure for a few minutes or replace (but do not lock) the lid and simmer until done.

While the beans are cooking, coarsely chop the greens. Swish them in several changes of water to remove all dirt. Drain.

Bring 1 cup water to a boil in a large skillet or saucepan that has a cover. Add the greens. Cover and steam over medium-high heat until they are tender, usually 5 to 7 minutes (kale and chard) or 10 to 15 minutes (collards). Add more water during this period if they become dry. Drain the greens.

If the stew is too thin, mash some beans against the side of the cooker and stir them in. Slice the remaining sausage and add it to the stew along with the cooked greens. Season with salt and pepper to taste plus enough vinegar to sharpen the flavors. Simmer uncovered until the sausage is hot, 3 to 5 minutes. Ladle into large bowls. Pass a bottle of hot sauce at the table.

Variations

• Instead of using a hearty green, substitute 12 ounces chopped fresh spinach or a large bunch of chopped arugula. There's no need to precook: just stir it into stew after pressure release and simmer until tender.

• COOK-ALONG POTATOES: Cook 2 large whole scrubbed potatoes with beans. After cooking, dice and stir into stew.

• Pan-fry sausage slices before adding them to stew.

• Use diced sausage to season stew, but serve stew with whole grilled sausages.

PRESSURE POINT

• If using a 4-quart cooker, divide recipe in half, but use 1 tablespoon of oil to control foaming.

254

Madras Chickpeas with Spinach

SERVES 6

For optimum results, season this flavor-packed vegetarian curry with a spice blend you know and enjoy. I use a mild Madras-style curry blend and then add cayenne when I'm in the mood for more heat. One good brand of Madras curry powder is Merwanjee Poonjiajee & Sons, available in gourmet shops and many supermarkets. This curry blend and some others contain salt, so it's best to add any additional salt after cooking.

Serve it over basmati rice, and pass bowls of mango chutney and eggplant or lime pickle on the side.

---

16 minutes high pressure plus natural pressure release

1¹/2 cups (about 10 ounces) dried chickpeas, soaked overnight in ample water to cover
1 cup chicken or vegetable broth
1 can (14 ounces) coconut milk
2 tablespoons Madras-style mild curry powder, plus more to taste
2 packages (10 ounces each) frozen chopped spinach
2 large (about 1 pound total) onions, peeled and cut into eighths
One can (15 ounces) diced tomatoes with chiles (including liquid)
Salt
Pinch of cayenne or crushed red pepper flakes
¹/4 cup chopped fresh cilantro

Drain the chickpeas. In a 6-quart or larger cooker, blend the broth, coconut milk, and curry powder. Set over high heat. Add the chickpeas, spinach, and onions. Pour the tomatoes on top. Do not stir after adding the tomatoes.

Lock the lid in place. Over high heat bring to high pressure. Reduce the heat just enough to maintain high pressure and cook for 16 minutes. Turn off the heat. Allow the pressure to come down naturally. Remove the lid, tilting it away from you to allow steam to escape. If the chickpeas are not quite tender, replace (but do not lock) the lid and simmer until done.

Stir the curry well and add cayenne, more curry powder if necessary, and salt to taste. The curry will thicken as it stands, but if you wish to thicken it immediately, mash some chickpeas against the side of the cooker with a fork and stir them in. Stir in the cilantro.

Serve in large, shallow bowls or lipped plates.

Variations

• Cook chickpeas with ¹/₂ pound vegetarian meat substitute, such as Smart Ground or Veat!

• Add ¹/₃ cup raisins after pressure release.

Transformation *(Follow basic recipe except as noted.)*

• CHICKPEA, SPINACH, AND LAMB CURRY: Add 1¹/₂ pounds lamb shoulder, cut into 1-inch cubes, along with chickpeas.

PRESSURE POINTS

• If using a 4-quart cooker, divide recipe in half.

• The acid in tomatoes can prevent beans from cooking properly. Soaking chickpeas overnight assures that they will become uniformly tender.

256

Black Beans with Soft Tortilla Chips

SERVES 4

This homey stew calls for stirring tortilla chips into a potful of just-cooked black beans. The chips absorb the bean broth and soften, thickening the stew and contributing their irresistible corn flavor.

What makes the dish especially fun to eat is the array of accompaniments served in bowls on the side. Be sure to offer fresh, crisp items—like radishes or chopped red onion—as well as salty ones—like a sharp cheese or olives.

25 minutes high pressure plus natural pressure release

6 cups water

1¹/₂ cups dried black beans, picked over and rinsed

1 cup coarsely chopped onions

4 whole cloves garlic, peeled

1 tablespoon oil (needed to control foaming)

¹/₂ teaspoon salt

1 to 2 teaspoons chili powder

1 to 1¹/₂ teaspoons dried oregano

8 loosely packed cups tortilla chips (regular or oven-baked)

2 cups coarsely chopped tomatoes

¹/₄ cup sour cream, for serving

Lime wedges, for serving

FOR THE SUGGESTED ACCOMPANIMENTS

Crumbled feta or shredded sharp cheddar

Chopped radishes or red onions

Chopped jalapeño peppers

Shredded romaine lettuce

Chopped pimento-stuffed green olives

Thinly sliced scallions

Diced avocado, sprinkled with salt and lime juice

Combine the water, beans, onions, garlic, oil, and salt in a 4-quart or larger cooker.

Lock the lid in place. Over high heat bring to high pressure. Reduce the heat just enough to maintain high pressure and cook for 25 minutes. Turn off the heat. Allow the pressure to come down naturally. Remove the lid, tilting it away from you to allow steam to escape. If the beans are not uniformly tender, return to high pressure for 1 to 3 more minutes and again allow the pressure to come down naturally, or cover and simmer until done.

Stir in the chili powder and oregano to taste. Simmer uncovered over low heat. Add the tortilla chips and tomatoes. Stir occasionally until the chips soften, 2 to 3 minutes. Add salt to taste. (It's likely to need at least 1 teaspoon.)

Ladle into large, shallow bowls while still quite soupy—the stew will continue to thicken on the plate. Top with a tablespoon of sour cream and serve two lime wedges with each portion. Serve your choice of accompaniments on the side.

258

Tip: When you reheat leftovers, thin with water or broth.

Variations
• Instead of chili powder, use 1 to 2 teaspoons mashed chipotle in adobo.
• Offer shredded roast chicken or pork as one of the accompaniments.

Vegetables

For additional vegetable recipes, consult the Index.

I love vegetables and all of my recipes include them in abundance. In soups and stews they are usually supporting players, but in this chapter they steal the show.

There are two approaches to pressure cooking vegetables. The first is to steam them in a basket above water. Use this method when you want to cook sliced vegetables quickly and maintain maximum flavor.

The second approach is to boil vegetables directly in water. This method makes sense when you are cooking whole root vegetables like beets and potatoes, which cook faster and more evenly when boiled rather than steamed.

Vegetables A to Z (see pages 263 to 270) suggests which approach is most appropriate for each vegetable and offers details about preparation and timing.

BASIC PRESSURE-STEAMED VEGETABLES

Pour 1 cup water into the cooker. Set a footed collapsible steaming basket in place. Alternatively, use the trivet and steaming basket that came with your cooker. (The vegetables should be above the water level.)

Prepare the vegetables as required for even cooking. Place them in the basket.

Lock the lid in place. Over high heat bring to high pressure. Reduce the heat just enough to maintain high pressure and cook for the time recommended on the Vegetable Timing Chart (see page 271).

If the vegetables are not sufficiently tender, replace (but do not lock) the lid and steam over high heat until done.

PRESSURE POINTS

• Do not fill the cooker more than two-thirds full.

• When you wish to steam two different vegetables together, consult the Vegetable Timing Chart on page 271 to determine how to slice them for even cooking. For example, if you cut parsnips into $1/2$-inch chunks and potatoes into $1/2$-inch slices, they will both be done in 5 minutes under high pressure.

• The more vegetables you cook, the longer the cooker will take to come up to pressure. However, cooking time under pressure remains the same.

VEGETABLES A TO Z

This alphabetical reference contains cooking times and preparation tips for vegetables that cook well under pressure. I haven't included entries for vegetables like asparagus or corn that cook quickly by standard means and can easily be overcooked in a pressure cooker.

Unless otherwise indicated, all estimated times refer to minutes under high pressure followed by quick-release. When a 1- or 2-minute range is given for whole vegetables, use the longer time for larger specimens. For example, cook an 8-ounce artichoke for 10 minutes and a 9-ounce one for 11. When a range is given for slices or chunks, use the shorter time for firm-cooked vegetables and the longer time for those you plan to mash or puree. Vegetables with approximately the same cooking time may be steamed together.

When measuring chunks and slices, it's handy to know that the length from the tip of your thumb to the first knuckle is approximately 1 inch. I use the word "chunk" to refer to a roughly shaped morsel of approximately the dimensions suggested. It's not necessary to cut vegetables into tidy cubes.

263

Artichokes

Large (8 to 9 ounces): 10 to 11 minutes
Medium (6 to 7 ounces): 6 to 8 minutes
Small (3 to 4 ounces): 4 to 5 minutes
Baby (1 ounce): 3 to 4 minutes

Preparation: Slice off stems so that each artichoke sits flat. Snap off any bruised or browned petals around the base. Slice off the top $1/2$ to $3/4$ inch of each artichoke.

Turn each artichoke upside down and bang the top firmly against the counter to release any dirt. To remove the choke (optional), pry open inner petals and use a melon baller or grapefruit spoon to scrape it out.

Testing for Doneness: You should be able to pull out an inner leaf with little resistance, and the flesh should be tender enough to easily scrape off with a knife.

• There isn't sufficient room in the cooker for a steaming basket when cooking large and medium artichokes, so set them directly in 1 cup water.

• Small and baby artichokes fair better steamed in a basket above water.

• Four medium artichokes fit in a 4- or 6-quart cooker (squeeze together if necessary). Cook up to 6 in an 8-quart cooker; set 4 on the bottom and stack 2 more on top, pyramid fashion.

• Artichokes heavier than 9 ounces do not cook evenly in the pressure cooker: the outer leaves overcook by the time the inner leaves and heart are tender.

Beets

Large, whole (7 to 10 ounces): 25 to 28 minutes
Medium, whole (5 to 6 ounces): 20 to 22 minutes
Small, whole (3 to 4 ounces): 11 to 13 minutes
Peeled, halved, and cut into 1/4-inch slices: 3 to 5 minutes

Preparation: For whole beets, trim off long roots or stems, but leave about a half inch intact to prevent the beets from bleeding. Scrub the beets but leave skin intact to protect flavor and color; skins will slip off easily after cooking, while the beets are still warm. For sliced beets, peel before cooking.

Testing for Doneness: The beets should be easy to pierce to the center with a thin skewer.

PRESSURE POINTS

• Steam sliced beets in a basket above water.

• Cook whole beets directly in 2 to 3 cups water. They don't need to be completely submerged to cook evenly.

Cabbage (Green)

2- to 3-pound cabbage, quartered: 3 minutes
Quartered, cored, and thinly sliced: 2 to 3 minutes

Preparation: Remove bruised outer leaves. If cooking in quarters, retain the core intact to keep leaves attached.

• Do not be concerned if the cabbage exceeds the cooker's maximum fill line. It shrinks considerably as the cooker comes up to pressure.

Carrots
Baby-cut: 4 to 5 minutes
Medium, cut into 1-inch chunks: 6 to 7 minutes
Medium, cut into ¼-inch slices: 4 to 5 minutes

PRESSURE POINTS
• Carrot slices and chunks hold their shape beautifully, even when cooked longer than necessary.
• When a dish containing carrots requires longer than 10 minutes to cook (including natural release time), leave the carrots whole and slice them after cooking.

Cauliflower
Medium, whole (2½ pounds untrimmed weight): 4 to 5 minutes
Large florets (about 2½ inches across the top): 1 minute

Preparation: For whole cauliflower, trim the leaves off the base. Use a paring knife to pry out about 1 inch of the core, leaving the florets attached.

265

Tip: For best results, cook cauliflower whole and cut it up afterward.

PRESSURE POINTS
• Cook whole cauliflower partially submerged in 1 cup water.
• Steam florets above water. Even large florets easily get overcooked; they are then best used in a puree.

Celeriac
1-inch chunks: 6 to 7 minutes
½-inch slices: 4 to 5 minutes

Preparation: Peel or pare off the coarse brown skin. (It's not necessary to remove every last bit). Cut in half, then slice or dice.

Collards

Chopped: 3 to 4 minutes

Preparation: Chop off and discard the bottom few inches of the stems. Thinly slice remaining stems and coarsely chop the leaves. Rinse thoroughly in several changes of water to release all sand.

Tip: Avoid steaming collards above water as they are likely to taste bitter.

PRESSURE POINTS

• Cook in 1 cup liquid.

• Although collards become tender quickly under pressure, they stand up well to longer cooking.

Eggplant

1½-inch chunks: 2 to 3 minutes

Preparation: Peel before cooking. With the exception of small Japanese eggplants, the skins do not become tender in the short time it takes eggplant to cook under pressure.

PRESSURE POINT

• Pressure-steam eggplant only if you intend to make a puree; cooked eggplant does not hold its shape.

Green Beans

Whole or cut into 2-inch lengths: 2 to 3 minutes

Preparation: Trim ends.

Kale

Leaves coarsely chopped, stems thinly sliced: 2 minutes

Preparation: Chop off and discard the bottom few inches of the stems. Thinly slice remaining stems and coarsely chop the leaves. Rinse thoroughly in a several changes of water to release all the sand.

Tip: Avoid steaming kale above water as it is likely to taste bitter.

PRESSURE POINTS
• Cook in 1 cup liquid.
• Although kale becomes tender quickly under pressure, it stands up well to longer cooking.

Parsnips
1-inch chunks: 5 to 6 minutes
   Preparation: Trim and scrub or peel. Cut into relatively even chunks.

Tip: Although unpeeled parsnips look scruffy, the vegetable's flavor is enhanced when the peel is left intact.

PRESSURE POINTS
• Pressure-steam parsnips only if you intend to make a puree; cooked parsnips do not hold their shape well.
• Whole parsnips don't cook evenly; the outside tends to be overcooked by the time the inside is done. For best results, cook parsnips in chunks.

Potatoes (Boiling, Yukon Gold, Waxy)
Whole, large (8 to 11 ounces): 28 to 32 minutes
Whole, medium (5 to 6 ounces): 15 to 17 minutes
Whole, small (2 to 3 ounces): 9 to 10 minutes
1-inch chunks: 6 to 7 minutes
$\frac{1}{2}$-inch slices: 5 to 6 minutes
$\frac{1}{4}$-inch slices: 3 to 4 minutes

PRESSURE POINTS
• Cook whole potatoes in 2 to 3 cups water. They do not need to be completely submerged to cook properly.
• When pressure-steamed whole with their skins intact on top of a roast or stew, potatoes don't get overcooked, so you can include

them right from the start when cooking ingredients that take longer than the times recommended.

Potatoes (New)
Whole, medium (2 ounces each): 8 to 9 minutes
Whole, small (1 ounce each): 5 to 6 minutes

PRESSURE POINTS
• Cook whole potatoes in 2 to 3 cups water. They do not need to be completely submerged to cook properly.
• To prevent skins from splitting, subtract 3 minutes from timing and let the pressure come down naturally.
• When pressure-steamed whole with their skins intact on top of a roast or stew, potatoes don't get overcooked, so you can include them right from the start when cooking ingredients that take longer than the times recommended above.

Potatoes, Russets (Idaho Baking)
Whole, medium (8 to 10 ounces): 26 to 30 minutes
1-inch chunks: 7 to 8 minutes
$1/2$-inch slices: 5 to 6 minutes
$1/4$-inch slices: 3 to 4 minutes

Tip: To maximize taste, cook whole potatoes with their skins intact. The skins slip off easily after cooking, while the potatoes are still warm.

PRESSURE POINTS
• Cook whole unpeeled potatoes in 2 to 3 cups water.
• When pressure-steamed whole with their skins intact on top of a roast or stew, potatoes don't get overcooked, so you can include them right from the start when cooking ingredients that take longer than the times recommended above.

Potatoes, Sweet
2-inch chunks: 9 to 10 minutes
$1/2$-inch slices: 4 to 5 minutes

PRESSURE POINTS

• Do not attempt to cook whole sweet potatoes in a pressure cooker. They burst open and the flesh begins to spill out before the center is fully cooked.

• Pressure steam sweet potatoes only if you intend to mash or puree them; cooked sweet potatoes do not hold their shape.

Rutabaga

1-inch chunks: 9 to 10 minutes

1/2-inch dice: 6 to 7 minutes

   Preparation: Before cooking always pare or peel off waxed skin and the thin green layer underneath.

Tip: To avoid a challenging hacking job, buy a small rutabaga.

Squash, Winter

Acorn, halved: 6 to 7 minutes

Pattypan, whole: 10 to 12 minutes

All winter squash, 1 1/2-inch chunks: 3 to 4 minutes

Tip: Peeling squash is optional. The pressure cooker does a good job of tenderizing the hard skin.

Turnips, White

Medium, whole (12 ounces): 24 to 26 minutes

1 1/2- to 2-inch chunks: 7 to 8 minutes

   Preparation: Always peel turnips before cooking. The peels are often bitter.

Tip: For optimum taste and texture, steam turnips whole or in large chunks. If cut too small, they become watery.

Zucchini and Yellow Squash

Whole, medium (about 1-inch diameter): 4 minutes
1-inch chunks: 2 minutes

Tip: Steam zucchini whole for best taste and texture.

Vegetable Timing Chart

Vegetable	Minutes High Pressure + Quick-Release
Artichokes	
Large (8 to 9 ounces)	10 to 11
Medium (6 to 7 ounces)	6 to 8
Small (3 to 4 ounces)	4 to 5
Baby (1 ounce)	3 to 4
Beets	
Large, whole (7 to 8 ounces)	25 to 28
Medium, whole (5 to 6 ounces)	20 to 22
Small, whole (3 to 4 ounces)	11 to 13
Peeled, halved, and cut into $1/4$-inch slices	3 to 5
Cabbage (Green)	
2- to 3-pound, quartered	3
Quartered, cored, and thinly sliced	2 to 3
Carrots	
Baby-cut	4 to 5
Medium, 1-inch chunks	6 to 7
Medium, $1/4$-inch slices	4 to 5
Cauliflower	4 to 5
Medium ($2^1/2$ pounds untrimmed), whole	
Large florets (about $2^1/2$ inches across the top)	1
Celeriac	
1-inch chunks	6 to 7
$1/2$-inch slices	4 to 5
Collards	
Chopped	3 to 4
Eggplant	
$1^1/2$-inch chunks	2 to 3

Green Beans

Whole or cut into 2-inch lengths	2 to 3

Kale

Chopped	2

Parsnips

1-inch chunks	5 to 6

Potatoes (Boiling, Yukon Gold, Waxy)

Whole, large (8 to 10 ounces)	28 to 32
Whole, medium (5 to 6 ounces)	15 to 17
Whole, small (2 to 3 ounces)	9 to 10
1-inch chunks	6 to 7
1/2-inch slices	5 to 6
1/4-inch slices	3 to 4

Potatoes, New

Whole, medium (2 ounces)	8 to 9
Whole, small (1 ounce each)	5 to 6

Potatoes Russets

Whole, medium (8 to 10 ounces)	26 to 30
1-inch chunks	7 to 8
1/2-inch slices	5 to 6
1/4-inch slices	3 to 4

Potatoes, Sweet

2-inch chunks	9 to 10
1/2-inch slices	4 to 5

Rutabaga

1-inch chunks	9 to 10
1/2-inch dice	6 to 7

Squash, Winter

Acorn, halved	6 to 7
Pattypan, whole	10 to 12
All Winter Squash, 1 1/2-inch chunks	3 to 4

Turnips, White

Medium, whole (12 ounces)	24 to 26
1¹/₂- to 2-inch chunks	7 to 8

Zucchini and Yellow Squash

Whole (about 1-inch diameter)	4
1-inch chunks	2

Vegetables

Stuffed Artichokes

SERVES 4

A simple stuffing of seasoned bread crumbs tucked into the petals adds good flavor to this fun-to-eat vegetable. Serve one artichoke per person as an appetizer, either hot or at room temperature.

By the way, don't ever buy an artichoke that doesn't talk back to you: fresh artichokes squeak audibly when squeezed.

11 minutes high pressure

1 cup fresh bread crumbs
$1/3$ cup grated romano cheese
$1/4$ cup chopped fresh parsley
1 teaspoon minced garlic or $1/2$ teaspoon granulated
Freshly ground pepper
4 large (8 to 9 ounces each) artichokes
2 to 3 tablespoons olive oil
Lemon wedges, for serving

To prepare the stuffing: In a small bowl, combine the bread crumbs, cheese, parsley, garlic, and pepper to taste.

To trim each artichoke: Slice off the stem so that the artichoke sits flat. Snap off any bruised or browned petals around the base. Slice off $1/2$- to $3/4$-inch from the top of the artichoke.

Turn each artichoke upside down and bang the top firmly against the counter to release any dirt. To remove the choke (optional), pry open the inner petals and use a melon baller or grapefruit spoon to scrape it out.

Again turn the artichoke upside down on the counter and press firmly to separate the petals. Sprinkle about one-fourth of the bread crumb mixture among the petals of each artichoke.

Pour 1 cup water into a 4-quart or larger cooker. Set the artichokes directly in the water, side by side. (You may have to squeeze them to fit.) Spoon the oil into the crevices between the petals.

Lock the lid in place. Over high heat bring to high pressure. Reduce the heat just enough to maintain high pressure and cook for 11 minutes. Turn off the heat. Quick-release the pressure. Remove the lid, tilting it away from you to allow steam to escape.

Test for doneness: You should be able to pull out an inner leaf with little resistance, and the flesh should be tender enough to easily scrape off with a knife. If the artichokes are not done, replace (but do not lock) the lid and steam over high heat for a few more minutes.

Use tongs to transfer the artichokes to plates. Serve with the lemon wedges.

Transformation *(Follow basic recipe except as noted.)*
• ARTICHOKES WITH VINAIGRETTE: Omit bread crumb stuffing. After cooking, serve artichokes with individual bowls of Lemon-Dill Vinaigrette (see page 289) for dipping petals.

PRESSURE POINTS
• You can fit 4 large artichokes in a 4- or 6-quart cooker and six in an 8-quart cooker (4 on the bottom and 2 stacked on top pyramid-fashion).
• Artichokes larger than 9 ounces do not cook evenly in a pressure cooker: outer leaves overcook by the time inner leaves and heart are tender.

275

Quick-Pickled Beets in Horseradish Dressing

SERVES 4 AS A SIDE DISH

When I visited my sister Aria Cahir in Seattle, she gave me a taste of her balsamic-pickled beets and I immediately asked her for the recipe. I couldn't believe how simple they were to prepare: just chop up cooked beets and toss them in some balsamic vinegar and a little olive oil.

You can stop right there and serve the pickled beets as a condiment, but I'm always looking for ways to make a good thing better. So I turned the beets into a side salad by adding a dressing made of sour cream and horseradish.

If possible, select beets of roughly the same size. If the size varies widely, give the large ones a head start. Then bring down the pressure, add the smaller ones, and continue cooking. Avoid cutting the beets for even cooking as they will lose flavor and bleed like crazy.

---

13 to 28 minutes high pressure (depending on size of beets)

---

1 pound beets
1^1/$_2$ tablespoons balsamic vinegar
1 tablespoon olive oil
1 teaspoon sugar

FOR THE HORSERADISH DRESSING
^{1}/$_4$ cup sour cream
1 to 1^1/$_2$ tablespoons prepared horseradish

If the beets need trimming, remove most of the roots and stems, but leave about a half inch intact to prevent the beets from bleeding. Scrub the beets but leave the skins intact. Pour 3 cups water into a 4-quart or larger cooker. Add the beets.

Lock the lid in place. Over high heat bring to high pressure. Reduce the heat just enough to maintain high pressure and cook

Pressure Perfect

for 13 minutes (small beets, about 4 ounces each), 22 minutes (medium, about 6 ounces each), or 28 (large, about 9 ounces each). Turn off the heat. Quick-release the pressure. Remove the lid, tilting it away from you to allow steam to escape.

Drain the beets. While they are still warm, slip off the skins. Slice or dice the beets and place them in a storage container. Add the vinegar, oil, and sugar and toss to coat. Marinate for 1 hour or refrigerate overnight.

When ready to serve, blend the sour cream and horseradish. Pour the dressing over the beets and toss to coat.

Variations
• When you toss beets in vinegar, add ½ teaspoon caraway or anise seeds.
• Use walnut oil instead of olive oil.

Transformations *(Follow basic recipe except as noted.)*
• PICKLED BEETS AND ONIONS: While beets are cooking, cut a small onion in half lengthwise, then slice thinly. Toss with 3 tablespoons white distilled vinegar and set aside for 30 minutes. Drain off vinegar. After beets are diced, toss in pickled onions. Serve as a condiment or toss with Horseradish Dressing.

• PICKLED BEETS WITH TOASTED PINE NUTS: Omit Horseradish Dressing. Toss Quick-Pickled Beets with ¼ cup toasted pine nuts (see page 19). Serve as a condiment. Makes 3 generous cups.

• FLAMBOYANT BEET AND GRAIN SALAD: Omit Horseradish Dressing. Finely chop 2 pickled beets and toss with 3 cups cooked rice or barley until grains turn pinkish. Add ¼ cup toasted pine nuts and 1 bunch watercress that has been coarsely chopped. Dress with 2 tablespoons olive or canola oil and 3 to 4 tablespoons freshly squeezed lemon juice. Add salt to taste. Garnish with navel orange or tangerine segments. Serves 6 to 8 as a side dish.

• PICKLED BEET "WAFERS" WITH GORGONZOLA AND WALNUTS: Omit Horseradish Dressing. Cut cooked beets into scant ½-inch slices. After marination, mash Gorgonzola (or other blue-veined cheese) on top of each slice. Press coarsely chopped toasted walnuts into cheese. Serve as an hors d'oeuvre.

• BEET DRESSING: Omit Horseradish Dressing. Puree 1 cup Quick-Pickled Beets with ¼ cup chopped walnuts. Thin with beet cooking liquid as needed. Toss into green salads or hot, cooked grains. Add salt to taste.

PRESSURE POINT
• You can cook as many beets as will fit in your cooker without exceeding maximum fill line. You don't need to increase the 3 cups water.

Sweet-and-Sour Red Cabbage with Apple Rings

SERVES 4 TO 6

Here is a twist on the classic cabbage-apple combination. Instead of fresh apples, which become very soft under pressure, use dried apple rings, which maintain their dense texture and provide a nice contrast to the tender cabbage. The flavors of this dish improve after standing for a few hours or overnight refrigeration.

Cooked red cabbage has a gorgeous purplish hue that makes this dish an ideal adornment for holiday meals; it goes especially well with roast chicken or turkey. Serve hot or at room temperature.

---

3 minutes high pressure

3/4 cup water

3 tablespoons apple cider vinegar, plus more to taste

2 tablespoons honey

1/2 teaspoon caraway seeds

1/2 teaspoon salt

2 pounds red cabbage, quartered, cored, and thinly sliced crosswise (about 13 cups)

1 cup tightly packed dried apple rings

1 to 2 tablespoons butter (optional)

In a 4-quart or larger cooker, combine the water, vinegar, honey, caraway seeds, and salt. Add the cabbage and distribute the apple rings on top.

Lock the lid in place. Over high heat bring to high pressure. Reduce the heat just enough to maintain high pressure and cook for 3 minutes. Turn off the heat. Quick-release the pressure under cold running water. Remove the lid, tilting it away from you to allow steam to escape.

If the cabbage is not sufficiently tender, replace (but do not

Vegetables

lock) the lid and steam for a few minutes in the residual heat. Stir in the butter (if using). Add salt to taste and vinegar, if needed for a more piquant flavor. To serve, drain with a slotted spoon or serve with the cooking liquid in small bowls.

Variations

• Instead of dried apples, use 2 fresh apples, peeled, quartered, and cored.

• Cook cabbage with 2 medium onions, thinly sliced.

• Substitute ½ cup raisins for dried apples.

• Omit caraway seeds and stir in ½ to 1 teaspoon dried dill after cooking.

• Omit honey and stir in black currant preserves to taste after cooking.

PRESSURE POINT

• If using a 4-quart cooker, do not be concerned if mixture exceeds maximum fill line. Cabbage will shrink as pressure builds, leaving sufficient room for cooker to function properly.

Cauliflower and Sweet Potato Curry with Mango Chutney–Yogurt Sauce

SERVES 4 TO 6 ENTREE PORTIONS

Here is a quick-to-prepare mixed vegetable curry that appeals to vegetarians and nonvegetarians alike. Patak's Mild Curry Paste, a zesty blend of about a dozen different seasonings, is the "secret" ingredient that contributes complex flavor in a flash. Patak's is available in many supermarkets and specialty food stores.

Consider the Mango Chutney–Yogurt Sauce essential: It adds a slightly sweet, creamy finish to the dish. Serve the curry over white or brown basmati rice.

---

4 minutes high pressure

---

1 medium cauliflower (about 2^1/$_2$ pounds)

2 cups water

5 tablespoons Patak's Mild Curry Paste (curry powder doesn't produce good results)

^{1}/$_2$ teaspoon salt, plus more to taste

1 medium onion, coarsely chopped

1^1/$_2$ pounds orange-fleshed sweet potatoes, peeled and cut into ^{3}/$_4$-inch chunks

10 ounces fresh or frozen cut green beans

1 cup plain yogurt

1^1/$_2$ cups cooked chickpeas or one can (15 ounces), drained and rinsed

^{1}/$_3$ cup toasted almonds (see page 19) or roasted cashews

3 tablespoons chopped fresh cilantro

FOR THE MANGO CHUTNEY–YOGURT SAUCE

1 cup plain yogurt (whole-fat or low-fat)

1^1/$_2$ tablespoons sweet mango chutney

Trim the leaves off the base of the cauliflower. Use a paring knife to pry out about 1 inch of the core, leaving the florets attached.

Pour the water into a 6-quart or larger cooker and blend in the curry paste and salt. Stir in the onions. Bring the mixture to a boil. Set the whole cauliflower in the curry liquid. Scatter the sweet potatoes and green beans around the cauliflower and on top.

Lock the lid in place. Over high heat bring to high pressure. Reduce the heat just enough to maintain high pressure and cook for 4 minutes. Turn off the heat. Quick-release the pressure under cold running water. Remove the lid, tilting it away from you to allow steam to escape.

Ladle out about 1 cup cooking liquid and blend in the yogurt. Use a long knife to slash the cauliflower into large pieces. Gently stir in the yogurt mixture, chickpeas, nuts, and cilantro. Many of the sweet potatoes will break down to thicken the sauce. Add more salt to taste. Let the curry rest for 3 to 5 minutes.

Meanwhile, prepare the Mango Chutney–Yogurt Sauce: Blend the yogurt and mango chutney in a small bowl. Serve the curry in large, shallow bowls over rice. Garnish individual portions with a generous spoonful of the sauce and sprinkle with cilantro. Pass the remaining sauce at the table.

Variations

• Reduce water to ½ cup and add 1 can (about 14 ounces) coconut milk.
• Omit green beans and stir in 1 cup frozen green peas along with chickpeas.
• Toast one or more of the following spices (see page 19): 1 tablespoon black mustard seeds, 1 teaspoon whole fennel seeds, and 1 teaspoon whole cumin seeds. Stir them in after slashing cauliflower.
• Add ⅓ cup raisins after releasing pressure.
• Instead of mango chutney, blend yogurt with Patak's Eggplant (Brinjal) Pickle to taste for a savory, spicy-hot sauce.

Transformation *(Follow basic recipe except as noted.)*
• CAULIFLOWER, SWEET POTATOES, AND STRING BEANS WITH ASIAN PEANUT SAUCE: Use vegetable broth instead of water and omit curry paste. Use 2 tablespoons soy sauce instead of salt.

Blend in ⅓ cup creamy peanut butter instead of yogurt. Season with 1 to 2 teaspoons grated fresh ginger and a pinch of cayenne (optional). Along with chickpeas, add 1 small diced red bell pepper. Use roasted peanuts instead of almonds. Just before serving, stir in ½ cup thinly sliced scallion greens and 1 to 2 tablespoons freshly squeezed lime juice. Season to taste with additional soy sauce. Omit the Mango Chutney–Yogurt Sauce.

PRESSURE POINT
• If using a 4-quart cooker, substitute 1 small cauliflower (2 pounds maximum) and reduce sweet potatoes to 1 pound.

Eggplant Caponata

SERVES 6 TO 8

To my mind, eggplant is at its culinary best in this classic Italian combination of tomatoes, raisins, and balsamic vinegar.

Serve the caponata cold as a vegetable side dish (it goes nicely with fish) or as part of an antipasti platter. Or use it as a spread on toasted Italian bread that's been rubbed with garlic and drizzled with olive oil. It can be refrigerated for up to 5 days. In fact, the taste improves with age.

---

4 minutes high pressure

---

2 tablespoons olive oil

2 cups coarsely chopped onions

2 large ribs celery, cut into 1/2-inch chunks (include some leaves, if available)

3 to 4 tablespoons balsamic vinegar

1 1/2 pounds eggplant, peeled and cut into 3/4-inch chunks

One can (28 ounces) crushed tomatoes in puree OR one can (28 ounces) plum tomatoes (with liquid), plus one can (6 ounces) tomato paste

1/2 cup raisins

1 teaspoon salt

Generous 1/4 teaspoon ground cinnamon

3 tablespoons capers, including some brine

3 tablespoons toasted pine nuts (see page 19), for garnish (optional)

Heat 1 tablespoon of the oil in a 6-quart or larger cooker. Add the onions and celery and cook over medium-high heat, stirring frequently, for 1 minute. Stir in 3 tablespoons of the vinegar. Add the eggplant and pour the tomatoes on top. (If using whole plum tomatoes, crush them in your hand and distribute heaping table-spoonsful of the tomato paste on top.) Do not stir after adding tomatoes. Sprinkle on the raisins, salt, and cinnamon.

Lock the lid in place. Over high heat bring to high pressure.

(It may take longer than usual since the pot is so full.) Reduce the heat just enough to maintain high pressure and cook for 4 minutes. Turn off the heat. Quick-release the pressure under cold running water. Remove the lid, tilting it away from you to allow excess steam to escape.

Stir in the capers and the remaining tablespoon vinegar, if needed to balance the flavors and give the mixture a piquant edge. Add the remaining tablespoon oil and stir just enough to break down some of the eggplant and thicken the mixture slightly. If the eggplant is not meltingly soft, replace (but do not lock) the lid and steam in the residual heat for a few minutes.

Serve warm, at room temperature, or chilled. The caponata will thicken further as it cools. Garnish with pine nuts, if you wish.

Variation
• After cooking, stir in ½ cup chopped green Sicilian olives or Greek calamata olives.

Transformations *(Follow basic recipe except as noted.)*
• CHICKPEA CAPONATA: Cook eggplant with 1½ cups cooked chickpeas or 1 can (15 ounces), drained and rinsed. This dish is substantial enough to serve as a vegetarian entree on a bed of rice or other cooked grains.
• PASTA CAPONATA: After adding vinegar, stir in 1 cup water and 8 ounces bowties, spirals, or other short dried pasta that normally cooks within 9 to 12 minutes. Add eggplant and proceed as directed. After cooking, stir well when you add capers and oil, taking care to release any pasta clinging to bottom of cooker. If pasta is not quite tender, replace (but do not lock) the lid and let it steam in residual heat until done but still chewy. (If not serving immediately, transfer pasta to a bowl or storage container to avoid overcooking.) Just before serving, stir in 1 cup finely diced celery and 2 to 3 tablespoons minced fresh basil or parsley. Serve hot or at room temperature. (Texture of pasta is best when dish is freshly made.) Serves 4 as an entree or 8 as a side dish.

PRESSURE POINTS

• If using a 4-quart cooker, cut recipe in half.

• It's necessary to peel eggplant since the skin doesn't become tender under pressure.

• No liquid is needed aside from the vinegar because tomatoes, onions, celery, and eggplant release sufficient liquid to bring cooker up to pressure.

Creamy Mashed Potatoes

SERVES 6

There are as many recipes for "the best" mashed potatoes as there are folks who love them. Here's the approach that makes me croon.

For the lightest, fluffiest mashed potatoes, use starchy russets. Pass the cooked potatoes through a food mill or a ricer—an inexpensive gadget that looks like an overgrown garlic press. If you don't own a food mill or a ricer, use a potato masher.

---

8 minutes high pressure

---

3 pounds russet (Idaho baking) potatoes, peeled, and cut into 1-inch chunks
1 teaspoon salt, plus more to taste
4 to 5 tablespoons butter
$2/3$ to 1 cup heavy cream or half-and-half
Freshly ground pepper (optional)

Pour 1 cup water into a 4-quart or larger cooker. Add the potatoes and sprinkle with salt.

Lock the lid in place. Over high heat bring to high pressure. Reduce the heat just enough to maintain high pressure and cook for 8 minutes. Turn off the heat. Quick-release the pressure. Remove the lid, tilting it away from you to allow steam to escape. If the potatoes are not fork-tender, replace the cover and steam for a few more minutes over high heat.

Drain the potatoes in a large colander. Set the cooker over low heat. Melt 4 tablespoons of the butter and stir in $2/3$ cup of the heavy cream. Pass the potatoes through a ricer or the medium blade of a food mill directly into the butter-cream mixture.

Using a whisk or slotted spoon, stir briskly to achieve a light, creamy texture. Add more cream to thin and more butter for added richness, if desired. Season to taste with salt and pepper (if using). Serve immediately.

Variation

• Instead of cream, use potato cooking liquid, 2 percent milk, or buttermilk. (The latter will give potatoes a slightly tangy taste.)

Transformations *(Follow basic recipe except as noted.)*

• MUSTARD MASHED POTATOES: Blend 1½ tablespoons Dijon mustard (preferably whole grain) and 2 tablespoons sour cream into ⅓ cup half-and-half or milk. Stir into melted butter before adding riced potatoes.

• GARLIC MASHED POTATOES: Cook 5 to 10 peeled cloves of garlic with potatoes. Pass garlic through food mill or ricer along with potatoes.

• CHEESY MASHED POTATOES: Reduce butter to 2 tablespoons, and use milk instead of cream. After adding riced potatoes to milk, stir in 1 cup grated sharp cheddar, Monterey Jack, or fontina cheese.

• PARMESAN MASHED POTATOES: Substitute olive oil for butter and ⅓ to ½ cup potato cooking liquid for heavy cream. Blend ½ to ¾ cup grated parmesan cheese (or a mixture of parmesan and romano) into riced potatoes.

• SOUR CREAM AND CHIVE-FLECKED MASHED POTATOES: Substitute ½ cup sour cream for heavy cream. Use cooking liquid, as needed, to thin. Stir 3 tablespoons snipped chives into mashed potatoes.

• RUSTIC SMASHED POTATOES: Do not peel potatoes. After cooking, add unpeeled potatoes to butter-cream mixture and smash with a potato masher.

PRESSURE POINT

• If you use a 6-quart or larger cooker, this recipe can be doubled or tripled.

Last-Minute Potato Salad with Lemon-Dill Vinaigrette

SERVES 4 TO 6

This recipe is for a European-style potato salad with a simple vinaigrette dressing. Be sure to use waxy potatoes, which hold their shape better than russets or other baking varieties.

Serve the salad warm or at room temperature. For a casual, impromptu meal, accompany with bratwurst or smoked sprats and some good dark bread.

---

3 minutes under pressure

---

2 pounds Yukon Gold or other waxy potatoes, scrubbed or peeled, halved lengthwise and cut into ¼-inch slices
1 cup diced celery
½ cup finely chopped red onion
2 tablespoons capers (chop if large)

FOR THE LEMON-DILL VINAIGRETTE
⅓ cup olive oil
3 tablespoons freshly squeezed lemon juice, plus more to taste
½ teaspoon dried dill
1 teaspoon salt, plus more to taste
Freshly ground pepper

Pour 1 cup water into a 6-quart or larger cooker. Set a collapsible steaming basket in place. Spread the potato slices out in the basket.

Lock the lid in place. Over high heat bring to high pressure. Reduce the heat just enough to maintain high pressure and cook for 3 minutes. Turn off the heat. Quick-release the pressure. Remove the lid, tilting it away from you to allow steam to escape. If the potatoes are not fork-tender, replace (but do not lock) the lid and steam over high heat for another minute. Take care not to overcook.

Transfer the potatoes to a bowl or storage container. Add the celery, onion, and capers.

Prepare the Lemon-Dill Vinaigrette: Combine the ingredients in a small jar and shake well. While the potatoes are still warm, gently toss in enough Lemon-Dill Vinaigrette to thoroughly coat the mixture. Add more salt, pepper, and lemon juice to taste.

Variations
• To soften the "bite" of red onion, briefly soak in cold water. Drain well before adding to salad.
• Use thinly sliced scallion greens instead of red onion.
• Instead of dried dill, use 2 to 4 tablespoons chopped fresh dill.
• Substitute 2 pounds whole small (1-ounce each) new potatoes and cook for 6 minutes under high pressure. After cooking, leave whole or cut into chunks.
• Instead of capers, use ½ cup marinated artichoke hearts, drained and coarsely chopped.
• Add grated zest of 1 lemon.
• Toss in a cup or two of Quick-Pickled Beets (page 276).

Transformations *(Follow basic recipe except as noted.)*
• AMERICAN POTATO SALAD: Omit capers. Instead of Lemon-Dill Vinaigrette, use ¾ cup mayonnaise blended with 2 tablespoons cider or red wine vinegar, 2 tablespoons minced fresh parsley, 2 teaspoons whole grain mustard, and 1 to 2 tablespoons sweet pickle relish (optional). Allow cooked potatoes to cool slightly before tossing with dressing. Served warm or chilled.
• SOUTHWEST POTATO SALAD: Use diced red or green bell pepper instead of celery and minced jalapeño pepper instead of capers. For vinaigrette, substitute freshly squeezed lime juice for lemon juice and ¼ cup chopped fresh cilantro for dried dill.

PRESSURE POINT
• If using a 4-quart cooker, set potatoes on a rack instead of a steaming basket.

Root Vegetable Puree

SERVES 6 TO 8

Pureed root vegetable medleys are a delightful alternative to mashed potatoes. You can be quite relaxed about the proportions, but I suggest including at least 25 percent russet (Idaho baking) potatoes for good body and an earthy flavor base.

Each pound of vegetables yields about 2 cups puree. Here are some good combinations:

2 pounds each potatoes and carrots
2 pounds potatoes, 1 pound parsnips, and 1 pound carrots
2 pounds potatoes, 1 pound carrots, and 1 pound white turnips
2 pounds each potatoes and celeriac

7 minutes high pressure

4 pounds potatoes and assorted root vegetables (see list above), peeled, trimmed, and cut into 1-inch chunks
1 teaspoon salt, plus more to taste
4 tablespoons butter
2/3 to 1 cup heavy cream or half-and-half
1 to 2 teaspoons prepared horseradish
Freshly ground pepper (optional)

Pour 1 cup water into a 6-quart or larger cooker. Add the potatoes and place the other vegetables on top. Sprinkle with salt.

Lock the lid in place. Over high heat bring to high pressure. Reduce the heat just enough to maintain high pressure and cook for 7 minutes. Turn off the heat. Quick-release the pressure. Remove the lid, tilting it away from you to allow steam to escape.

If the vegetables are not fork-tender, replace (but do not lock) the lid and let the whole batch continue to steam in the residual heat until done. Drain the vegetables in a large colander.

Melt the butter in the empty cooker over medium-high heat. Reduce the heat to very low. Stir in 2/3 cup of the heavy cream.

Pass the vegetables through the medium blade of a food mill directly into the cooker.

Using a whisk or slotted spoon, stir briskly to achieve a light, creamy texture. Add more cream, if needed. Season with salt and pepper and enough of the horseradish to add a subtle flavor dimension. Serve immediately.

Variations

• Use rutabaga instead of carrots or turnips. Peel, halve, and cut into 1/2-inch slices.
• Add 1 or 2 peeled, cored apples when cooking carrots, parsnips, or rutabaga. Sweeten puree with a tablespoon or two of honey. Omit horseradish.
• Use buttermilk or yogurt instead of heavy cream.
• Thin puree with chicken broth or milk instead of heavy cream.
• Season puree with ground cardamom, freshly grated nutmeg, or chopped fresh herbs. Omit horseradish.
• Use 2 to 3 tablespoons rosemary, basil, or other herb-infused olive oil instead of butter (or in combination).

Transformations *(Follow basic recipe except as noted.)*

• ROOT VEGETABLE SOUP: Thin leftover puree with chicken or vegetable broth and serve hot, garnished with Herb Croutons, page 37.
• SMASHED ROOT VEGETABLES: Instead of using a food mill, smash cooked vegetables into hot butter-cream mixture with a potato masher.

PRESSURE POINT

• If using a 4-quart cooker, reduce to 3 pounds root vegetables. Reduce butter to 3 tablespoons and heavy cream to 1/2 cup.

Mashed Sweet Potatoes with Sage and Ginger

SERVES 6 TO 8

It's common to think of sweet spices like cinnamon and cloves when seasoning sweet potatoes. Actually aromatic herbs like sage and thyme work equally well, a reminder that this gorgeous vegetable is more versatile than we might have thought.

Serve as you would mashed potatoes, alongside a roast or stew.

---

5 minutes high pressure

---

4 pounds sweet potatoes, peeled, halved lengthwise, and cut into
   $1/2$-inch slices
3 to 4 tablespoons butter
$3/4$ to 1 teaspoon dried sage
$1/4$ to $1/2$ teaspoon ground ginger
Salt
$1/4$ cup toasted pine nuts or pecans (see page 19)

Set a rack on the bottom of a 6-quart or larger cooker. Pour in 1 cup water and add the sweet potatoes.

Lock the lid in place. Over high heat bring to high pressure. Reduce the heat just enough to maintain high pressure and cook for 5 minutes. Turn off the heat. Quick-release the pressure. Remove the lid, tilting it away from you to allow steam to escape.

The slices should be uniformly tender and easily pierced in the center with the tip of a paring knife. If not, replace (but do not lock) the lid and steam over high heat for another minute or two. Drain the potatoes in a large colander. Remove the rack from the cooker.

Melt the butter in the cooker over medium-high heat. Reduce the heat to very low. Stir in $3/4$ teaspoon sage and $1/4$ teaspoon ginger. Add the sweet potatoes and mash with a potato masher. Season well with salt. Add more sage and ginger to taste. Serve hot, garnished with pine nuts.

Transformations *(Follow basic recipe except as noted.)*
• MASHED SWEET POTATOES WITH ROSEMARY OIL AND LEMON ZEST: Reduce butter to 2 tablespoons, and omit sage and ginger. Mash potatoes with 1 to 2 tablespoons rosemary-infused olive oil (Consorzio is a good brand) and zest of 1 large lemon.
• MASHED SWEET POTATOES WITH SAGE AND CHILI: Instead of butter, use 3 tablespoons olive oil. Omit ginger and add 1½ to 2 teaspoons chili powder. Just before serving, stir in grated zest of 1 lime. Instead of pine nuts, garnish with toasted pumpkin seeds.
• MASHED CANDIED SWEETS: Omit sage and ginger and substitute ¼ to ½ cup brown sugar and ½ teaspoon ground cinnamon. Instead of pine nuts, garnish with toasted walnuts or pecans.
• OLD-FASHIONED CANDIED SWEETS: Omit the sage, ginger, and pine nuts. Set a layer of cooked, drained sweet potatoes in an ovenproof casserole. Sprinkle with 2 to 3 tablespoons brown sugar and dot with butter. Repeat layering potatoes, brown sugar, and butter. Pour ¼ cup apple juice or water over potatoes, cover, and bake in a 350-degree oven until very soft, about 35 minutes. Raise heat to 425 degrees Fahrenheit. Uncover and cook until bubbly and lightly browned on top.
• CANDIED SWEETS WITH MARSHMALLOWS: Follow recipe above but scatter 1 cup miniature marshmallows between layers.

PRESSURE POINT
• If using a 4-quart cooker, reduce to 3 pounds sweet potatoes and season to taste.

Five-Minute Tomato Sauce

MAKES ABOUT 1¹/₂ QUARTS

Here's a quick and satisfying all-purpose sauce. Unlike long-simmering versions that reduce and thicken, a PC tomato sauce loses very little liquid as it cooks. To compensate, it's necessary to use a thick tomato product like crushed tomatoes with added puree. If your market doesn't carry it, use plum tomatoes in juice in combination with tomato paste.

---

5 minutes high pressure

---

1 to 3 tablespoons olive oil
1¹/₂ cups coarsely chopped onions or leeks
1 cup finely diced celery
1 medium green bell pepper, seeded and finely chopped
1 cup dry red wine or dry vermouth
6 to 10 cloves garlic, peeled, or 1 teaspoon garlic powder
Two cans (28 ounces each) crushed tomatoes in puree OR
    2 cans (28 ounces each) plum tomatoes (with liquid), plus
    2 cans (6 ounces each) tomato paste
¹/₄ cup chopped fresh parsley
2 teaspoons Italian Herb Blend (page 18 or storebought)
Salt and freshly ground pepper
Pinch of sugar (optional)
Pinch of crushed red pepper flakes (optional)

Heat 1 tablespoon of the oil in a 4-quart or larger cooker. Add the onions, celery, and green pepper and cook over medium-high heat, stirring almost constantly, until the onions begin to soften, about 2 minutes. Stir in the wine, taking care to scrape up any browned bits sticking to the bottom of the cooker. Bring to a boil and cook until reduced by half, 1 to 2 minutes. Add the garlic.

Pour both cans of crushed tomatoes in puree on top. (If using whole plum tomatoes, crush them in your hand and distribute heaping tablespoonsful of the tomato paste on top.) Do not stir after adding the tomatoes.

Lock the lid in place. Over high heat bring to high pressure. Reduce the heat just enough to maintain high pressure and cook for 5 minutes. Turn off the heat. Quick-release the pressure by setting the cooker under cold running water.

Stir in the parsley, Italian herbs, and salt and pepper to taste. Add enough oil to balance the tomatoes' acidity. Season with the sugar and red pepper flakes (if using). Cook at a gentle boil until the flavor of the dried herbs infuses the sauce, about 2 minutes.

Tip: The sauce freezes well.

Variations
• Add 6 ounces sliced mushrooms when you add tomatoes.
• Stir in ½ cup chopped fresh basil instead of parsley.

Transformations *(Follow basic recipe except as noted.)*
• TOMATO SAUCE WITH MEAT OR FRESH SAUSAGE: After heating oil, brown 1 pound ground chuck, ground pork, or fresh Italian sausage (sweet or hot; casings removed). Break up clumps before adding onions.
• PUTTANESCA SAUCE: After adding tomatoes, scatter 4 or 5 chopped anchovy fillets on top. After cooking, stir in 2 to 3 tablespoons chopped capers and ¾ to 1 cup Mediterranean olives along with herbs.

PRESSURE POINTS
• When bringing up pressure over high heat, sugars in tomatoes have a tendency to scorch on bottom of pressure cookers that aren't well insulated. For this reason, avoid stirring after adding tomatoes.
• If your cooker's bottom doesn't have an aluminum sandwich, or if you are cooking on an electric or high-BTU stove, set a heat diffuser under cooker before bringing up pressure.
• It's best to chop green bell peppers finely for pressure cooking; large pieces shrivel and skins remain tough.

Desserts

If you are surprised to find a dessert chapter in this book, you are not alone. Once they think about it for a minute, most people are easily convinced that the pressure cooker can produce a quick dried fruit compote or applesauce, but cheesecake? It seems you'll need to make one to believe that it's possible. Enjoy!

Rice Pudding

SERVES 5 TO 6

Rice pudding is the ultimate comfort food. With this easy recipe and the Transformations, I hope you'll feel comforted on a regular basis.

First cook the rice until soft in a generous amount of water. Then add milk and boil while stirring—as you would when finishing a risotto. The starch released into the milk makes this egg-free pudding creamy and custardy, even when it's made with skim milk.

---

8 minutes high pressure

To Cook the Rice

2¹/₂ cups water

1 cup long-grain white rice

1 tablespoon butter (needed to control foaming)

¹/₄ teaspoon salt

To Finish the Pudding

1¹/₂ cups milk (whole, 2 percent, or skim)

¹/₂ cup sugar, plus more to taste

¹/₃ to ¹/₂ cup raisins

1 teaspoon vanilla

Ground cinnamon, for garnish (optional)

In a 3-quart or larger cooker, combine the water, rice, butter, and salt.

Lock the lid in place. Over high heat bring to high pressure. Reduce the heat just enough to maintain high pressure and cook for 8 minutes. Turn off the heat. Quick-release the pressure under cold running water. Remove the lid, tilting it away from you to allow excess steam to escape.

Stir in the milk, taking care to release any rice that is clinging to the bottom of the cooker. Stir in the sugar and raisins to taste. Boil over medium-high heat while stirring until the pudding develops the consistency of loose oatmeal, usually 4 to 6 minutes. Stir in the vanilla.

If you like a slightly soupy rice pudding, transfer the mixture to a medium bowl or individual ramekins at this point. For a more solid rice pudding, continue cooking another minute. (Keep in mind that the pudding will thicken considerably as it cools.) Garnish with a light sprinkling of cinnamon, if you wish. Serve warm, room temperature, or chilled.

Variations
- Use half-and-half instead of milk.
- Substitute soy milk for dairy. Since soy milk is usually sweetened, you will probably need to use less sugar.
- Omit raisins.
- Use another variety of white rice, such as arborio or jasmine.
- Top with fresh fruit and serve for breakfast.

Transformations *(Follow basic recipe except as noted.)*
- TROPICAL RICE PUDDING: Use coconut milk instead of dairy and add 2 tablespoons rum. Substitute dried, snipped mango or pineapple for raisins. Garnish with freshly grated nutmeg instead of cinnamon.
- MAPLE-WALNUT RICE PUDDING: Sweeten with $1/4$ to $1/3$ cup maple syrup instead of sugar. Stir in $1/2$ cup toasted walnuts (see page 19) along with vanilla.
- CHOCOLATE CHIP RICE PUDDING: Reduce sugar to $1/4$ cup. Add $1/2$ cup semisweet chocolate chips instead of raisins. After transferring hot pudding to a bowl, stir in another $1/4$ cup chocolate chips.
- CRANBERRY-ORANGE RICE PUDDING: Use dried cranberries instead of raisins. Along with vanilla, stir in 1 teaspoon grated orange zest and a pinch of cardamom.

PRESSURE POINT
- Rice foams when it cooks, sometimes splattering starch across lid. If necessary, thoroughly clean area under and around pressure regulator with a toothbrush.

301

Desserts

Lemon Cheesecake

SERVES 6 TO 8

You'll have fun telling your guests that this cheesecake was "baked" in a pressure cooker. They probably won't believe you.

"Wow!" exclaimed one friend who tried the recipe. "Making cheesecake is reason enough to invest in a pressure cooker. You can be sure I'll never make cheesecake in the oven again." "It must be the fastest cheesecake on earth," said another.

You may enjoy eating the cheesecake warm, when its texture is reminiscent of a soufflé. For the traditional dense version, allow the cheesecake an hour to cool to room temperature, then at least 4 hours to chill in the refrigerator.

Steam the cheesecake in a 7-inch springform pan. If you can't find one in a local kitchenware store, order it by mail (see page 317).

---

15 minutes high pressure plus natural pressure release

FOR THE CRUST
1 teaspoon softened butter for greasing the springform pan
1/2 cup chocolate wafer or graham cracker crumbs

FOR THE FILLING
16 ounces regular cream cheese, at room temperature (see Tips)
1/2 cup sugar
2 large eggs
1 tablespoon freshly squeezed lemon juice
1 to 2 teaspoons grated lemon zest
1/2 teaspoon vanilla

FOR THE OPTIONAL GARNISH (CHOOSE ONE)
Berries, cherries, or sliced fresh fruit
Cherry Pie Filling (storebought, from a can)

To prepare a foil strip to lower the cake into the cooker: cut off a 1 1/2-foot-long piece of standard-width aluminum foil. Double it twice lengthwise to create a long strip. Set aside.

Grease the bottom and sides of the springform pan with butter. Coat the sides with the crumbs and distribute the remaining crumbs on the bottom.

Using an electric mixer or a food processor, blend the cream cheese and sugar until smooth. Blend in the eggs, lemon juice and zest, and vanilla. (Do not overwork batter.) Pour the batter into the prepared pan.

Pour 2 cups water into a 6-quart or larger cooker. Set a trivet on the bottom of the cooker to raise the cheesecake above the water. Center the uncovered pan on the foil strip and lower it onto the trivet. Fold down the ends of the strip so that they don't interfere with closing the cooker.

Lock the lid in place. Over high heat bring to high pressure. Reduce the heat just enough to maintain high pressure and cook for 15 minutes. Turn off the heat. Allow the pressure to come down naturally. Remove the lid, tilting it away from you to allow steam to escape.

Let the steam subside before lifting the pan from the cooker with the aid of the foil strip. Set on a wire rack to cool. If there is a small pool of condensed water in the middle of the cake, blot it up with a paper towel. Serve warm or cool to room temperature, cover with plastic wrap, and refrigerate for at least 4 hours or overnight. Release and remove the rim of the springform pan. Serve the cheesecake on the base of the pan, with your garnish of choice.

Tips: Don't substitute reduced fat cream cheese; it contains more water, which will prevent the cake from setting properly. The cheesecake freezes very well. Defrost it at room temperature or in the microwave.

Variation
• Make crust from amaretti or chocolate graham crackers ground into crumbs.

Transformations *(Follow basic recipe except as noted.)*

• MOCHA CHIP CHEESECAKE: Omit lemon juice and zest. Dissolve 1 1/2 teaspoons instant coffee powder in 1 tablespoon warm water and blend into cream cheese mixture. Stir in 1/2 cup miniature semisweet chocolate chips. Instead of fruit garnish, press 1 tablespoon chips into top of cheesecake while it is still warm.

• CAPPUCCINO CHEESECAKE: Follow instructions for Mocha Chip Cheesecake but omit chocolate chips—or use just a few to decorate top.

• CHOCOLATE-MARBLE CHEESECAKE: Omit lemon juice and zest. Melt 1/2 cup semisweet chocolate chips and let cool slightly. Blend 3 tablespoons batter into melted chocolate. Pour remaining batter into prepared pan. Drop tablespoonsful of chocolate batter onto cheesecake. With flat side of a knife, gently swirl dots through batter in figure-eight motions to create a marbled effect. Garnish is optional.

• LEMON CHEESECAKE WITH FRUIT SWIRL: After pouring cheesecake batter into pan, dot top with 6 tablespoons fruit preserves, at room temperature. With flat side of a knife, gently swirl dots through batter in figure-eight motions to create a marbled effect. Increase cooking time to 20 minutes high pressure. No need for a garnish: this cheesecake looks pretty without it.

PRESSURE POINT

• A 4-quart cooker is not tall enough to accommodate a springform pan sitting on a trivet.

Orange Ricotta Cheesecake

SERVES 6 TO 8

This cheesecake is lighter than the Lemon Cheesecake (page 302) but equally well received. The texture is best after chilling for at least 4 hours, preferably overnight.

25 minutes high pressure plus natural pressure release

FOR THE CRUST
Cooking spray or butter for greasing the springform pan
2 tablespoons melted butter
1/2 cup cookie crumbs (made from amaretti, chocolate wafers, or graham cracker)
1/3 cup toasted pine nuts or walnuts (see page 19), finely chopped

FOR THE FILLING
One container (15 ounces) whole- or skim-milk ricotta
3 ounces regular cream cheese, at room temperature (see Tips)
1 cup sugar
4 large eggs
1/4 cup sour cream or plain yogurt
2 tablespoons all-purpose flour
1 tablespoon grated orange zest
Shaved chocolate or chocolate chips, for garnish

To prepare a foil strip to lower the cake into the cooker, cut off a 1 1/2-foot-long piece of standard-width aluminum foil. Double it twice lengthwise to create a long strip. Set aside.

Coat the bottom and sides of a 7-inch springform pan with the cooking spray.

To make the crust, combine the melted butter, cookie crumbs, and toasted nuts. Press them onto the bottom and sides of the springform pan.

To make the filling, use an electric mixer or food processor to blend the ricotta, cream cheese, and sugar until smooth. Blend in the eggs, sour cream, flour, and orange zest. (Do not overwork the batter.) Pour batter into the prepared pan.

Pour 2 cups water into a 6-quart or larger cooker. Set a trivet in the bottom of the cooker to raise the cheesecake above the water. Center the uncovered pan on the foil strip and lower it onto the trivet. Fold down the ends of the strip so they don't interfere with closing the cooker.

Lock the lid in place. Over high heat bring to high pressure. Reduce the heat just enough to maintain high pressure and cook for 25 minutes. Turn off the heat. Allow the pressure to come down naturally. Remove the lid, tilting it away from you to allow steam to escape.

Let the steam subside before lifting the pan from the cooker with the aid of the foil strip. Cool to room temperature on a wire rack. Cover with plastic wrap and refrigerate for at least 4 hours or overnight. Release and remove the rim of the springform pan. Serve the cheesecake on the base of the pan with the chocolate garnish of your choice.

Tips: Avoid reduced-fat cream cheese; it contains more water, which will prevent the cake from setting properly. This version doesn't freeze well. The texture becomes grainy.

Variations
• Use lemon zest instead of orange.
• Instead of garnishing with shaved chocolate, use a 4-ounce can of drained mandarin orange segments.

Transformation *(Follow basic recipe except as noted.)*
• CHOCOLATE-MARBLE RICOTTA CHEESECAKE: Melt ½ cup semisweet chocolate chips and let cool slightly. Blend 3 tablespoons batter into melted chocolate. Pour remaining batter into prepared pan. Gently drop tablespoonsful of chocolate batter onto cheesecake. With flat side of a knife, gently swirl dots

through batter in figure-eight motions to create a marbled effect.

PRESSURE POINT

• A 4-quart cooker is not tall enough to accommodate a spring-form pan sitting on a trivet.

Little Chocolate "Pots"

SERVES 4 TO 6

"It's like eating molten chocolate," said my chocoholic friend after savoring these pots de crème, a classic French dessert. I have adapted the recipe from *Short and Sweet,* a charming dessert cookbook by Melanie Barnard.

You'll need six ¹/₂-cup or four ³/₄-cup heatproof ramekins to make this hard-to-stop-eating dessert.

---

12 minutes high pressure plus natural pressure release

1¹/₂ cups half-and-half
6 tablespoons sugar
1 cup semisweet chocolate chips
4 large egg yolks
2 teaspoons vanilla
Sweetened whipped cream, for garnish (optional)

Combine the half-and-half and sugar and heat in a microwave for 2 minutes (or gently heat in a saucepan, stirring until the sugar dissolves).

Place the chocolate chips in a bowl and pour the hot half-and-half over them. Let the mixture sit for 1 minute. Whisk in the egg yolks and vanilla until thoroughly blended. Divide the mixture among the ramekins.

Pour 2 cups water into a 6-quart or larger cooker. Set a trivet in place and set a steaming basket or rack on top of the trivet. Place a layer of ramekins in the basket and then, if necessary, stack a second layer, pyramid-style.

Lock the lid in place. Over high heat bring to high pressure. Reduce the heat just enough to maintain high pressure and cook for 12 minutes. Turn off the heat. Allow the pressure to come down naturally. Remove the lid, tilting it away from you to allow steam to escape.

After the steam has subsided, lift the basket or individual

ramekins from the cooker with tongs and set on a wire rack to cool. Serve warm or at room temperature with whipped cream if desired.

Variations
• Garnish each portion with fresh raspberries or mint leaves.
• Blend a drop or two of mint extract (go easy!) into batter.

Chocolate Chip Bread Pudding

SERVES 6 TO 8

This is an easy-does-it, agreeable dessert that eliminates much of the hassle of making bread pudding. There's no need to let the bread dry out, no need to cut off the crusts, and no need to let the pudding sit before you cook it—though it's fine to assemble it in advance, if that's more convenient.

You'll need a round, heatproof casserole that fits into the cooker with a little room to spare around the edges. A 5- to 7-cup porcelain soufflé dish or round Pyrex casserole works well.

Spoon out the pudding while it is still warm or chill it and slice into wedges. The pudding is quite rich, so plan on serving dainty portions.

Avoid any temptation to substitute milk for the half-and-half in this recipe. With a thinner liquid, the pudding weeps, creating a moat of clear liquid around the perimeter—a sad affair.

20 minutes high pressure plus natural pressure release

3 to 4 tablespoons butter at room temperature, plus more for greasing the casserole
6 slices good-quality white sandwich bread
3 large eggs
1 1/2 cups half-and-half (fat-free is fine but don't substitute milk)
1/3 to 1/2 cup sugar
1/8 teaspoon salt
2 teaspoons vanilla
1/2 cup semisweet chocolate chips
2 tablespoons toasted slivered almonds (see page 19), for garnish
Sweetened whipped cream or vanilla ice cream, for garnish (optional)

To prepare the foil strip to lower the casserole into the cooker, cut a 1 1/2-foot-long piece of standard-width aluminum foil. Double it twice lengthwise to create a long strip. Set aside.

Grease the bottom and sides of a round, heatproof casserole with butter. Set aside. Generously butter both sides of the bread. Stack the slices and cut them in half.

Lightly beat the eggs. Whisk in the half-and-half, sugar, salt, and vanilla. Distribute 4 tablespoons of the mixture on the bottom of the prepared casserole. Arrange four pieces (two slices) of bread in the casserole and pour about one-third of the remaining egg mixture over them. Pierce the bread with a fork in a few places to encourage absorption. Sprinkle with 2 tablespoons of the chocolate chips. Make two more layers of bread, egg mixture, and chocolate chips, using a fork to pierce the bread and gently press down the layers as you go. Distribute the remaining 2 tablespoons chocolate chips among those already scattered on top.

Pour 2 cups water into a 4-quart or larger cooker. Set a rack or trivet in the bottom of the cooker to lift the pudding off the bottom. Center the uncovered casserole on the foil strip and lower it onto the rack. Fold down the ends of the strip so that they don't interfere with closing the cooker.

Lock the lid in place. Over high heat bring to high pressure. Reduce the heat just enough to maintain high pressure and cook for 20 minutes. Turn off the heat. Allow the pressure to come down naturally. Remove the lid, tilting it away from you to allow steam to escape.

Let the steam subside before lifting the casserole from the cooker with the aid of the foil strip. Set on a wire rack. Use a knife or spatula to gently spread the top layer of chips into a frosting.

Let the pudding rest for at least 5 minutes before serving. Serve warm or chilled, garnish with the toasted almonds and whipped cream or ice cream (if using).

Variations
• Cut 5 to 6 slices challah or panettone into scant ½-inch-thick slices and use instead of white bread.
• Use raisin bread instead of white.

Transformations *(Follow basic recipe except as noted.)*

• MOCHA CHIP BREAD PUDDING: Eliminate vanilla and substitute 1½ teaspoons instant coffee powder.

• CRANBERRY-ORANGE BREAD PUDDING: Add 2 teaspoons grated orange zest to egg mixture. Substitute dried cranberries for chocolate chips.

Easy Applesauce

The best thing about making homemade applesauce is that you can cook the apples with their skins intact, giving the mixture a pale, rosy hue. You can also use a mixture of apple varieties to create custom flavors—tart or sweet, as you please.

In this recipe, the pressure cooker and a food mill do most of the work. If you don't own a food mill, make Chunky Applesauce (see Transformations).

Up to high pressure plus natural pressure release

1 cup water
3 pounds apples, rinsed and quartered (coring not necessary)
Sugar (optional)
Freshly squeezed lemon juice (optional)

313

Pour the water into a 6-quart or larger cooker. Add the apples.

Lock the lid in place. Over high heat bring to high pressure. As soon as the cooker reaches high pressure, turn off the heat. Allow the pressure to come down naturally, about 10 minutes. Remove the lid, tilting it away from you to allow steam to escape.

Let the apples cool slightly. Pass the apples and cooking liquid through a food mill. Add sugar to taste and lemon juice, if needed to intensify the flavors. Refrigerate until needed, up to 10 days, or freeze up to 4 months.

Variations

• Cook apples with a cinnamon stick that's been broken in half.
• Sweeten with maple syrup rather than sugar.

Transformations *(Follow basic recipe except as noted.)*

• CHUNKY APPLESAUCE: Peel and core apples. After cooking, stir well.

• APPLESAUCE WITH RHUBARB: Reduce apples to 2 pounds and add 1 pound rhubarb stems cut into 1/2-inch slices.

• CRANAPPLE SAUCE: Reduce apples to 2 1/2 pounds. Add 2 cups fresh cranberries before adding apples.

• PEAR SAUCE: Substitute ripe pears for apples. After cooking, season to taste with freshly grated ginger, if you wish.

• SAVORY APPLESAUCE WITH SAGE: Season applesauce with fresh or dried sage. Serve warm, with roast pork or turkey.

PRESSURE POINTS

• If using a 4-quart cooker, reduce apples to 2 pounds for a yield of about 3 cups.

• If using an 8-quart cooker, increase apples to 5 pounds, if you wish, for a yield of about 6 1/2 cups.

• Apples foam when cooking under pressure. Do not fill cooker more than halfway in a jiggle-top cooker or two-thirds in a second-generation cooker. Do not quick-release pressure.

314

Pears and Figs in Mulled Wine

SERVES 6

This warming dessert evokes lit candles and a gay holiday spirit. Serve the compote in small bowls with a dollop of sweetened whipped cream, or use it as a topping for vanilla or butter-pecan ice cream.

---

4 minutes high pressure

---

1 cup red wine
1 cup water
1 stick cinnamon, broken in half
6 thin slices unpeeled orange, seeded and cut in half
6 plump dried figs, halved (use loose pear-shaped figs, not the leathery ones strung on a rope)
1/2 cup dried cranberries or cherries
3 ripe but firm Bosc or Bartlett pears, halved and cored

In a 4-quart or larger cooker, combine the wine, water, cinnamon, orange, figs, and cranberries. Arrange the pears on top.

Lock the lid in place. Over high heat bring to high pressure. Reduce the heat just enough to maintain high pressure and cook for 4 minutes. Turn off the heat. Quick-release the pressure by setting the lid under cold running water. Remove the lid, tilting it away from you to allow excess steam to escape.

Stir gently. Serve hot, warm, or chilled.

Variations
• Use additional water instead of wine.
• Garnish with toasted pine nuts (see page 19) or slivered almonds.

315

Dried Fruit Compote
with Crystallized Ginger

SERVES 6

Serve this lovely fruit combo warm with a scoop of good-quality vanilla ice cream. Or try it for brunch, topped with a generous spoonful of yogurt and your favorite granola.

---

5 minutes high pressure

---

4 cups water

12 dried figs, halved

1^1/2 cups tightly packed mixed dried fruits, such as prunes, apricots, peaches, or apple rings

^{1}/2 cup dried cherries or cranberries

^{1}/2 cup almonds (no need to blanch) or hazelnuts

2 tablespoons crystallized ginger

Place the water, figs, mixed dried fruits, cherries, almonds, and ginger in a 4-quart or larger cooker.

Lock the lid in place. Over high heat bring to high pressure. Reduce the heat just enough to maintain high pressure and cook for 5 minutes. Turn off the heat. Quick-release the pressure by setting the cooker under cold running water. Remove the lid, tilting it away from you to allow steam to escape.

Allow the compote to cool slightly. Serve warm with a scoop of ice cream on top.

Transformation (*Follow basic recipe except as noted.*)

• STEWED PRUNES WITH ANISE AND ORANGE: Substitute 4 cups dried pitted prunes for figs and mixed dried fruit. Cook with 1 teaspoon whole anise seeds. After cooking, stir in 1 navel orange, peeled, seeded, and coarsely chopped.

Mail-Order Sources

COOKWARE

Zabar's
www.zabars.com
800-697-6301
Carries a variety of pressure cookers at discount prices and also
stocks all of the Useful Accessories listed on page 17.

La Cuisine
800-521-1176
www.lacuisineus.com
Sells an Italian enameled cast-iron heat diffuser with detachable
handle.

SPECIALTY INGREDIENTS

Ethnic Grocer
800-523-1961
www.ethnicgrocer.com
Search this virtual store by country or by ingredient.

Gold Mine Natural Food Company
800-475-3663
Superb organic beans and grains and a range of excellent
Japanese soy sauces.

Penzeys
800-741-7787
www.penzeys.com
High-quality spices and dried herbs, excellent prices, and a
catalog that contains a world of flavors.

MEAT

Niman Ranch
510-808-0340
www.nimanranch.com
Sells beef, pork, and lamb raised on natural feed, free of growth
hormones. A favorite source for chefs.

Directory of Pressure Cooker Manufacturers and Distributors

Contact the manufacturers and distributors below to obtain product information and customer service.

Aeternum (Miracle Exclusives)
800-645-6360
www.miracleexclusives.com

Fagor
800-207-0806
www.fagoramerica.com

Hawkins Futura
800-675-4416
www.pressurecooker.us

Innova
800-767-5160
www.innova-inc.com

Kuhn Rikon
800-662-5882
www.kuhnrikon.com

Magafesa
888-787-9991
www.magafesausa.com

Manttra
877-962-6887
www.manttra.com

Mirro
800-527-7727
www.wearever.com

Presto
800-877-0441
www.gopresto.com

Salton/Farberware
800-233-9054

www.salton-maxim.com

Silit
800-233-9054
www.natural-lifestyle.com

Sitram
800-515-8585
www.cookware.com

T-Fal
800-395-8325
www.t-falusa.com

WMF
800-999-6347
www.wmf-usa.com

Troubleshooting

On occasion the pressure cooker's behavior may puzzle you. Here are some problems you may encounter followed by explanations and potential solutions. Those cooking on electric stovetops will also find pertinent suggestions in special situations, page 20.

If you continue to have difficulty with your cooker, contact the manufacturer's customer service department. You'll find a Directory of Pressure Cooker Manufacturers and Distributors on page 319.

The cooker is taking a long time to come up to pressure.

> You are cooking a larger quantity of food than usual. Be patient.
>
> There is insufficient liquid in cooker. Release pressure and add more liquid.
>
> The cooker is filled beyond the recommended capacity and there isn't sufficient space for the steam pressure to gather. Release pressure and remove some of the ingredients.
>
> The lid isn't locked properly.
>
> Jiggle-Top Cooker: The vent pipe is clogged with a particle of food. Quick-release the pressure under cold running water and clean the vent according to manufacturer's instructions.
>
> Second-Generation Cooker: The pressure regulator may be stuck. Tap the top of the regulator lightly with a spoon to release. If this doesn't help, quick-release the pressure and make sure the regulator is screwed in tightly.

Water is dripping down the sides of the cooker.

> The gasket isn't forming a tight seal. Try oiling it. If that doesn't work, purchase a new one.

Liquid or foam is spouting from the vent.

> Immediately turn off the heat. Do not attempt to move the cooker until the pressure comes down naturally. Consider the following possibilities:
>
> The cooker is filled beyond capacity. Cook the ingredients in two batches.
>
> You are cooking foaming foods and have forgotten to add oil. Stir in 1 tablespoon oil, clean the area around the pressure regulator, and resume cooking.

The lid won't come off even though all of the pressure has been released.

> A vacuum has been created inside the cooker. Either wait until the cooker cools entirely or bring it back up to pressure and quick-release. If the lid still does not come off, contact the manufacturer.

Food forms a crust or burns on the bottom of the cooker.

Your cooker doesn't have a well-constructed bottom. Try the following:

> Use a heat diffuser (see page 17).
> Bring the ingredients to a boil before locking on the lid.
> Increase the liquid slightly the next time you cook the recipe.
> Bring up the pressure over medium rather than high heat. Although the cooker will take longer to come up to pressure, time under pressure remains the same.

Timing Charts at a Glance

Meat Timing Chart

All timings are calculated for natural pressure release except as noted. When cooking frozen meat, add 5 minutes high pressure for each inch of thickness. For detailed information on individual cuts and testing for doneness, refer to Meat Cuts and Making Them Pressure Perfect, pages 71 to 91.

Pounds or Thickness	Minutes High Pressure + Natural Release	Serves
BEEF		
Brisket		
1¹/₂ to 2 pounds	45	2 to 3
2 to 3 pounds	45 to 55	3 to 4
3 to 4 pounds	55 to 60	4 to 6
4 to 5 pounds	60 to 70	6 to 8
Chuck Roast (boneless, more than 2 inches thick)		
2¹/₄ to 3 pounds	35 to 45	5 to 6
3 to 4 pounds	45 to 55	6 to 8
4 to 5 pounds	55 to 65	8 to 10
Chuck Steak (less than 2 inches thick)		
¹/₂ to 1 inch	15 to 20	6 ounces/person
1 to 1¹/₂ inches	20 to 25	6 ounces/person
1¹/₂ to 2 inches	25 to 30	6 ounces/person

Corned Beef		
1¹/₂ to 2 pounds	45	2 to 3
2 to 3 pounds	45 to 55	3 to 4
3 to 4 pounds	55 to 60	4 to 6
4 to 5 pounds	60 to 70	6 to 8
Flanken	25	1 pound/person
Oxtails	30	1 pound/person
Round/Rump Roast		
2¹/₄ to 3 pounds	35 to 45	5 to 6
3 to 4 pounds	45 to 55	6 to 8
4 to 5 pounds	55 to 65	8 to 10
Shanks, Cross-Cut		
1 to 1¹/₂ inches (³/₄ to 1 pound)	25	1 shank/person
1¹/₂ to 2¹/₂ inches	25 to 35	¹/₂ shank/person
Short Ribs/ Flanken	25	1 pound/person
Stew Meat (1- to 1¹/₂- inch cubes)	16	6 ounces/person
LAMB		
Breast/Riblets	20 + quick-release	1 pound/person
Chops: *see* **Shoulder Chops**		
Leg (boneless, 1¹/₂-inch cubes)	6	6 ounces/person
Neck Shoulder Slices (bone-in stew meat)		
1 inch	16 + quick-release	1 pound/person
2 to 3 inches	23 + quick-release	1 pound/person

Riblets: see Breast		
Shanks		
1/2 to 1 pound	25	1 shank/person
1 to 1 1/2 pounds	30	1 shank/person
Shoulder (boneless, for stew)		
1- to 1 1/2-inch cubes	12 to 16	6 ounces/person
Shoulder Chops		
1/2 to 3/4 inch	10	1 chop/person
1 inch	11	
Stew Meat: see Leg and Shoulder		
PORK		
Ribs (bone-in and boneless)	15 + quick-release	1 pound/person
Shoulder Arm Picnic (bone-in)		
3 1/2 to 4 pounds (trimmed weight)	50 to 55	3 to 4
4 to 5 pounds (trimmed weight)	55 to 65	4 to 5
Shoulder Blade Roast or Picnic Shoulder (boneless)		
3 1/2 to 4 pounds (trimmed weight)	45 to 50	6 to 8
4 to 5 pounds (trimmed weight)	50 to 60	8 to 10
Shoulder Steaks/Chops		
1/2 to 3/4 inch	4 to 5	6 ounces/person
3/4 to 1 inch	5 to 6	6 ounces/person
1 1/4 to 1 1/2 inches	7 to 8	6 ounces/person

Timing Charts at a Glance

Stew Meat **(1-inch cubes)**	8	6 ounces/person
VEAL		
Breast **3 to 4 pounds**	40 to 50	1 pound/person
Shanks **(osso bucco)** 3/4 to 1¼ pounds	18 to 20	1 shank/person
Shoulder Roast **(boneless)** 2¼ to 3 pounds 3½ to 4 pounds	45 50 to 55	4 to 6 7 to 8
Shoulder Steak/ **Chop (bone-in)** ½ inch 3/4 to 1 inch	6 8	10 ounces/person 10 ounces/person
Stew Meat **(1½-inch cubes)**	8	6 ounces/person

Poultry Timing Chart

Note: When cooking frozen chicken parts, add 1 extra minute. When cooking a whole frozen chicken, add 1 extra minute per pound. When cooking frozen turkey parts, add 4 minutes for every 1 inch of thickness.

	Minutes High Pressure + Release Method	Serves
CHICKEN		
Whole		
3 pounds	18 + natural release*	3 to 4
4 pounds	20 + natural release*	4 to 5
Breast halves		
bone-in	7 + 4 natural release, then quick-release	1 pound serves 2
boneless	4 + 4 natural release, then quick-release	3/4 pound serves 2
Drumsticks	8 + 4 natural release, then quick-release	1 pound serves 2
Thighs		
bone-in	8 + 4 natural release, then quick-release	1 pound serves 2
boneless	4 + 4 natural release, then quick-release	3/4 pound serves 2
Thighs and Breast boneless, cut into 1-inch pieces	4 + quick-release	1 pound serves 2 to 3
CORNISH HEN		
Whole		
1 pound	6 + 6 natural release, then quick-release	1
1 1/2 pounds	8 + 6 natural release, then quick-release	2

327

TURKEY		
Breast Roast **boneless**		
2 to 2¹/₂ pounds	20 + natural release†	4 to 6
Drumstick (small)		
1 to 1¹/₄ pounds	12 + natural release	1
Thigh **bone-in**		
¹/₂ to 1 pound	12 to 14 + natural release	1
1 to 1¹/₂ pounds	14 to 16 + natural release	2
boneless		
7 to 10 ounces	8 + natural release	1 to 2
Tenderloin, **cut into 1-inch** **chunks**	4 + quick release	1 pound serves 2

*Temperature at thigh joint should read at least 170 degrees Fahrenheit.
†Temperature in thickest part should read at least 160 degrees Fahrenheit.

328

Fish Timing Chart

This chart works for firm-fleshed fish steaks or fillets, such as salmon, cod (scrod), or halibut.

Thickness*	Minutes High Pressure + Quick-Release
$3/4$ inch	4
1 inch	5
$1^1/4$ inches	6
$1^1/2$ inches	7

*Time for thickest portion.

Fish Packet Timing Chart

This chart works for any fish steak or fillet that flakes easily, such as scrod, salmon, pollack, tilapia, or orange roughy.

Thickness*	Minutes High Pressure + Quick-Release
$1/4$ inch	6
$1/2$ inch	8
$3/4$ inch	10
1 inch	13
$1^1/4$ inches	14
$1^1/2$ inches	15

*Time for thickest portion.

Whole Grains Timing Chart

All timings are based on quick-releasing pressure by setting the cooker under cold running water. If using an electric cooker, subtract 5 minutes from cooking time and allow the pressure to come down naturally for 10 minutes, then quick-release any remaining pressure.

15 Minutes*	18 Minutes	25 Minutes	35 Minutes
brown rice (short- and long-grain; basmati)	pearl barley	wild rice	kamut
calusari red rice (Christmas rice)	black barley	rye berries	oat groats
black japonica rice			spelt
wehani rice			wheat berries

*This timing also works for packaged brown rice blends that usually call for 45 minutes cooking time.

Bean Timing Chart

For firm beans, to be served on their own or in salads, cook for the minimum suggested time. For bean soups, stews, or purees, cook for the maximum suggested time. Allow 15 to 20 minutes for the natural pressure release, which is essential to completing the job properly. Allow extra time for any additional cooking that may be needed.

Always add 1 tablespoon oil to control foaming; 2 tablespoons oil for limas and soybeans. Do not fill the cooker more than halfway when cooking beans.

1 Cup Dried Beans	Minutes High Pressure* + Natural Release	Yield in Cups
Adzuki (Azuki)	16 to 21	2
Black (Turtle)	22 to 25	2
Black-Eyed Peas	6 to 8	$2^1/_4$
Cannellini	28 to 32	2
Chickpeas (Garbanzos)	32 to 35	$2^1/_2$
Cranberry (Borlotti)	28 to 34	$2^1/_4$
Flageolet	28 to 34	2
Great Northern	25 to 30	$2^1/_4$
Lentils (brown or French green)	1[†] to 5	2
Lentils (red)	5[‡]	2
Lima (large)[§]	9 to 10	$2^1/_2$
Lima (baby)	13 to 15	$2^1/_2$
Navy (pea)	22 to 25	2

Timing Charts at a Glance

Peas (split, green or yellow)	10 to 12	2
Pinto	19 to 22	$2^{1}/_4$
Red Kidney	25 to 30	2
Romano (Roman)	25 to 30	2
Small Red Beans	26 to 30	2
Soybeans (beige)§	28 to 35	$2^{1}/_4$
Soybeans (black)§	32 to 37	$2^{1}/_2$

*For soaked beans, cut cooking time in half.
†After 1 minute high pressure, allow pressure to come down naturally for 8 minutes, then quick-release any remaining pressure.
‡Red lentils do not hold their shape when cooked, so you can use the quick-release method.
§Use 2 tablespoons oil per 1 cup beans to control foaming.

Vegetable Timing Chart

Vegetable	Minutes High Pressure + Quick-Release
Artichokes	
Large (8 to 9 ounces)	10 to 11
Medium (6 to 7 ounces)	6 to 8
Small (3 to 4 ounces)	4 to 5
Baby (1 ounce)	3 to 4
Beets	
Large, whole (7 to 8 ounces)	25 to 28
Medium, whole (5 to 6 ounces)	20 to 22
Small, whole (3 to 4 ounces)	11 to 13
Peeled, halved, and cut into $1/4$-inch slices	3 to 5
Cabbage (Green)	
2- to 3-pound, quartered	3
Quartered, cored, and thinly sliced	2 to 3
Carrots	
Baby-cut	4 to 5
Medium, 1-inch chunks	6 to 7
Medium, $1/4$-inch slices	4 to 5
Cauliflower	4 to 5
Medium ($2^1/2$ pounds untrimmed), whole	
Large florets (about $2^1/2$ inches across the top)	1
Celeriac	
1-inch chunks	6 to 7
$1/2$-inch slices	4 to 5
Collards	
Chopped	3 to 4
Eggplant	
$1^1/2$-inch chunks	2 to 3

Green Beans	
Whole or cut into 2-inch lengths	2 to 3
Kale	
Chopped	2
Parsnips	
1-inch chunks	5 to 6
Potatoes (Boiling, Yukon Gold, Waxy)	
Whole, large (8 to 10 ounces)	28 to 32
Whole, medium (5 to 6 ounces)	15 to 17
Whole, small (2 to 3 ounces)	9 to 10
1-inch chunks	6 to 7
1/2-inch slices	5 to 6
1/4-inch slices	3 to 4
Potatoes, New	
Whole, medium (2 ounces)	8 to 9
Whole, small (1 ounce each)	5 to 6
Potatoes Russets	
Whole, medium (8 to 10 ounces)	26 to 30
1-inch chunks	7 to 8
1/2-inch slices	5 to 6
1/4-inch slices	3 to 4
Potatoes, Sweet	
2-inch chunks	9 to 10
1/2-inch slices	4 to 5
Rutabaga	
1-inch chunks	9 to 10
1/2-inch dice	6 to 7
Squash, Winter	
Acorn, halved	6 to 7
Pattypan, whole	10 to 12
All Winter Squash, 1 1/2-inch chunks	3 to 4

Turnips, White

Medium, whole (12 ounces)	24 to 26
1^1/$_2$- to 2-inch chunks	7 to 8

Zucchini and Yellow Squash

Whole (about 1-inch diameter)	4
1-inch chunks	2

Timing Charts at a Glance

Index

Index

Index

Index

341

Index

cook-along, lamb shanks with
white beans with, 116–17
in five-minute tomato sauce,
295–96
lima bean soup with tomatoes and,
247
lima beans with tomatoes and,
245–47
mashed potatoes with, 288
roasting, 18
German-style pot roast, 98–99
German-style split pea soup with
knockwurst or franks, 46–47
ginger:
crystallized, dried fruit compote
with, 316
grating fresh, 18
mashed sweet potatoes with sage
and, 293–94
and plum sauce, delectable meats
in, 107–10
goulash with potatoes, 122–23
grain blends, 204
grapes:
in brown rice Waldorf salad with
orange-marmalade dressing,
212–13
chicken salad with tarragon-
mayonnaise dressing and, 159
Greek flavors, tabbouleh with,
215–16
Greek-inspired tomato sauce,
ground lamb meatballs with,
138–39
green beans:
in cauliflower and sweet potato
curry with mango chutney–
yogurt sauce, 281–83
cauliflower and sweet potatoes
with Asian peanut sauce and,
282–83
cook-along, Parmesan chicken
packet with, 161–62
cooking tips, 266

ham:
hock, in black bean soup with avocado salsa, 51–53

risotto with Gruyère, peas and,
198–99
Southern split pea soup with,
45–47
high-altitude cooking, 21
hominy stew, Southwest pork and,
127–28
horseradish cream sauce, beef in,
102–3
horseradish dressing, quick-pickled
beets in, 276–78
hummus:
basic, 240–41
jalapeño, 241
parsley, 241
red pepper, with toasted cumin
seeds, 241

Indian-inspired chicken salad with
mango-yogurt dressing, 159–60
Italian herb blend, 18
Italian meatloaf, 135

jambalaya:
chicken, 190–91
seafood and chicken, 190–91

kabocha squash, 229
kale:
beans with sausage and, 253–54
cooking tips, 266–67
and potatoes with kielbasa, 130

lamb:
barley risotto with, 200–202
in beer-braised ribs in barbecue
sauce, 111–13
biryani, 193
curried, with potatoes, 144–45
curry, chickpea, spinach and, 256
in curry in a hurry, 124–26
cuts and cooking tips, 79–83
and lentil stew with minted
yogurt, Moroccan, 131–32
meatballs with Greek-inspired
tomato sauce, 138–39
with pasta, North African, 221–22
Scotch broth, 202

lamb (*continued*)
    shank casserole, bean and, 118
    shanks or chops in gingered plum
      sauce, 107–110
    shanks with white beans, 116–18
    stew, rustic, 120
    timing chart, 93–94
leek(s):
    in chunky fish chowder, 41
    cleaning and chopping, 19
    in potato corn chowder, 41
    and potato soup, rustic, 40–41
    in vichyssoise, 41
lemon:
    cheesecake, 302–4
    cheesecake with fruit swirl, 304
    -dill vinaigrette, last-minute
      potato salad with, 289–90
    mashed sweet potatoes with
      rosemary oil and, 294
    -oregano vinaigrette, lima bean
      salad with zucchini, corn and,
      246–47
    zesting, 19
lentil(s):
    French green, 216
    stew, Moroccan chicken and, 132
    stew with minted yogurt,
      Moroccan lamb and, 131–32
    tabbouleh, 215–16
lentil soup:
    chickpea and, with basil pesto,
      Provençal, 49–50
    with chickpeas and mint-feta
      pesto, 48–50
    with chickpeas and winter squash,
      49–50
    with corn and cilantro pesto,
      49–50
    five-minute red, 46–47
lima bean(s):
    with butter and fines herbes,
      246
    salad with zucchini, corn and
      lemon-oregano vinaigrette,
      246–47
    soup with tomatoes, garlicky,
      247
    with tomatoes, garlicky, 245–47

lime-cilantro cream, shredded meat
    tacos with, 146–49
lime-cilantro vinaigrette, Southwest
    chicken salad with, 160
little chocolate pots, 308–9

Madras chickpeas with spinach,
    255–56
maple-walnut rice pudding, 301
marshmallows, candied sweet
    potatoes with, 294
meat:
    cuts and cooking tips, 68–91
    timing chart, 92–95
    see also shredded meat; *specific*
      meats
meatball(s):
    ground lamb, with Greek-inspired
      tomato sauce, 138–39
    in mock lasagna, 138–39
    porcupine, 137, 139
    Stroganoff, 138
    Stroganoff, with broad noodles,
      138–39
    with tomato sauce, jiffy, 136–39
    and tomato sauce, pasta with,
      138–39
    in un-stuffed cabbage in sweet-
      and-sour tomato sauce, 140–42
meatloaf:
    with cheddar-smashed potatoes,
      133–35
    "frosted," 135
    Italian, 135
    Parmigiana, 135
    stuffed, 135
    Tex-Mex, 135
meat sauce, pasta with, 220–22
meat timing chart, 92–95, 323–26
Mexican chicken soup with avocado
    and corn, 33–34
Milanese, risotto, 198
minestrone with basil pesto, 42–44
minted yogurt, Moroccan lamb and
    lentil stew with, 131–32
mint-feta pesto, lentil soup with
    chickpeas and, 48–50
mocha chip bread pudding, 312
mocha chip cheesecake, 304

moo shu chicken or pork with flour tortilla "pancakes," mock, 149

Moroccan chicken and lentil stew, 132

Moroccan lamb and lentil stew with minted yogurt, 131–32

mushroom(s):
    and barley soup with beef, 30–31
    in chicken cacciatore, 164–66
    double-mushroom barley soup, 31
    gravy, brisket with, 99
    gravy, pot roast with, 96–99
    porcini risotto, 199
    sauce, chicken noodle "casserole" with, 226–27
    sauce, pasta with, 221–22
    shiitake, Asian orzo risotto with, 231
    wild, orzo risotto with, 230–31
    ziti with, 224–25

mussels, rice with, 194–95

mustard:
    -honey sauce, ribs with, 113
    -honey sesame sauce, ribs with, 113

mustard gravy, beef in beer and, 100–103

mustard mashed potatoes, 288

niçoise, bean salad, 248–50

noodles:
    broad, meatball Stroganoff with, 138–39
    chicken "casserole" with mushroom sauce and, 226–27
    chunky chicken soup with, 32–34
    chunky turkey soup with, 34
    turkey "casserole" with, 227
    see also pasta

North African lamb with pasta, 221–22

nut(s):
    in brown rice Waldorf salad with orange marmalade dressing, 212–13
    in cauliflower and sweet potato curry with mango chutney–yogurt sauce, 281–83
    in chicken biryani, 192–93
    in chicken salad with grapes and tarragon-mayonnaise dressing, 159–60
    -cranberry and brown rice pilaf, 209–11
    -cranberry and brown rice stuffing, 210–11
    festive rice with fruit and, 187–88
    and fruit tabbouleh, 215
    in Indian-inspired chicken salad with mango-yogurt dressing, 159–60
    maple-walnut rice pudding, 301
    in penne with winter squash and ricotta, 228–29
    pickled beets with toasted pine nuts, 277
    pickled beet "wafers" with Gorgonzola and walnuts, 277–78
    toasting, 19

oats, rolled, in meatloaf with cheddar-smashed potatoes, 133–35

olives, black:
    in chicken cacciatore, 164–66
    in fish packet with puttanesca sauce, 172–74

onions:
    in barley risotto with lamb, 200–202
    in beef, mushroom and barley soup, 30–31
    in chicken biryani, 192–93
    in chicken cacciatore, 164–66
    in classic beef stew, 119–21
    in curry in a hurry, 124
    in eggplant caponata, 284–86
    in five-minute tomato sauce, 295–96
    in garlicky lima beans with tomatoes, 245–47
    in goulash with potatoes, 122–23
    in lamb shanks with white beans, 116–18
    in lentil soup with chickpeas and mint-feta pesto, 48–50

Index

Index

350

chunky fish chowder, 41
chunky turkey noodle, 34
creamy celery with fennel, 39
curried carrot, 38–39
curried coconut split pea, 46–47
curried coconut with sweet potatoes and chickpeas, 36
double-mushroom barley, 31
elegant bean soup du jour, 54–56
five-minute red lentil, 46–47
garlicky lima bean, with tomatoes, 247
German-style split pea with knockwurst or franks, 46–47
hearty beef borscht with sour cream–dill topping, 27–29
lentil, with chickpeas and mint-feta pesto, 48–50
lentil with chickpeas and winter squash, 49–50
lentil with corn and cilantro pesto, 49–50
minestrone with basil pesto, 42–44
multi-bean, 237
pasta e fagioli, 55–56
potato-cheddar, 41
potato corn chowder, 41
Provençal lentil and chickpea with basil pesto, 49–50
pureed summer borscht, 29
red lentil, five-minute, 46
root vegetable, 292
rustic bean with pesto, 55–56
rustic leek and potato, 40–41
sage-scented butternut squash, with herb croutons, 37–39
Scotch broth, 202
Southern split pea with ham, 45–47
split pea, *see* split pea soup
sweet potato, 38
tabbouleh, 216
turkey, barley and vegetable, 31
Ukrainian-style borscht, 29
vichyssoise, 41
see also broth

sour cream:
and chive-flecked mashed potatoes, 288
-dill sauce, sauerkraut with smoked pork chops, sausage, potatoes and, 114–15
-dill smashed potatoes, fish with, 170–71
hearty beef borscht with dill and 27–29
lime-cilantro, shredded meat tacos with, 146–49
Southern split pea soup with ham, 45–47
Southwest:
bean and tuna salad, 249–50
chicken salad with lime-cilantro vinaigrette, 160
pork and hominy stew, 127–28
potato salad, 290
Spanish rice with chicken and sausage, 189–91
specialty rice, 207, 209, 212, 214
spices, toasting, 19
spinach:
brown rice pilaf with raisins, chickpeas and, 210–11
chickpea and lamb curry with, 256
Madras chickpeas with, 255–56
risotto with chickpeas, raisins and, 199
split pea soup:
curried coconut, 46–47
with ham, Southern, 45–47
with knockwurst or franks, German-style, 46–47
squash, winter:
in barley and winter vegetable risotto, 201–2
butternut, risotto with, 198
chunky chicken soup with beans and, 33–34
cooking tips, 269
lentil soup with chickpeas and, 49–50
penne with ricotta and, 228–29
soup, sage-scented butternut, with herb croutons, 37–39
in vegetable biryani, 193

Index

353

Index